WILDCAT
HAVEN

by the same author

THE BIG MAN
IT SURE BEATS WORKING
ALONE IN THE WILDERNESS
MY WILDERNESS WILDCATS
LIANE, A CAT FROM THE WILD
BETWEEN EARTH AND PARADISE
GOLDEN EAGLE YEARS
A LAST WILD PLACE
OUT OF THE WILD
ON WING AND WILD WATER

WILDCAT HAVEN

The complete story of
My Wilderness Wildcats and
Liane, a Cat from the Wild,
revised and updated

Mike Tomkies

JONATHAN CAPE
THIRTY-TWO BEDFORD SQUARE LONDON

First published 1987
Text and photographs copyright © 1987 Mike Tomkies
Jonathan Cape Ltd, 32 Bedford Square, London WC1B3EL

British Library Cataloguing In Publication Data

Tomkies, Mike
Wildcat haven: the complete story of my wilderness
wildcats and Liane, a cat from the wild. – Rev. and updated
1. European wildcat
I. Title. II. Tomkies, Mike. My wilderness wildcats.
III. Tomkies, Mike. Liane, a cat from the wild
599.74'428   QL737.C23

ISBN 0224 02502 3

Typeset by Computape (Pickering) Ltd, North Yorkshire
Colour separations and printing by
Chorley & Pickersgill Ltd, Leeds
Text printed by Butler & Tanner Ltd,
Frome and London

Contents

1 · A Bundle of Contradictions

As Highlander Allan MacColl walked along a lonely track eight miles from my isolated waterfront cottage, a sudden flurry in a steep-sided ditch made him look down. What he saw there astonished him. Spitting and hissing, two wildcat kittens had backed into a corner, their mouths open, tiny fangs bared, claws out, ready to fight for their immature lives with all the ferocity that characterizes their kind. Allan caught a glimpse of a big cat with long striped bushy tail slinking away with more kittens through the undergrowth above the ditch. Peeling off his jacket, he threw it over the two spitting kits and, after a struggle, caught them.

He put his angry captives on to soft sacking in a grocery box in his van and drove them home.

A few weeks later, as the last of the 570 miles from London slid away beneath my Land Rover, and I negotiated the single-track roads which fell precipitously through the mountains or wound beside the wild wooded lochs, I looked forward to merging once more into the tranquillity of the remote Highland area in Western Scotland which had then been my home for nearly five years. I would call in at Allan MacColl's village shop to stock up with supplies before embarking on the final stage of the journey to my remote outpost halfway up a roadless, 18-mile freshwater loch.

My six-week return visit to Canada had been an extraordinary experience. I had trekked with an Indian hunter after wild mother grizzlies with cubs, stalking close enough for photos, but trying not to provoke a charge. I had also chased on foot behind a pack of trained hounds over miles of mountainous terrain to photograph and radio-collar mountain lions. After those hard, blistering days, I was conscious now of a feeling of anticlimax.

It was a fine but cloudy day, with a strong southerly breeze. At the MacColl shop door I paused to look up the loch to where the waters vanished four miles away in a fold in the mountains. I hoped the good weather would last for I had to go more than twice that distance to reach home. Even from the wood where I left my boat and parked the Land Rover, I still faced a six-mile walk if it cut up too rough for a laden boat. The hike led through woods with many windfalls, along high ledges and rocky foreshore, across several bogs and large areas of two-foot-high tussocks whose grassy crowns hid the treacherous gullies between them. Although I had frequently made the double trek with full pack, tired as I now was I did not relish the idea of covering the route on foot carrying 80lbs of supplies.

As I checked the shopping against my list, Ian MacColl (Allan's brother), who was a field officer with the Red Deer Commission, talked to me about the wildcat kittens.

'He'd probably let you have them, if you've a mind to it,' he said.

With my head still full of my exciting trip, I expressed only mild interest. I had never liked cats much, for they always seemed to me faithless creatures, whose love for their owners was of the cupboard variety, only coming home for food and warmth, and to have their heads tickled or to be stroked before going their own independent ways again. I was more of a dog man myself, proof of which, all 6ft 4ins nose-to-tail-tip of him, was now reposing outside the shop in the Land Rover.

Moobli had come to me as an 11-week-old pup from a breeder in Sussex who was renowned for her large, powerful, amiable Alsatians. When I moved to my present home, I had felt the need for a really good dog, not only as a companion but also to help me track the wildlife that passed through my woods, so I could record exact movements for my studies. Moobli was so far proving ideal. Like any big aristocratic dog sure of its place, he was tolerant towards various sheepdogs and tiny terriers, but he was still only eight months old. I felt sure that Moobli and wildcats would not be a wise mixture to have around my lonely home. Besides, I doubted that

Allan's kits could be true wildcats. I had never heard of anyone catching even very young wildcats by hand, and felt they were almost certainly the progeny of a domestic cat gone wild, a common occurrence in the Highlands.

Yet to go straight home without even bothering to take a look at the kittens would have been downright rude. I drove to Allan's seaside cottage where, dark-haired and burly, he greeted me with a big affable grin. I already had much to thank him for, as it was he who had first told me about the wilderness dwelling that was now my home. He took me to the shed where the kittens were housed.

'They were truly wild when I picked them up,' he said. 'If they had been any older I would have needed thick gloves.'

He took the kittens out of a wooden box with both hands. They spat and hissed when they saw me, a looming stranger, and struggled, flaring loudly. One bit his thumb and he let them go. Immediately they hit the ground they scattered in opposite directions into the undergrowth, disappearing completely, like wisps of smoke. That one glance told me these were not ordinary cats. They were beautiful, with dramatic markings – two light tawny tigers with striped legs, bright blue eyes turning to greeny gold, and thick black-tipped tails. Allan said the wildlife park 100 miles to the east would gladly have them, but the problem was taking them there. While busy with his mobile grocery van in the tourist season, he had no spare time.

As we rounded up the kittens, grabbing them firmly by the scruffs of their necks so that they couldn't twist their heads round to bite, they made an odd loud squawking sound with wide-open mouths, rather like the noise ducks make when startled or seized. I was surprised, for I had heard young cougars make exactly the same sound, though louder, when first handled by men.

'I slept with them the first few nights, trying to tame them a little,' Allan said with a grin. 'I heard you should do that. It was a wee bit of a task coaxing them to lap warm milk and eat meat at first. I don't think they were quite weaned.' He scratched his head. 'Well, I kept them for you anyway. But if you don't want them, we can let them go again later.'

Touched by his kindness, I thanked him and asked if I could have a little while to think about it. Rearing a pair of wildcats which could grow to anything between 8 and 16lbs was not something to undertake lightly.

In the pine and larch wood where I parked my Land Rover, I heaved my boat right way up and, after laying a track of branches over the rocky shore, hauled it into the water. Before I finished loading up, Moobli leaped into the boat and stood in the bow, his usual place, looking at me solemnly, anxious to please. His philosophical expression was not only endearing, it reflected his gentle nature, for although his bark was already deep enough to scare a cougar, he seldom used it. He was the quietest dog I had ever known.

After the first three miles, the stiff southerly wind forced its way down the valley of a high mountain saddle on the right and sent curling waves slapping along the side of the heavily laden boat, throwing high spumes of spray over us. I headed into the waves until I was abreast of a 40yd-long spit of gravel which ran into the loch from the north bank, then turned north-east with the waves until I reached the slight lee of a gravelly beach two miles from home. There, I throttled down the engine, drifting near the shore. Moobli remembered this as the start of his exercise run. He put his huge paws on the side, peered at the rising ground below the surface and, when he judged it shallow enough, leaped out with a huge splash. Then, shaking himself vigorously on shore like a small bear, he set off alongside the moving boat. Heavily built though he was, all his flesh was fluid muscle and he could cover that last two miles, over terrain in which no man could run, in about 10 minutes.

I arrived shortly before him, and in the now-calm waters edged the boat gently against the grassy bank below the ash and alder trees and stepped ashore into the paradise I call Wildernesse. Gazing around after my longest absence was like seeing it for the first time.

To the west stood a four-acre wood in full summer bloom. Behind its southern fringe of scaly red-barked Scots pines, the land rose to a rocky 30ft escarpment from whose ledges sprang birches, rowans and twisted oaks. Areas of mushy swamp, tussock grass and broad mossy tables cushioned thickly with needles lay between the profusion of larch, ash and silver and Douglas firs, some of which reared over 100 feet into the sky. At the top was an open undulating area where pines competed with larch, and red deer had their winter rubbing posts.

I had completely renovated the old, south-facing gamekeeper's cottage after hauling paint, timber and other materials up the loch by boat and raft. Before it lay a one-and-a-half-acre patch that had

been verdant pasture when I left, for I had cut away the early
bracken. Now, I noted wryly, the bracken was again in complete
control, some of it six feet high. To the east of the cottage and
starting from right next to it, stood a larger triangular wood of oak,
ash, holly, rowan, hazel bushes and birch trees, dominated by a
huge Norway spruce that was a full 15 feet round the butt. Along
my waterfront, 60 yards from the cottage, a screen of alder and ash
trees fringed and framed the shimmering waters of the loch, which
from my door stretched in a spectacular view for a full four miles
before the first bend below the big mountain. Immediately behind
the cottage the land began to rise to the first 400ft ridges, which
were but the prelude to the rolling hills behind them which rose to
1500 feet, then dropped down into a misty glen and a river before
rising almost sheer again to the long 2000ft-high saddle of Guardian
Mountain.

It was a lovely kingdom, one that really extended for 15 miles, for
mine was the only home along that length of roadless shore. It also
stretched back to the north for a good six miles of glens and mountains before striking a road. It was one of the largest uninhabited
areas left in the British Isles – a kingdom of red deer stags that
roared in the autumn as they rounded up their harems of hinds, of
golden eagles, ravens, buzzards, kestrels and sparrowhawks, of
foxes and badgers, of otters which had their holts along the rocky
shores, of roe deer which sheltered in and shared my woods with a
pair of red squirrels.

Meadow-brown butterflies and sooty-black sweep moths flitted
about the grasses. In the clearings speckled wood butterflies hopped
and dropped through the humming summer air. A lone cormorant
winged powerfully westwards over the loch surface, looking as if it
would crash at any moment into a wave.

As the silent peaceful spell of Wildernesse enveloped me once
more, I was joined by Moobli, panting heavily after his run, and in
that carefree moment I ran with him to the south-east corner of my
land on the lochside. Then we walked beneath the stately beeches
along the banks of the burn which was the main vein of the mountains for some eight miles. A hundred yards north-east of the
cottage, we came to the waterfalls. Here the burn flows over four
deeply stepped pools, drops down a 10ft waterfall into the pool
from which I pipe my water, then cascades 30 feet in three separate
forks on to a tangle of great gnarled rocks. Tiny ferns spring from

the many grottos in the rocks and in the sunlight the splashing water forms myriad rainbows from the spray.

Over the next few days I slashed the bracken back from the front area for, where this weed flourishes, nothing else will grow. I tried to avoid the foxgloves where so many bees come for nectar, and also the birch, oak and hazel seedlings which I would thin out later when I had decided how I wanted the forest to encroach.

The vegetable garden, a 21ft-square patch which I had laboriously cleared of more than two tons of rocks, and had fertilized with last year's autumn leaf compost and seaweed brought up in the boats, was now a weed-covered wilderness of its own. All the radishes had gone to seed, so had the lettuces, but the cabbages, sprouts and kale (which last all winter and can stand frost) were fine. I weeded the whole patch. All my carefully sown peas had gone and the tiny diggings along their rows showed that mice and voles had had them. Mice too had gnawed their way through the doors and into the house – to eat and litter the kitchen floor with last year's crop of hazelnuts. It was then I remembered the wildcat kittens.

I thought of them again the following morning as I took Moobli on an inspection of the woods. The eastern edge of the 30ft rock escarpment finished in a tumble of huge jagged boulders, forming a bridge with the marsh, and these merged into a tangle of criss-crossed windfall trunks of fir, larch and oak, through which brambles with new-forming blackberries and necklaces of honeysuckle competed for space.

In places inaccessible to man there were many dry rock ledges covered with moss. To a professional forester interested mainly in rows of close-stacked, fast-growing conifers, the whole of the west wood would have seemed a mess. I was more interested in enhancing the wildlife. I intended to plant new broadleaf trees, for the young seedlings often failed to regenerate naturally in my woods, due not only to the deer but also because mice and voles ate them. I often saw voles scudding like brown bullets through their grass tunnels. These little creatures can multiply to plague proportions, 500 to an acre, and do great damage in woods by eating seed and seedlings and stripping young trees of their bark, as well as competing with deer for green grass. As I looked at the dry grottos between the boulders, and the astonishing array of sheltered retreats in the wood, I made up my mind. Wildcats thrive on voles, among their other prey of mice, hares, rabbits and birds. Here seemed to be a perfect wildcat habitat.

The main problem was to ascertain, if possible, that Allan's were pure wildcats. Consulting my few reference books, I was astonished to discover that the only two things all naturalists agreed upon were that the true Scottish wildcat, *Felis silvestris grampia*, was still rare, surviving only in isolated pockets in remote parts of the Highlands (the species had been near extinction in the early part of this century), and that the animal was totally untamable. The rest was a mass of contradictory evidence:

> Wildcats are larger and more strongly built than domestic cats; they are sometimes smaller and lighter.
> Wildcats have short truncated striped tails; they have long bushy ones.
> Wildcats never purr; they purr like domestic cats but louder.
> Wildcats bury their droppings like domestic cats; they never do.
> Wildcats are faithful to one mate for life and never mate with domestic cats turned feral; they readily do, but the hybrids are infertile.
> Wildcats have shorter small intestines than domestic cats; this theory is nonsense.
> Wildcats eat no vegetable matter; they sometimes do.
> Wildcats have two, occasionally three breeding periods a year; they have only one.
> Wildcat females rear their young away from the males, which are liable to kill and eat the kittens; the male sometimes helps to feed the family.

The more I read the more interested I became. It had been thought that domestic cats were descended from one of the two North African cats, *Felis lybica* and *Felis margarita* (the earliest records of domesticated cats come from the early Egyptians, and then later from other parts of the Mediterranean), and that they were unrelated to European and Asian wildcats, *Felis silvestris silvestris*. There is an opposite view, however, that domestic cats are descended from crosses between *Felis s. s.* and species like *Felis lybica*.

It was surprising to learn that the precise origin of the domestic cat remains unknown. They are believed to have been brought to

Britain and Western Europe by Phoenician traders some 1200 years B.C., and later by the Romans to keep rats and mice down in corn stores. The first mention of *cattus* in literature was made by Palladius in A.D. 350 as being 'useful in granaries'. However, the pure wildcat of Scotland, Europe and Asia was an indigenous prehistoric animal descended from the extinct ancestor species *Felis lunensis*. Its bones have been found in Pleistocene deposits up to 2 million years old, along with those of the mammoth, great cave bear and cave lion. Its pure form and structure today have not altered one whit since then. I was fascinated.

On July 23 Moobli and I boated up the loch against strong wester-lies and went to see Allan and the kittens again. Two gamekeepers and a local man who had studied indigenous wild creatures all his life were convinced they were pure Scottish wildcats. As I looked at the two little monsters in their box, healthy, flaring and spitting at the two humans gazing down at them, Allan echoed my own thoughts:

'Not much is known about wildcats. If you could tame them a wee bit and get them to live around your wild place up the loch, you might find them rewarding to study.'

He had heard of an American naturalist who had offered £200 each for wildcat kittens on Skye the year before. Here, where I lived in south Inverness-shire, was one of the last strongholds of the species. By the kind of miraculous luck that occasionally comes to a beginner, I had even managed to photograph a huge old tom wildcat as it stood full-length on a rock less than half a mile from Allan MacColl's home. Later, using the photo as a guide, I had measured the image on the rock and had estimated the cat to be nearly 4 feet long. It was just possible that these two kits were his progeny.

I told Allan I was grateful that he had kept them so long for me, and would be happy to take them. We put them into a large wooden box with two wire netting sides that I used for small injured birds. I was reaching for my cheque book when Allan swiftly put out his hand to stay my arm.

'Please, I don't want anything for them,' he said. 'If you can look after and study them, they're yours.'

I stammered my thanks and took the box to my boat, where I placed it on the deck in light rain. As we rode the waves up the loch, the kittens stretched their little 13-inch bodies against the wire

netting and watched the lone larches of Green Isle, the great grey
dead tree snags on Heron Island and the wild woods of sessile oak
and birch passing by. I heard strange whistling sounds – '*wheeou
wheeou*' – rather like weak buzzard calls. At first it sounded as if
they came from the air above, although there was no bird to be
seen, and then from the near-by land. Then I realized the kits were
making them, through barely opened mouths. They were eerie,
high-pitched sounds, not piercing yet far-carrying, and distinctly
ventriloquistic. I thought they were probably special calls young
wildcats make to summon their mothers from a distance without
attracting predators. I had never heard kittens make such a noise
before. The inside of their mouths was a far brighter red than that
of domestic kittens.

At home I set the box-cage on a stand in the 14ft-square kitchen.
When my hand went near they both reared high on their forelegs at
the back of the box and spat, growling like two tiny whirring
dynamos. Puny though their spits were, the kits were being as
fierce as they knew how. I sorted out two plastic bowls for food
and milk and opened a tin of cat-food. As soon as I prised up one
corner of the netting and they scented the meat – instant attack!
Yowling and growling in their high treble voices, they jammed
their heads against the stout wire and slashed out at the food with
the claws on their unusually big feet. I withdrew my hand just in
time.

Immediately the larger kit, with a slightly broader head, ousted
the other, chewing the meat while it growled and flared at the
other's attempts to get a share. With the milk it was slightly
different, for the bigger kit would not let the other near until it had
some in its belly, but then it did relinquish king position a little, and
the smaller kit shoved its head in. They both lapped greedily with a
noisy ticking sound. I tried to push their heads away from the bowl
but they resisted with amazing strength, forcing their skulls against
my fingers as they continued drinking.

As soon as they had fed and drunk their fill, they relaxed a little,
just flaring slightly as I passed to and fro while stacking away
supplies. After supper I checked them against the wildcat descrip-
tions I had gathered: the light tawny rufous fur, the dark grey-black
leg stripes, the dark lines down the back that would eventually
merge, the malformed M on the forehead, the twin stripes running
back from the eyes, the ringed tail ending in a black tip, the black

15

furred feet and soles, horn-coloured claws, large canine teeth — all seemed to fit.

When I stole in at dusk and again after dark, they were curled round each other, keeping themselves warm on the hay in the darkest corner. One always faced outwards, with an eye half open and its bright red tongue sticking out slightly.

As I dressed early next morning I had an idea. A sweater of mine was of the same rusty brown hue as the one Allan usually wore, and I put it on in the hope it would make a difference to the kits' response. I was greeted with silence as I opened the kitchen door, then with a cacophony of squawls and '*mau*'s — a sound as in Mau Mau, without the preliminary '*ee*' of the domestic cat's '*miaow*'. They spat as I got close but not as loudly as yesterday. Perhaps they did associate the sweater with the strange creature which had been feeding them since they lost their mother. Again the smell of meat and milk sent them into a frenzy. They flattened their heads against the netting and reached out with their claws. Once more the bigger animal ousted the smaller until it had eaten its fill.

After breakfast I let them free in the big kitchen to see how Moobli would react to them. I thought he would have to be trained not to chase them. The kits crept instinctively towards the walls. When they discovered the iron fender before the fireplace, they scrambled clumsily over it and peeped at us from behind its protection. Astonishingly, Moobli took them in his stride. I sat with one arm lightly round him, so he would not feel jealous, and he gazed at the little kits with as much interest as I did. He showed no belligerence at all. When he moved forward cautiously to sniff them, and they spat and struck out at him with their claws, he just looked pained and retreated with a whine of disappointment.

We stayed still while the kits investigated this new world, sniffing everything and moving their heads up and down as they peered at us. I saw in the sunlight from the window that the bright blue of their eyes was being edged out from the pupils by a greeny-gold colour. These piebald eyes gave them a comical look.

From the start, the kittens displayed totally different characters. The smaller, weaker one was shy and secretive, yet more fierce at human approach. She had a slinky, feminine look and always flared and tried to bite when being picked up. The bigger one was more easy going, always investigating strange objects, and would only crouch down with flattened ears when my hand went near. I soon

16

realized one could not dither when picking them up; if they saw the hand coming slowly, both would retreat and spit. If I spoke soothingly first, then grasped them quickly, firmly yet gently, by the scruff of the neck as close to the head as possible, I could usually succeed without being bitten. Once grasped, the big kitten went limp, but the smaller one squawked loudly.

Inspired by their wild beauty, and wanting to call them something distinctive, I hit on the name Cleopatra. Cleo would be the thinner, wilder one, and the bigger (also a female) would be Patra. So CleoPatra would be a good collective name for the two in the diaries I intended to keep about them.

As they spent the whole morning asleep, curled round each other, I wondered if they liked comfort as much as domestic cats. I took them into my bedroom and let them go on the thick woollen bedspread. To my surprise they instantly flattened themselves on the open exposed surface, crawled to the edge, keeping as close as two striped moles, dived clumsily for the floor and shot for refuge beneath the bed. I had quite a tussle and wore thick gloves to get them back into their box.

To help strengthen their legs after being cooped up in boxes, I fed them at midday with meat dangling from string. Both kits leaped up for it as best they could and I rewarded them after the first few jumps by letting the meat drop. Instantly they fell on it with loud whirring growls. Even at this age their fierceness told me they would never be household pets. Their bites and scratches were little worse than catching one's hand on barbed wire, and I doubted they weighed much more than a pound apiece. Mature wildcats vary from 8 to 16lbs and are reputed to be able to kill animals of more than their own weight. I decided to bring them up as naturally as possible and let them run free in the perfect habitat around my home.

In the afternoon I transferred them to an old woodshed that nestles away from the prevailing winds at the back of my L-shaped cottage, and started to feed them at night by the light of a paraffin Tilly lamp. I had no electricity at the cottage, and hoped that when they became mature they would associate the lamplight in my study window with the food and protection I had given them when young.

Again they fought each other over food. I realized that I would have to feed them separately – a good use for all the empty rustless tobacco tins hoarded in the workshop. After boiling and scrubbing several of them, I gave each kit a separate tin for food and milk – four in all. Immediately they stopped scrapping and went for different tins.

It soon became clear that while they would fight to reach food first, they would not fight *over* it, like dogs, or try to grab it from each other. The first cat to get at the food owned it. They were not proprietary over particular tins, and even though I always tried to feed Cleo on the right, Patra on the left, if one left anything it would permit the other to sneak over and steal it. Once, when Patra was filching Cleo's meat in this way, I tried to push her head away. Immediately she attacked and slashed out with her claws, trying to pull my finger back for a bite. Momentarily peeved, I gave her behind a light flick to let her know who was boss. It only made her fiercer. There was clearly no canine masochism here, and punishment, however slight, from a superior force only increased their natural savagery. It had been a foolish thing to do.

Although I made a bed of hay in a deep tea chest for them, the kits jumped out of it and climbed up to some sacking that lay between three logs which accidentally formed an open-ended square. There they were three feet off the ground and could clearly see any approaching danger.

Over those first few days, Moobli sat just outside the shed and watched them with me, only sniffing at them from a few feet away, as if registering the scent in his mind. They seemed less scared of him than of me. If they ran away from the woodshed and got lost, at least Moobli might be able to track them with his excellent nose.

2 · My Wilderness Wildcats

It was proving to be a wet summer, and the wildcat kittens were spending most of the daytime in the shed. On the first sunny day after a week of rain, I took axe and saw to the west wood with the intention of topping up my supply of firewood. I took only wind-falls and cut no growing trees. By taking logs that lay jammed across other trunks on the ground, not only did I get drier firewood, but I left the decaying timber on the forest floor. These ground logs were inhabited by over 200 species of insects and invertebrates which, along with fungi, helped to break up the wood and leaf litter into the humus all plants need. They also provided food for woodpeckers, frogs, mice, shrews, voles, birds and other small mammals. On these creatures preyed the owls, hawks, foxes, badgers and one day, I hoped, my wildcats.

When I came back with my second loaded pack and a log under each arm I found the kittens had left the shed. Perhaps they had been disturbed by my work and would return when I had finished. By stacking old and new wood right up to roof level at the back, I made more room in the shed than before. I went back at dusk after an hour's writing but the kits were still not there. I began to worry that I might have scared them away for good. I held their bed sacking to Moobli's nose and told him to track the pussy coots – which, by the strangely perverse idea association that comes to folk living alone with animals, had now become their slang name.

19

Moobli immediately put his nose to the ground, zig-zagged about a few times, then began bulldozing through the bracken that dominated the north hill behind the cottage. It was then I discovered that while the kits accepted Moobli watching them inside the shed, meeting him in the open was entirely different. Almost immediately Cleo shot out of the bracken like a small striped rocket, paused when she reached the open, looked quickly about her, then in two long bounds reached a broken knothole at ground level on the shed corner and vanished inside. Then Moobli started whining. He had found Patra too, but she was standing her ground, at bay amid thick bracken. With ears flattened, her eyes narrowed and pitch black with expanded pupils, tail fluffed up like a flue brush, she was growling like a high-pitched motor, ready to claw him if he came any closer.

'No!' I commanded. 'Get back!'

Moobli backed off a few feet. Again I realized his whining was not prompted by anger, nor was it a prelude to attack – for he could have finished either kitten off with one swift chop – but came from disappointment that they found him terrifying and didn't want to play! When we both retreated a few steps and Patra felt safe again, she also took off for the shed and squeezed through the knothole. I enlarged this hole as they were probably using it as a regular exit and entrance at night.

Moobli's attitude towards the kittens and theirs to him was now most important. I did not want to punish him when he caught up with them outside, for that might have made him jealous and induced him to seek revenge when I was not close by. Besides, his natural urge to track after them was worth cultivating. At the same time, the best way to get them to accept our presence without alarm or dashing for cover, was for us to take no notice and to carry on with whatever we were doing. Slowly Moobli learned not to make quick sudden movements near the kits, and sometimes, instead of flying into the shed, they just retreated behind a loose board or into a pile of timber by the cottage's west wall and watched our activities with interest.

Patra was the first to lose a little of her fear. Within two weeks she knew I was the source of regular food and watered milk and that, despite his size, even in the open Moobli meant no harm and always backed away from them on my command. Cleo remained far more wary. Once when they were back in the shed at dusk, Moobli put his nose to the knothole as Cleo, unseen, was crouching behind it. She snarled, spat and swiped out at him.

One early August morning I walked to the far end of the east wood and cut three 10ft logs from a larch that had fallen across the secondary burn and jammed over a large rock, so that its 40ft top reared upwards threateningly over the forest floor. After carrying the logs up to the house, itching from midge bites, I went to cool off in the waterfalls. As I stood there, swiftly refreshed in the cold mountain waters, I noticed there were several natural holes under the banks. Beneath them were slabs of moss-covered rocks that lay unevenly on top of each other. It seemed a perfect area for wildcats to hunt.

I carried the kits in their box to the waterfalls and put them on a large log near the bank. They hated it! The splashing noises and the rushing water, so soothing to human ears, scared them. They flattened their ears, jumped off the logs and scattered for cover under the bank, away from the awful noise. Although wildcats are said to swim readily when mature, so as to reach small islets to hunt or when danger threatens, water was something the kits would have to be introduced to slowly, in their own good time.

They quickly forgot the experience on the way back and looked at the passing woodland with great interest. To see if they could climb, I held Patra, the most forward of the two, against a thick-barked larch trunk. She clung on instinctively with her claws, but did not seem to know how to move down and had too little strength to haul herself upward to the first branch. She just stayed there and '*mau*'d. When I set them both on top of a branch nearly eight feet high, they showed no alarm whatever at the unaccustomed height and began raising and lowering their heads, peering at the oak trees halfway up the north hill. Cleo suddenly looked up into the sky, her elliptical pupils closing to mere slits. High overhead a young buzzard was soaring westwards. There was nothing wrong with their eyesight.

By this time, their attitudes at feeding time had begun to change. If I put one bowl of meat down a fraction before the second, the first kit to reach it no longer tried to claw the other as she came near but merely growled and shot out an accurate clawless paw, placing it firmly on the other kit's head, to stop it coming any closer. Three evenings after the waterfall visit, both kits jumped down from their bed to greet me when I went in with their food. Cleo grabbed her meat and with high whirring growls dashed between the logs with it. Momentarily irked by what seemed her constant wild ingratitude, I decided to experiment. Pretending not to be looking at her, I waited until she dropped the main piece of meat and was chewing a morsel, then I snatched the big chunk back. There was no retaliation. It was suddenly gone and she showed no anger. I then gave it to Patra, who also took it between the logs. This time I was slower in snatching it back. Patra, usually the tamer, went for me, spitting like a firecracker and lashing out with her claws, drawing blood.

I determined to find out if Patra's attack had been due to a different temperament. I gave her another piece of meat and when she was chewing it with her side teeth I made a light fast grab for the piece she had left on the log. With her eyes averted as she chewed, she did not even see it go. When she did notice it was gone, she behaved, like Cleo, with no animosity at all. Their reactions were purely defensive. They would try to stop the meat going if they saw the threat, but once it was gone there was no thought of vengeance. That is quite unlike canine behaviour. Although I brought up Moobli to let me take his food away while he was eating, an untrained dog will certainly attack during the taking *and* after it has gone. The revenge motive did not appear to exist in my wildcats' make-up, either towards me or each other.

Cleo was the first to catch wild prey and I was lucky enough to witness it. I was looking through the rear bedroom window when I saw her stalking through the long grass in front of the bracken on the north hill. Crouched low, her eyes glaring like twin headlamps, black-pupilled despite the daylight, she moved stealthily towards a disturbance between a mass of buttercup leaves below a bramble bush. Moving one foot at a time, her front elbows protruding above her back, rolling forward on her long rear hocks as if they were the runners of a slow-motion rocking horse, she edged forward until some two feet away. Then, gathering her rear legs carefully beneath her, her tail not twitching like that of a domestic cat, she sprang, hit the unsuspecting field vole a terrific stunning whack with her right paw, impaling it on her claws, brought her left paw up, then brought the vole back to her mouth for the death bite. As she bit she flicked her head right and left. The vole shot a foot away but she was on it again as it landed. It was all over in a second. Then with flattened ears she ran with it in her jaws to the gap between the woodshed and the cottage wall and ate it, starting with the head.

There was no attempt to cripple the vole with a bite and then to play with it while it was still alive, as a domestic cat will do. Cleo was about ten weeks old and it was a deadly efficient kill.

That night I gave Patra a dead woodmouse which I had trapped in the kitchen. She sniffed, touched it with a paw, then walked away. She did not appear to know what it was or what to do with it. Although she was bolder, bigger and could often bully her sister's head out of her own milk tin, she was more backward than Cleo as far as wild hunting instincts were concerned.

As the dull wet August continued, and ominous drips on the wooden ceilings told me that the corrugated iron roof had sprung a couple of leaks, I decided to perform my annual blitz on repairs. I drove the 44 miles to the nearest town and bought supplies and materials.

As I performed acrobatic contortions on the roof – fibre-glassing the leaks, cementing the chimneys and painting them – I caught occasional glimpses of the kits prowling through the bracken forests of the north hill. Moobli crept near and quietly sat down, watching me and them, panting contentedly in the warm sunshine, grinning at them in proffered friendship. They now seemed to be accepting that he was not too much of a threat.

In the third afternoon on the roof I became aware that all had gone quiet, like the silence one suddenly notices among children, when one wonders what they are up to. I climbed down my scaffold-ladder device and peered in at the windows. They were all in the kitchen: Cleo and Patra were eating the scraps from Moobli's bowl and he was sitting on his bed, watching them with a fond paternal air, as if they were his cats, his pups!

When I crept through the back door Cleo panicked, darted this way and that, and then shot outside. Patra crouched down low over the bowl, perhaps because Moobli had followed the fleeing Cleo and was now stationed at the door. As I muttered the usual soothing pussy coot phrases, she allowed me to pick her up by the neck scruff for the first time since she was really small. I carried her outside and placed her against the unusually gnarled bark of an old ash tree. This time she climbed up a little way, jerkily, before I lifted her off again and put her into the woodshed with Cleo. That night, after feeding them and spending some time in soothing talk, I managed to pick Cleo up too, although she disliked it and scratched me. I was surprised to find that, though smaller and thinner, she felt heavier than

23

Patra. Her flesh was all muscle and sinew, whereas Patra had plenty of fat. Cleo also had thicker and bigger claws.

For two days I suffered odd attacks of stomach cramps. I had noticed that the kits also seemed subdued and had not left the woodshed at all. Clearly something was wrong, and I decided to check the water supply. I walked up past the waterfalls to the pool where the siphon pipe was wedged under rocks. The decomposing carcass of a large deer hind was lying athwart the brink of the pool and was wedged right on top of the pipe. We were all slowly being poisoned.

With a short rope I hauled it away over the rocks. The stench was appalling. The deer's cheeks fell off, exposing the teeth in an awful laugh. I barely got the corpse into a dry recess between the rocks before I had to give up. Later I disinfected the area and poured disinfectant down the pipe, which I blocked up to let the fluid do its work. For three days I carried water in buckets from the loch, then let the tap run all night to clear out the disinfectant.

Next morning the flow had dried up completely. Now something was blocking the pipe. I undid the joints outside and saw the distorted head of a dead eel. I felt sorry for it as I dug it out of the pipe. After surviving several years in the higher reaches of the burn, it had been on its way for a spell back in the loch before migrating across the Atlantic to spawn in its birth place, the Sargasso Sea. It had travelled far, survived much, and it seemed a shame that its life had to end this way, in an artificial human creation. As it had swum about the pool, looking for a way down the falls, it had followed the gentle flow of water down the luring round hole of the pipe, only to be slowly drowned by the water piling up behind it when it hit the restriction at the far end.

As eels frequently fill their gills with water and travel overland at night in summer dew, I wondered if they ever provided food for nocturnal prowling wildcats. I nailed the dead eel to a chopping block near the woodshed and retired to the workshop window to watch.

Cleo was first to emerge. She pushed her head through the knot-hole entrance, sniffing the air. Then looking carefully about her, she stalked towards the eel, sniffed, then seized it in her teeth. She tried to pull it off the nail, so as to run into hiding with it. Then, realizing it would not budge, she started to chew it with her carnassials. She had recognized it instantly as food. Just then Patra also came out

24

sniffing, but as she crept towards her sister, Cleo let go of the eel, flared and stamped her right paw down hard a few inches away from the eel, a gesture that said unmistakably 'Stay away!' Following the wildcat law of first come, first served, Patra kept her distance. I went out, scaring both cats back into the shed, cut the eel in half and shared it between them.

In fine weather, I usually left the back door ajar to allow Moobli free run around the house at night, for true to his breed he never showed any inclination to wander alone in the hills. One morning I found both cats had come in and climbed into the old bath where I kept the animals' sterilized meat sausages and were busily guzzling away. Contrary to much zoological belief, it was clear that wildcats have excellent scenting power, and in the wild probably rely on it to find carrion when times are hard in winter.

By the end of August both kits were spending more time out in the bracken jungles, and sometimes came back with dead shrews, which they seldom ate because of the distasteful scent glands on the little insectivores' flanks. These active hunting days in the finer weather seemed to make them wilder and hungrier. Now they instantly went for my fingers with their claws the second I put their tins down. To stop this, I upturned the tea chest they had spurned as a bed chamber and, using it as a table, sorted out their four bowls on its surface. Meanwhile, they stalked to and fro beneath, '*mau*'ing their hunger, standing anxiously on their haunches like otters, milling their claws around in the air below me. Then, unable to wait a second longer, Patra leaped up on to the chest and hissed at my fingers as I mixed the meats. When I tried to brush her off with my thick sweatered elbow she resisted and went on the attack, knocking over the milk. They could be as fierce as they liked, I wasn't having them attack me directly. I seized her thick bushy tail and with a quick movement hauled her off the chest. She was on the floor before she had time to dig in her claws. Again there was no revenge; she just kept milling around with Cleo and '*mau*'ing for the food which I put beside them quickly. If they were as fierce as this at feeding time now, I would need to put their food out behind a protecting screen when they were full grown in a year's time.

One late August morning I pushed my typewriter away and went out to lie in the hot sun. Suddenly I heard a loud buzzing noise. Thinking it was just one of the big blue Aeshna dragonflies which often flew close with rattling wings, I opened an eye. It was a giant wood wasp, a thick-bodied, two-inch-long yellow and black insect which was rare in my part of Scotland. I sat up, hoping to catch it for a photo. Cleo leapt up into the air twice, batting out with her paws, and caught it. As I got up she ran away. I took my photo and then put the big harmless wasp on to the bark of a pine tree which was dying after being used as a red deer rubbing post, and on which I hoped it would lay its eggs. Later the photo and sighting were recorded at the British Museum of Natural History in London. Wildcats, it seemed, had uses I had never dreamed of!

As Cleo and Patra were now becoming more adventurous, I took them one calm day to the loch shore and then ran back to the house with Moobli. From the window I watched Patra creeping through the undergrowth, from wads of rushes to bramble bushes, behind bracken patches, keeping well away from the path and all open areas, taking nearly half an hour to cover the sixty yards of strange territory in the glare of daylight, before she reached the safety of the shed.

Cleo stayed by the shore. At dusk, I found her nine feet up an ash tree, clinging to the trunk. Moobli whined when he saw her plight, which only started her '*mau*'ing loudly. She could not turn round and had not discovered how to back down. We went a distance away and watched her work out how to do it. She relaxed one front foot at a time, lowering it a few inches, then reached lower for new footholds with her back feet. When she was only two feet from the ground she decided it was safe enough to take a chance. She looked at the ground intently, put right foot over left and sprang down, landing awkwardly for a cat. Then she ran like a hare straight up the path and into the shed, which clearly she had spotted from her perch up the tree. Although Patra had proved she could climb a little nearly two weeks earlier, this was probably the first time Cleo had ventured to do so, hence her hesitant clumsiness.

Later I heard a slight noise in the kitchen and crept slowly outside to peer in through the kitchen window. Patra was helping herself to the pickings from Moobli's bowl, while he sat on his bed with an intent but doting look. To my further surprise, she walked up to him and they rubbed noses. I never saw it happen again. What had caused such an extraordinary temporary affinity between two such disparate animals I will never know. But several times, when both kittens had been in the kitchen in the early morning taking scraps from his bowl, they had let him step between them and lick up a few crumbs too.

Neither wildcat would let either Moobli or me take or go near food when it was in their bowls. It seemed they both knew now that Moobli would not hurt them, at least inside the house. So far, it appeared he had tamed them as much as, if not more than, I had.

After two nights of lashing rain at about this time, I saw that two windfall larches were causing a blockage in the small run-off burn along the east side of the west wood, flooding a small bed where two uncommon water avens had found a foothold. I rather liked my little water avens with their beautiful, nodding red bell-like heads, for they added a fine dash of colour to the woodside in summer. Dead larches are not much use, even for insect larvae, so I cut up the trees for firewood.

The young cats were away all afternoon as I stacked the logs in the shed. When I went out at dusk with their meal and gave the usual food call – 'Mau, the pussy coots!' – and banged the tin lids together, they both came streaking in from the bracken like striped missiles. Although they did not approach close or walk about with tails up, rubbing against me like domestic cats, it was wonderful to see them come to my call for the first time. Cleo once even allowed me to stroke her, but when I picked her up she instantly scratched and bit my forefinger. I put her down fast. A few minutes later I went back with more food and she was amiable again. It had been a purely instinctive action and she bore no grudges. By now my fingers were lacerated all over from their claws and I wore sticking plaster in several places. Would they never be hand tame?

Both kits began to stay out more at night and slept in the shed by day. Often in the morning Moobli would find Patra in the big rhododendron bush by the path, crouching below the protective, twisted tangle of brown stems. It seemed she was establishing her first small territory, using the bush as headquarters from which to stalk in the dark. On one ocasion, when Moobli and I were indoors and Patra was sitting on some logs, I saw her ears prick up and she looked west. I could see and hear nothing, but a few minutes later a boat came up the loch. She had heard it long before I could. Good sight is usually the main sense attributed to wildcats but it seemed their hearing was equally keen – and of great value when hunting and trying to pinpoint the position of prey rustling about in thick herbage.

In late September the first autumn gales and driving rain began roaring in from the west, whipping the loch surface into a froth and stripping the first leaves from the trees. Alder leaves began to fill my boats and litter the shore. When the first hailstones fell, whole twigs of ash, made heavy by the wet, were torn away. Hazel leaves flapped against the windows and their nuts also began to fall. Occasionally the old ash trees behind the cottage shed small branches which thumped to the ground or fell with a clang on the iron roof.

One wild night I heard Moobli whining in the kitchen. He was at the closed back door, from behind which came loud '*mau*'s. When I opened it I found Patra outside. Bewildered by all the new noises of the storm, she had come to seek shelter in the kitchen. She had probably been coming more at night than Cleo when the door was left open, raiding the bowl of the monstrous but soft-hearted creature who, from long periods of just sitting near by and watching her, she knew meant her no harm. By now the wildcats' faces were changing with growing maturity: Cleo's slimmer and thoroughly feline with oval eyes, Patra's fatter, rounder and the tops of her eyelids almost straight, so that her eyes were like full moons with a slice taken off the top.

Returning from a supply trip one fine day, I found a rabbit that had been freshly killed by traffic on the road. As rabbits are among the favourite larger prey of wildcats, and there were many in the wood up the loch where I intended to release the cats, I decided to start training Cleo and Patra to hunt. I fixed a pulley on to a fence post 35 yards from the window of my heavy workbench. Then I wrapped cellulose tape round the line already on a fishing reel and wound a double line of 66lb breaking strain nylon line round both reel and pulley. By tying first a dead mouse and then the rabbit on the bottom line and reeling in and out, I could make the prey dance, run and bounce through the grass and bracken most realistically.

For three afternoons, at their normal feeding time towards dusk, I tried to teach the kittens to stalk in true wildcat style. Fast or slow, sudden jerky or smooth movements – all could be controlled by the speed of the reel. This naturally worked best with the mouse, for I could make it move and dart about faster.

At first the kits chased the mouse for all they were worth. On the third run Cleo, far keener, with her jet black pupils fully distended, caught the mouse with both sets of claws, snatched it back to her mouth and with two heavy tugs pulled it from the line. She ran into the bracken to eat it.

Hunting the rabbit was altogether different, even though I had fed them short rations the night before. At first both chased it with swiping claws but ran off again as soon as it stopped. On the second day they attacked it but later ignored it and went to investigate the squeaking pulley. So I oiled the pulley. Then they played games but not hunting games. They stood in the path of the moving rabbit, leaping out of the way at the last second and giving it a playful swipe as it went past. I tried letting the rabbit lie until they made a move towards it, then making it leap off. This brought a few more half-hearted attacks, mostly from Patra. She crouched behind tufts of grass and bracken, curled her feet beneath her, quivered, and made sudden dashes, but seldom made contact.

By the third evening they had lost all interest. I took the rabbit off the line. Although I had gutted it to preserve it longer, the carcass was beginning to smell. While I felt it likely that wildcats do eat carrion, their instincts would tell them that dead, slightly off meat would not get up and run. I also realized, by watching them, that for a wildcat every kill would be different from the last because of minute differences in terrain and the individual behaviour of the prey itself.

Even though I moved the pulley site about, the sight of the same rabbit always heading to the workshop window, fishing line fore and aft, the moving pulley – all became associated in their minds. They soon had it worked out as an artificial contrivance. It was interesting to see Patra make five attacks the first day, three on the second and two on the third, while Cleo made five attacks the first day, only two on the second and none at all on the third. Although slightly smaller and skinnier, Cleo was the more shrewd. I finally gave up teaching them to hunt when hordes of bluebottle flies chased the rabbit far harder than the cats.

Two evenings later, Cleo brought a dead common shrew back to the shed, as if to tell me 'We do know how to hunt, you know!' It had been slashed in the neck, almost certainly killed by claw stroke alone.

Nevertheless, I was disappointed by what I felt to be a poor showing towards the rabbit prey. The kits were reaching the age when they needed more roughage in fur and feather than I was able to give them, and I doubted if voles, mice and shrews, which only

Cleo seemed to be catching (though she never ate the shrews), would be enough when they were mature. Perhaps I'd spoiled them, and they would be unable to hunt large prey.

Something else happened late one afternoon to make me doubt the wisdom of having two growing wildcats loose around the home. I had a bird table a couple of yards from my study window. Few birds used it in summer, but as insects and vegetable food became harder to find chaffinches, great tits, blue tits, blackbirds and robins were all returning to it regularly. I was sitting at my desk when Cleo looked fixedly at the tail of a chaffinch protruding over the edge as it pecked into a hunk of brown bread, and made a clumsy leap. The bird escaped easily, leaving Cleo to hang for a moment from the table by her front claws. I opened the window and shooed her away. I had not thought about this danger to the birds around the table.

I grew even more concerned when on a trek to the east I found the remains of a deer calf and near by the unmistakable four-toed prints of a large wildcat. One of the legends attached to these creatures was that the big toms will often eat young kittens. Although wildcats are said to have a territory of roughly 150 acres, such generalizations about a solitary, largely nocturnal, predatory animal seem arbitrary, for a rough hunting area must depend entirely on the kind of terrain and available prey. A wildcat with a den in a wooded rocky ravine, flanked on each side by desolate bog and tussock country, might hunt nearly all its life in the ravine. Although these tracks were a mile and a half from the cottage, and I had never found prints or droppings nearer, much of the route back was flanked by cliffs close to the shore. It seemed to me quite possible that a big cat could make spasmodic raids from that far away.

As if to confirm my doubts during another spell of bad weather, both young cats came in the back door at night and broke into a new sterilized meat carton, ripping it open with their claws.

While they were often out in light rain, the autumn winds and swirling leaves certainly scared them, and they were now more belligerent at feeding times. On the day the first snow fell on the top of the big mountain, Cleo tried to bite my hand as I put the food down. I pushed her off with the toe of my boot, which she also swatted and clawed.

Next night Cleo again attacked before I could remove my hand. She growled and bit my right forefinger. Without thinking, I tapped her backside with the other hand. She let go, dropped to the floor and spat as I sucked my bleeding finger. Then she squeezed her flattened broad head sideways and slid between crevices in the logs, her body (with its pliable ribs) able to go anywhere her head could fit.

I was sorry then, and felt I had finally learned my lesson. Never, ever, get angry with a wild animal, no matter what it does to you, short of serious injuries of course. A wildcat acts instantly, upon pure instinct, without pause to reason first. It was foolish of me to have taken Cleo's latest attacks personally. Because I, too, had acted on mere instinct, I had undone weeks of work. There would clearly be many problems as they grew bigger, and from then onwards I wore thick gauntlets over leather gloves when I fed them.

I was by no means sure that I wanted to part with the wildcats, but I decided to write with a preliminary enquiry to Dr Michael Brambell, whose name I had found in the London Zoo's annual report. I knew that the Zoo was moving away from its old policy of keeping animals singly in cages, and was creating larger habitats with natural conditions, where breeding pairs or groups could live. I suggested that if later I felt my two females would not survive healthily in the wild, the Zoo might care to have both, or just one, from which to breed.

'I don't want to keep them as pets,' I wrote. 'If they have to be captive, they might well serve as inspiration and education to thousands of kids who know little of our wildlife heritage . . .'

Next day both cats were absent at feeding time. Only by working round the land in decreasing circles with Moobli could I herd them back into the shed area. Patra took one mouthful of food and ran between the logs. Cleo flatly refused to come in until I went away.

At dawn on the fifth day after my contretemps with Cleo I spotted her working through the blackberry thickets and the tangles of grass, soft rush and hogweed in front of the cottage. She had found a vole colony in the rocky tunnels below the topsoil.

I worked quietly outside, peeling logs, ignoring her completely. At night feed time she brought a vole into the shed as I stood outside, dropped it, ate her food, then picked up the vole again and took it into the logs to eat it. At least she had returned while I was near, but it took several more days, putting titbits of steak and liver in her bowl on the logs, to win back her trust, even to the low level at which it had been before.

31

On Saturday October 5 I boated up the loch for mail. Among the letters was one from London Zoo. The postmistress asked me how my wildcats were faring, and told me of a young man who had come to live in a glen a few miles to the south with a university grant to study wildcats. Back at home I opened Dr Brambell's letter.

'We cannot take your two wildcats. I have a male and really feel we should be finding somewhere with better accommodation for it.' He added that he knew of a Yorkshire gamekeeper who wanted to keep a species of wildcat, and had written to him suggesting the possibility of the Zoo's old male and also my two females. Could he put the man in direct touch with me?

At that moment, when I realized there was an increasing interest in this rare member of our fauna, my serious wildcat project was born. If my females did become too belligerent as they grew bigger, I could always build a large natural pen for them. Perhaps I could achieve something from the educational point of view by writing about them myself. I wrote back saying I would carry on with their care myself. Then I added:

'In fact, if the gamekeeper doesn't want the wildcat tom you have, and it is capable of reproducing, perhaps I could take him too.'

The thought of breeding wildcats intrigued me. What better home could the Zoo's old wildcat tom have than here in the wild woods at Wildernesse? Little did I realize what lay ahead.

Sylvesturr, sixteen pounds of wildness incarnate. A foot stamp and a loud spitting *'PAAAH!'* was his usual welcome.

above: My only photograph of the wildcat tom which could have been Cleo and Patra's father.

below: The late Geoffrey Kinns captures the magnificent defensive ferocity of a wildcat male at bay in an enclosure.

above: Cleo and Patra at seven weeks old. One kit sometimes put its paw on the other's head to stop it reaching the food.

below: A week later both kits proved they had no fear of heights.

above: At eleven weeks Cleo could climb confidently but seemed fearful about getting down.

below: Patra scented out a dead woodmouse I left near their woodshed quarters, while Cleo found and ate the eel.

3 · Spitting Image

During the short Indian summer of early October, the two cats took to sunning themselves in front of corrugated iron pyramids I had erected to keep my spare timber dry. Whenever Moobli or I came round the corner, they dived for cover beneath these sheets. If Moobli put his nose too close, Cleo growled and swiped out with her claws. By now Moobli was so used to this that he could antici-pate it and perform a swift little shuffle out of the way. Once, as he gazed at Patra in the sun, lying still several yards away so she would not panic, Cleo came up the path from the rhododendron bush and out of the long grass right in front of him. Surprised, he got to his feet. Neither cat would face Moobli in the open if there was time to run, so Cleo ran, and when she did he naturally followed. She scooted up an old fence post and balanced precariously on top, growling and flaring as Moobli whined and reared upwards from below. He was playing, she was not. I called him away and approached her with the thick gauntlets. Instead of spitting, she just crouched down with ears depressed. Reckoning she could not claw me without losing her balance, I seized her neck scruff without much protest and carried her inside the shed where Patra too had fled after Moobli jumped up. Cleo did not dive into the logpile but merely crouched there, looking at me, as if knowing I had saved her from danger.

That evening, as they lay in their bed together after their feed, both cats started licking each other while I stayed quietly near by. Suddenly I heard an odd clattering, almost purring sound, louder and slower than a domestic cat's, and with a faint whistling note to it. It was Cleo, sounding as if her voice box had broken loose. I had never heard either cat purr before. Taking advantage of her sudden good mood, I gingerly put out my gloved hand and, for only the second time, Cleo let me stroke her. What odd creatures they are, I thought. I hoped such progress would continue, because if they stayed wild the day would come when I could no longer handle them even with gloves. As yet they were only a little over five months old.

Later in October I received another letter from Dr Brambell:

I do not know if our wildcat is capable of reproducing. I have no reason to believe that it is not. If you have a cage to keep ours in beside yours but not with them until they have become familiar, I should think it might well work. I'd be very happy to get our wildcat rehoused and would only ask that you give him a good home.

Now I had a long journey ahead, for I felt it wiser to go down to London and fetch the cat in the Land Rover rather than have him sent up in the noisy cold guards van of a train. As I wrote my reply next day, there was a blurred streak outside the window. Patra, like Cleo earlier, had stalked round the cottage and had made a leap for the birds on the table. They escaped easily. As she swung to and fro on her front claws like a gymnast, I realized that this could be an increasing problem in the hard winter months. I had hoped the wildcats would wander widely for prey as they grew older, only returning at night to their familiar home in the woodshed. Cleo was now roaming alone and foraging further afield – we once surprised her in the west wood – but Patra seemed more inclined to stay around the cottage area.

A few nights later Patra leaped on to the lighted window sill to catch moths that were attracted by the bright paraffin lamp. She munched them up, wings and all, as if they were cornflakes. Later, with the light out, I saw Cleo also catching moths by moonlight. It seemed these insects were a part of their natural diet, at least while young.

In early November I began to make a small temporary run for the tomcat. Realizing that he would be bigger and stronger than the females, I constructed it with ash poles and one-inch wire netting, with the strong box I had used for bringing the kittens home fixed on one end for bed and shelter. At least it would hold him until I had made a large natural enclosure among the rocks, bushes and wild plants in what seemed a perfect spot just west of the cottage.

I had long ago worked out a plan for leaving the cats in the woodshed while I travelled south to collect the tomcat. Six pints of sterilized milk were mixed with water and put into a slightly tipped bowl, then covered partly with a plank so the cats could drink but not spill it. Near by was another bowl of pure water. I hung half-cooked sheep's hearts and liver on the walls at varying heights so that they would have to work for their food, and put beef and eight 15-ounce sterilized meat sausages around the logs. I would be away for only a week but they had enough food for a month, and in the cold weather the half-cooked meat would keep fresh for a long time. Then I locked the doors and widened their exit hole.

Next day the wind and rain turned to squalls of hail. With the box for the wildcat, sleeping bag, food and other gear I needed in London covered with a thick plastic sheet held down in the boat by rocks, Moobli and I waited until one heavy squall had passed and then, in the pocket of relative peace, set off. We covered three miles before the next squall hit us, and I was soaked when we reached the Land Rover in the wood six and a half miles away. The long drive to London seemed a welcome period of luxurious ease after such a boat trip.

On the fourth day I kept my appointment with Dr Brambell at the Zoo. The Curator of Mammals turned out to be a tall, broad-shouldered man who was full of enthusiastic plans for his new breeding units and the new gorilla and lion houses. He was a few years younger than me, and often spent holidays camping and boating in Scotland a few miles south of my home. After we had talked about animals for a while, he seemed satisfied I would take good care of the Zoo's only wildcat, and took me to meet the youngest head keeper, Nobby Clarke, a tall, dark-haired Cockney who was in charge of small mammals.

Clarke told me that the wildcat was getting on in age. He had been caught in the Highlands as a kitten, had spent two and a half years at the Welsh Mountain Zoo in Colwyn Bay, and had been taken in by London Zoo in April 1968. So he had been in captivity for nearly all his ten years.

I said I would pick him up the following Monday, and put down the stout wooden box I had brought for him. The two men looked at each other.

'Er, I don't think that box will be suitable,' Nobby Clarke said. 'We could perhaps let you have one of our special boxes if you'll send it back to us.' As I agreed he added, 'Would you like to see him first? I could show him to you now.'

I was certainly anxious to see the tomcat from which I hoped to breed before introducing him back to the wild. As we passed the glass front of his pen, I peered in eagerly, but the cat was not to be seen. He was in the den at the back.

'We always get him in there first, then shut the door while we clean out his cage or put his food in,' Clarke said.

I thought his tone of voice a trifle odd. We went along a corridor at the back of the cage block and stopped by a black door.

'He's in there.'

As the keeper raised the trapdoor of the cubicle, I bent down expecting to see a rather large type of tabby cat with a fine bushy tail. First I heard a growl that sounded as if it came from a small lion, then as my eyes came level – '*PAAAH!*' – a blast of hot steamy air shot past my face and I was looking into the great, mad, gold eyes of the Devil incarnate. The cat was well over 3 feet long, thick-bodied and broad-headed. He was standing at full stretch on powerful braced forepaws, one of which he had just smashed down in front of him to accompany what Dr Brambell called his spit. Spit? It sounded more like a small charge of dynamite going off! As I stared at the open mouth, the curled rasping red tongue, the fearsome array of brownish teeth and sabre-like canines, the flattened ears, I could have sworn I saw flames flickering behind those huge malevolent eyes.

'Holy crow!' I heard myself say in a far-off voice.

'I suppose you'll not be back for him on Monday,' Nobby Clarke said, seeing the shock on my face. I managed to recover.

'I'll be here,' I said, trying to look more confident than I felt. 'He'll be more of a handful than I expected, but I've come all this way, so I'll take him.'

'It'll be interesting,' the keeper remarked with masterly understatement when he heard that I hoped to pair the ferocious wildcat with one of my two females.

Later, as we discussed the wildcat's diet and the sort of draught-proof den I should make for him, both men agreed that, pound for pound, the wildcat tom was probably the fiercest animal in the Zoo. Not once, in all the years of his captivity, had he shown the slightest liking or even momentary toleration towards those who fed and cared for him.★

Clearly the small temporary run I had made back home would be hopelessly inadequate. Such an animal, as powerfully muscled as a small cougar, could have torn his way out of it with ease. While he was similar in colouring and shape to my ungrown females, there was a great difference in size, for he was an exceptionally large and magnificent specimen. Over the next three days I searched for and bought nearly £50-worth of thick green plastic-covered Rylock fencing for the tom's enclosure. I also had a roof-rack fitted to the Land Rover so that I could keep the inside clear of ropes, boat engine, tank, all my new supplies and gear, and the fencing itself. On the Monday I went to pick up the wildcat.

It had been put into one of the Zoo's big, barred, black animal boxes, complete with galvanized water and food containers. Both men wished me luck with the venture. As I left I thought I heard one of the under-keepers say, 'Is that bastard really going?'

I struggled over the asphalt with my unused box under one arm and the 16lb cat hissing and growling in the Zoo box clutched by the other. A stocky under-keeper who had worked with the tom offered to carry it for me.

'We called him Sylvester – after the cartoon cat,' he said. 'You'll need to be very careful. I went into his pen once and he dived at my head from a high tree branch. Would probably have scalped me, but I just got out fast enough and shut the door as he struck it.'

I knew then I would call him Sylvesturr, because of the awful low growl he was making . . . *'urrr urrr'*, like a dynamo throbbing deep in the bowels of the earth. I put him on the floor at the back of my vehicle, covered his box with a cloth, instructed Moobli not to bother him, and managed the 570-mile journey home in 14 hours.

★ In later correspondence Nick Jackson, Curator of the Welsh Mountain Zoo, informed me: 'He came to Colwyn Bay in an attempt to commence breeding, but as great difficulty was found in obtaining a female, and as his presence could not be justified from an exhibition point of view, it was decided to send him to a collection where he could be paired. He arrived in Colwyn Bay certainly not as a kitten but probably between one and two years old. During his stay here he proved to be a ferocious and highly secretive animal . . .'

It was hard driving in a loaded Land Rover, with foggy patches north of Preston which worsened around Glasgow. When we stopped on the big hill overlooking Loch Tulla, sleet was falling in the silent darkness. Sylvesturr clawed some liver from my gloved hands and ate with great relish, despite his growls. The journey did not seem to be upsetting him too much. After heating a can of soup, I put the bed down in the back. With Moobli's vast snoring form cramming me against the wall, and to the sound of Sylvesturr's low growls every time I moved, I managed some brief sleep.

The next day dawned with cold blue skies. When I approached with his breakfast, Sylvesturr gave a loud hiss and made his low growl, like distant thunder or the start of a minor earthquake. Already he was proving to be a cunning old cat for he had not once dashed about inside the box, trying to force a way out, nor had he fouled himself by disturbing the sawdust.

As we boated up the loch in the sunlight, the somnolent belligerent gloom that seemed to be his dominant expression lifted slightly. His great golden eyes glared between the bars as he watched the passing oaks and alders. His face registered the fact that he knew he was somewhere different. Perhaps the idyllic mountain landscape evoked memories of his long-ago kittenhood.

I carried Sylvesturr up the path. Patra sat at the top, as if to greet us, while the pink nose and long white whiskers of Cleo peeped from the edge of the rhododendron bush. They ran for cover as we approached. They still had some milk and water left, and there was red blood on the bone of the remaining meat. We could not have timed it better.

I swiftly made a temporary run from the stout wooden 2ft-square box, the aluminium frame of an old deck chair and stout half-inch wire netting. Then, wearing three sweaters, an old jacket and the thick gauntlets and gloves, and making sure that all gaps were blocked with spare netting, I tipped Sylvesturr into it. He landed with a loud hiss, went straight into the attack, spat and then huddled in the back of the box. I put a large beach towel over the sides of the netting, to darken it and make him feel more secure. Then I heaved the whole contraption into the wintry sunlight for warmth.

A few minutes later I saw Patra investigating this new cage, but a sudden spit – *'PAAAH!'* – sent her fleeing. Then Cleo, sniffing gently, moved close and gazed in with eyes like dark lamps. Apparently Sylvesturr tolerated her approach because he did not spit at her. I thought this extraordinary, for he had never seen another cat since his mother when he was a kitten, yet he appeared not to find the wilder Cleo disturbing.

When Moobli approached the cage, he went instantly on the attack – '*PAAAH!*' – slamming his right paw down on the ground, then clawing the netting with his left. Moobli leaped back several paces. Sylvesturr repeated the performance at my approach, and I noticed with a slight jump of the heart that his horn-coloured talons were over an inch long. Moobli started to bark, but the big cat stood his ground, braced at full height, glaring from me to the dog. I had no doubt that if the cage had not been there and he had gone too close, Moobli would have lost at least an eye. Unlike a truly wild wildcat, which, if it can, will flee and hide, Sylvesturr was used to humans, had found they were afraid of him, and so had become more dangerous to them or any dog he knew to be with them. I had to get things right from the start. Although I hated myself for it, I whacked Moobli hard with my hand, told him to stop barking and spent some time explaining to him that Sylvesturr was now one of us.

From that moment on, Moobli never again acknowledged Sylvesturr's presence. He looked through the big cat as if it was not there. Yet his fascination for the two young females, especially Patra, remained as strong as ever.

For four days I worked (mostly in the rain) to make a natural roofed enclosure for Sylvesturr in the sunny area west of the cottage, where there was a big natural rockery, with small hazel bushes, ferns, bracken, brambles and entwining honeysuckle. To give him both flat ground and the rocky habitat wildcats like, I cut right through the high rockery, heaving the boulders out with a crowbar. Then I drove in the side and end posts to a height of five feet. The den, some 3½ft long by 1½ft wide, was made with large smooth rocks, the earth lined with polyurethane chips to repel any moisture that might seep up. Gravel went on top of that, covered with brown dry bracken and masses of hay cut from the front pasture. The den roof was made of larch slabs, lined with hay and covered with Perspex sheets, then lined again with hay and topped with a sheet of aluminium, tipped slightly for draining. The whole den was then covered with armfuls of loose bracken. I made a stout wooden door with a curved entrance hole and slung it from the cats' hunter-training pulley so that I could raise or lower it from outside the pen. I also built wooden draught excluders to deflect the prevailing wind.

Right from the start, Sylvesturr proved to be a frightening creature. I could never move near him without seeing those great eyes upon me, watching every move. During fine spells I placed his cage so that he could watch me making his enclosure, watch me working with hammer, saw, pliers, or wielding the sledgehammer, skinning my hands as I heaved out the rocks, and stretching and digging the fencing into the ground. My slender hope was that after the drive, the boat trip and all this building work for him, he might recognize me as different from other humans whom he was prepared to attack. What a forlorn hope! As soon as I went near him he stood up with a growl. I had never seen such a glance as his, not even from an eagle. It was most disconcerting. He seemed even more wary of Moobli, spitting the moment he came into view. This surely was a hereditary fear dating from the time when wolves and more wildcats inhabited Britain. Just putting his meat into the cage was a tricky operation. The moment he scented it, he came out on the attack to get it, and I had to withdraw my hand fast through the roof flap.

He seemed almost too independent for his own good. How on earth was I to treat him if ever he became sick? Never, since he had been torn away from these wild hills as a small kitten, had he permitted a single human hand to touch him.

Transferring Sylvesturr from the heavy box-cage to the pen was tricky, and I don't mind admitting I muttered a silent prayer. I had to hold the whole contraption three feet off the ground, with the box end thrust into the triangular flap in the fencing. There was a gap below the box in the region of my groin through which he could thrust to escape. I had little faith in the flimsy wire netting, especially as it fell away slightly when I went to shake the fearsome creature out. Calling Moobli for support, I shook and shook as the wildcat growled and hissed with rage before finally landing on the ground. Instantly he glared round at me, spat loudly and launched a direct attack. I growled back even louder, from defensive fear. Then he saw Moobli and went for him through the fencing as I desperately struggled to retrieve the box-cage from the pen door and shut it all up. Suddenly the cat spotted the entrance to the den and shot quietly into it, his long bushy black and buff striped tail following like a snake. It was a success, without injury to any party.

When I went out two hours later Sylvesturr had gone. I checked every inch of the pen but there was no sign of him. By torchlight I eventually found that he had forced his way on to the top of the cardboard box that lined the den. In time his weight would crush it. I now had to get that box out again. Remembering what I had learnt with cougars in Canada, I hastily turned the box-cage into a cat trap, with a falling door at the back held up by a nail which would be whipped away by a mousetrap spring when anything took the bait. Poling a piece of plywood against the den's entrance hole, to keep the cat inside, I set the cage-cum-trap and at midnight found him safely caught in it. I carried him to the porch, intending next day to remove the cardboard box and make his den smaller and cosier.

By morning Sylvesturr had escaped. In the dark I had failed to hook the flap down properly and he had forced his way out between the roof and wall netting, despite a five-inch overlap. Now what? Thrusting Moobli's head into the trap for a good strong scent, I pointed to the ground and gave the usual command when making him follow animal trails in the woods and hills. Track it, Moobli. Track the pussy coots! This was only the second time I had asked him to track cats and I was afraid his dislike of Sylvesturr would make him refuse. Instead he instantly took off, zig-zagged with nose down round the pens and through the front pasture. Then he came back up from the shore and headed past some hazel clumps into the west wood. Within minutes he was by the big rocky cairn east of the rock escarpment – exactly the spot I had thought a wildcat would choose. When I caught up he was whining and pacing over the rocks by the hole from which came unmistakable growls and flares. Moobli would not put his nose into the entrance itself, nor was Sylvesturr going to come out now he was safe. I set the trap between the wood and his pen.

After a night of gales and hail showers, I hurried out anxiously. Cleo was in the trap. She had obviously scented the meat from the woodshed, a good 40 yards away. Worried about Sylvesturr being out without food in such weather after his sheltered zoo years, I blocked Cleo and Patra in the shed and set the trap again, this time near the dark shelter of the rhododendron bush by the path. I reckoned he might come back to the area where he had been fed during the first few days.

While dozing next morning, I heard a slight thud and rushed out half dressed. There was Sylvesturr perfectly caught, and all the meat gone. So he *had* come back around the area when he was hungry.

That was a small victory in itself. When he saw me, he raged up and down, then fled into the box again. I quickly made his den cosier by lowering the roof, putting wood at the back and stuffing all crevices with thick hay and bracken. Then I put the wildcat back into the pen. This time he ran straight into his den without even looking round, an example of what I found out later was an extraordinary memory.

Happier with the smaller den, he soon made a bowl in the hay in which to lie, long bushy tail curved round so that its thick black tip showed from beneath his chin. I watched him carefully through early December, wondering how he would adjust to the cold outdoors. Luckily the weather co-operated, for at first there were more sunny calm days than gale-ridden ones, the latter occurring only occasionally as if to serve as brief toughen-up courses. He usually ate just after sunset, taking the liver first then returning for the rest about an hour later. His appetite increased. I weaned him to life outside as gently as possible, erecting a screen in front of his den in the worst winds, cutting a hole in his food pan so rain water would drain out, or moving it under his den roof if rain was heavy.

Several times after dark I found him exploring his new territory, sniffing delicately at the posts, his long white whiskers twitching like feelers. Although I had put heavy wire liner along the fencing bottom and dug it six inches into the ground, setting rocks and logs round the outsides too, he never once tried to dig his way out. At first he darted back into his den when he heard us coming, but after a week he grew more confident. As his body stocked up against the cold and his tawny grey-striped coat grew thicker, he became more hungry. He was less afraid of the hissing paraffin lamp than of human or dog forms looming up in the dusk. His eyes proclaimed his age, for they flashed with a dull yellow against the light and the sides of his pupils were pitted in two places with black spots – quite different from the brilliant bluey-green flashes of Cleo and Patra's youthful eyes.

I could never be sure how he would react when I approached with his food. For several nights he advanced out of his den the moment he smelled the meat. First a muscular foreleg would emerge before a broad head. He would then look about him, hissing. He had a crazy, sideways glance that was the prelude to a swift attack. As I put the food through the fencing into his pan, he looked at it, rushed out in a furious attack, stopped an inch or two away from the fence and slammed down his foot with a blasting '*PAAAH!*'. He glared straight into my eyes for a second or two before seizing a piece of meat and running back with it. At other times he flew out, '*PAAAH!*', and stood his ground, guarding his meat with a big outstretched paw between it and myself, growling while he ate. Once he stalked the lamp and, after one bouncing bound, flew straight at the fencing and spat as he hit it a hard blow with extended claws that had a spread of almost two and a half inches.

While I did not wish to cow him, these attacks could not be allowed to continue. If I kept flinching as I did, he might continue with the habit when I released him in the wild. I took to standing my ground, knowing the fencing would hold him, and growling back while waving the light, which kept him away from my fingers.

Although it became clear over the first few weeks that Sylvesturr would never, in any sense, become even half tame, I felt a strong empathy with him. I was living totally alone, six and a half miles from my nearest neighbour, up a lonely loch where I never even saw another boat for eight months of the year. I lived in the wilds now because after many big city years in countries halfway across the world, rare wilderness wildlife had become all that really interested me. So, in some ways, Sylvesturr seemed almost a soulmate. For me, this fierce old wildcat became a symbol of independence. Unloved, unlovable, he would be a loner to the end. I *liked* him, admired his cussed, prehistoric magnificence. It seemed increasingly important to try to breed from him and, if it could be done safely, to release him and his progeny back into the wild.

Yet his irascibility was largely confined to humans and dogs. One afternoon I saw a feathered thorn-moth fluttering over the grass before his den. He watched it for a few seconds before coming out and putting his paw on it. He did it softly, not killing it, as if he just wanted to slow it down so he could see it better. There was an odd, almost kindly expression in his big eyes as he looked at it, and presently it fluttered up and away. It was probably the first moth he had ever seen, and he did not seem to regard it as food, as did young Cleo and Patra.

Although the two females occasionally walked outside Sylvesturr's pen, looking in at him with huge eyes, he showed little interest in them. His eyes followed their movements but he did not come out on the attack, or even move. Perhaps he regarded them as mere

43

attachments of man. Perhaps they were prowling for extra food. Certainly, after four days of heavy south-westerly gales and lashing rain, which scared the females, all the cats became hungrier and were eating almost two pounds of meat and cat food daily.

Cleo never entered the house now, though Patra would when I was not there, taking advantage of Moobli's liking for her. She once deceived him into thinking she would allow him to give her a lick, but her eyes were darting about for food, and as soon as she located the half-sausage in the sink, she was up after it and off so fast that Moobli hardly saw her go. Patra was cunning about the house and ate voraciously even when her stomach was distended. I felt she could possibly be partly tamed in time. But Cleo, never.

An hour after putting out Sylvesturr's food I used to peer round the cottage corner to make sure he had eaten it. One evening I saw Patra stealing along by his front fencing. She stopped in front of his half-full pan, and as he watched her through the curved hole of his door, she stretched in a paw and tried to scoop some food out with her claws. Instantly he shot out of the den, but instead of a loud '*PAAAH!*' and an enraged foot stamp, he put his head close to hers and delivered a discreet small spit. It was enough to terrify her. She might not have seen him coming for he moved like lightning, but the sight of the great head sent her scurrying back to the woodshed as fast as her legs would carry her. Sylvesturr then ate the rest of his food, between growls, out in the open. He was taking no more chances.

Next day, needing cat and dog food, and with mail to post, we fought our way down the windy loch. The waves were so rough I had to sit in the stern, constantly adjusting the engine throttle. At the village store I set my pack down by the Land Rover's rear wheel, went back for an extra purchase, forgot about the pack and reversed over it. Now I had to buy a new pack. As I also wanted a flash unit for my camera in order to photograph Sylvesturr, who seldom came out before dusk, there were good reasons for making a trip to the town over 40 miles away – a rare chore I usually put off as long as possible.

I did not go next day, however, as the first heavy snowfall of winter arrived, and went out tracking instead.

Following our wildcats' four-toed prints in the snow, I was surprised by how much ground they had covered in the night. One set followed the edge of the path, around the boats and along the shore for about 100 yards before turning back to the garden. From the shed more tracks led into the east wood, one set crossing a fallen tree that bridged the burn and covering 50 yards of the far shore. In front of the house the tracks criss-crossed. They had clearly hunted a long time in the bramble banks. Between them (though each hunted alone) they had covered over half a mile in the cold crisp snow. I found no trace of a kill. Both had walked round Sylvesturr's pen, and inside it his larger tracks showed that he too had been on the move. I had read somewhere that wildcats lie up in rain and snow, except when driven out by hunger, yet these three had been extremely active despite being well fed. There was still food left in Syl's pen.

Two days later, with drizzle melting the snow, we made it to the town. When I had completed the shopping I was hailed across the street by a man I knew as Willie, a Council worker who had a great admiration for Moobli and who owned two pet foxes. He offered to show them to me, and I went with him to the lochside where he lived in an old caravan, below the railway line. The foxes, sister and brother, were in a small run near by, from which he took them for walks as if they were pet dogs. They were beautiful creatures with thick red coats, black ears and feet, and they moved with the cat-like grace of raccoons. The bigger dog fox had lovely bright orange eyes, and when I put my hand down, he nuzzled it gently with his wet nose. I coveted them immediately and said he was lucky to have them.

Willie then told me that he had just retired, that a new by-pass road was about to be constructed beside the loch, and as a result he had had to leave his home. He was now living on a caravan site in a village some 11 miles to the north where there was nowhere to keep the foxes. He was coming back to the town each day to feed the foxes and take them for runs while he was trying to make up his mind what to do with them.

I found myself gabbling – I would be glad to take them, studying wildlife was my work, I would make a big natural run for them between two up-ended stumps in my east wood, they would be in a perfect wild environment away from the town ... I would gladly pay him for them, look after them well, let him know how they were faring ... And at the end of my peroration, Willie said he would be happy to let me take them the following week.

Two tame foxes, I thought, as we boated home in high winds.

What a windfall! It seemed our little run of bad luck was at an end. When I went to feed Sylvesturr three hours later, for the first time he did not spit, flare or growl. Instead, he just watched quietly as I put his food down. Maybe the deathly silence around the house had worried him and he was actually grateful that he was to be fed after all.

I started to build a 12-ft temporary run for the foxes from spare timber and fencing. It was bitterly cold in the gales and hail showers, but the work had to be done well, with the fencing stapled all along its length on every strut so the foxes could not dig their way out. I fixed an upward hinged gate at one end.

The late December day on which I went back to the town to fetch the foxes was a disaster from the start. After a calm dawn, the south-west gales started again half an hour before I hauled the boat down. Holding it against the waves with one hand while I loaded an empty calor gas container, fuel tank and pack with the other, I pulled a back muscle badly. We fought our way down the loch and got the anchor stuck under a tree root at the other end. Complicated prodding with a larch pole freed it, but resulted in icy water filling both my boots.

Willie looked pale and drawn when finally we met. His brother, near whom he now lived, had been killed in a car crash. I went with him to his butcher and bought nearly £7 worth of meat for the foxes and the cats. Then, as it was my last day out before Christmas, I asked him if he would mind waiting until I had bought last-minute supplies before we transferred the foxes to my Land Rover and discussed their future care.

Rain was pouring down as I returned to Willie, and someone had stolen my driving windscreen wiper. As I struggled to transfer the other over with a pair of pliers, Willie stood with the vixen in his arms, his face haggard and miserable. Now that the moment had come, he could not bear to part with his beloved foxes.

'Oh dear,' I said, despite my keen disappointment, 'you don't want to let them go, eh?'

Suddenly he seemed confused and, nervously shouting that I could pick them up some other time, he ran away through the rain like a gawky two-legged giraffe, with the shivering vixen in his arms, not towards the pen where the dog fox was pacing alone, but back towards the town.

I stood there drenched, miserable, furious with myself for not having taken the foxes first, so giving Willie no time to think. As I saw the poor man vanishing between the buildings, I knew in my heart I could not take the foxes if it meant his unhappiness. I drove sullenly back to the boat.

The anchor had dragged in the gale, and we arrived at the mooring to find the boat stern banging up and down on the gravelly shore. The journey up the loch was the worst of the year. In almost pitch darkness, we made our way by following the line of the hills, almost indiscernible against the sky. I kept the boat hugging the southern shore, then rode the alarmingly deep and fast-running waves across the loch at the last minute. Landing the boat and all the gear was a dangerous operation in the gloom. After hauling everything over to the landward side of the boat, I swung it round so that the keel and bow were thrust into the waves and leapt off, heaving my supplies ashore and then dragging the boat up the grass bank, one end at a time before the crashing waves filled it completely. Boat and engine weighed some 600 lbs, so this frantic activity did nothing for my strained back.

I walked up the muddy path in the wind and rain, drenched and trembling. All those risks, to return home foxless to another lonely Christmas in the wilds! Sylvesturr had resumed his usual belligerence and came straight out on the warpath with a foot stamp and a loud '*PAAAH!*' I stared at him for a moment.

'And *PAAAH!* to you too!' I yelled back, stamping my foot so hard on the ground that it shook.

His ferocious glare turned to one of astonishment, and for the first time he turned tail and shot back into his den.

Although I felt very depressed, there was one consolation. The new fox run turned out to be a blessing in disguise. Not only could I now use it to keep the females away from the bird table, it could become a forcing ground for a close introduction between them and Sylvesturr. By setting the pen endways to his in early spring – when I hoped the mating urge would come upon the wildcats – I could keep them close together and still protect the females from any possible attack. It would be a tricky operation, but I had plenty of time to work out the details.

On Christmas morning I made a rich dough of four pounds of wholemeal bread, prepared a small turkey and shoved them both in the Calor gas oven together. Then I took Moobli for a two-mile trek in the hills, despite the constant drizzle and cold south-east wind. After my own royal feast of turkey, I fed the animals like fighting cocks with it, and tried to make friends with Sylvesturr.

Before, I had always put all his food down at once, and depending on how hungry he was, he either came out on the attack to get it or stayed glaring from the den door, growling, until I had gone away. I wondered if this was because he regarded my continued presence as a threat. Perhaps he thought I might take it all away again. So I tried a new method. For over an hour I sat in the rain hunched in my grass-green oilskins, and slowly, one by one dropped titbits into his pan. At first he growled from the den door, but as I did not move he came out, grabbed the small portion and took it back inside. I persisted, with very small bits, and finally he realized I was only staying there to feed him. Suddenly he associated me with a constant food supply and relaxed enough to come and feed near me, munching away with his side teeth. Occasionally his great golden eyes would switch on to me warningly. His old teeth grated together as he chewed, and he went '*noine, noine, noine*' deep in his throat. In an affectionate voice, I imitated him, '*noine, noine, noine*'. The fact that he soon stopped doing it was worth his first look of disgust. Although it was gratifying to see him feed in the open near me for the first time without foot stamps or spits, I had no real wish to tame him for eventually I intended to let him go. I did not repeat the experiment.

On Boxing Day I put the two females into the fox pen with a thick wooden rubber-roofed den box I had made. Cleo accepted the fact that she could not escape after a careful look round and went to sleep in the box. Patra got her head stuck three times in the fencing squares as I watched from the bedroom window. The last time, she failed to get it back again and started bawling like a squawking duck. With gloved hands, I managed to get her head back through the fence wire as she sank her teeth into the gloves, luckily missing my fingers. After feeding them in the run I let them out again two hours later.

4 · *Touch and Go*

New Year opened on a sad note. I found a newly dead red deer hind, with a calf behind her, as if they had both fallen while running in echelon, their legs stretched out as if still pacing. Red deer were originally woodland animals before farming and forestry fencing forced them on to the bare Scottish hills. In cold wet winters, their strength sapped by poor food, warble fly holes in their coats, the oldest and youngest animals with severe infections of lung worms and nasal bot fly grubs rapidly weaken. They return to whatever woods they can find for shelter, finally dying from pneumonia.

There was no point in wasting the deer meat. The wildcats and Moobli ate a great deal between them, and the deer would save me long trips up the stormy loch. Making sure the calf was dead, I hauled it on to a downward slope and bled it while I skinned the hind, taking a shoulder and one haunch for dog and cats.

Her calf was very young, probably late-born in September or even early October, after its mother had perhaps come into a second season and mated with one of the young stags which take over when the master stags have left. I took the two haunches of the calf and left the rest for the wild predators. The two carcasses would provide much needed winter food for ravens, buzzards, crows, foxes and even badgers, which occasionally eat carrion, as well as the useful burying beetles and other small scavengers.

Although its strong gamey smell was unlike the beef and mutton

49

flank he had been used to, Moobli wolfed down his first venison with relish, and Cleo and Patra rushed off with their pieces to separate corners. Sylvesturr just sniffed and went back into his den. It was all gone, and some bone too, by morning. Within a few days he developed a strong appetite for venison. It seemed to make him fiercer too, for once again he started coming out on the attack at feeding times. If I dropped a large piece down first, he would make off with it while I put the rest down without risk to my hands.

I now studied his habits more closely. He showed no tendency to bury droppings, preferring to leave them on piles of old bracken rather than on earth or grass. Once every two days seemed the regular pattern. He could chew and swallow quite large pieces of bone without harm, like a dog. If there was too little roughage in his food or I could not catch a mouse or vole – the two females had virtually eradicated them from the area around the house – he chewed bracken and rush stalks and grass to provide his own. Vegetation, I noticed from his droppings, was an important part of his diet. I felt sure that wildcats subsisting largely on carrion in the depths of winter would also supplement their diet in this way. They would also need it to help clear through any pieces of bone.

I fed Cleo and Patra in the fox pen, so that they would become more used to it. Eventually Patra gave up her attempts to escape, sharing the sleeping box with Cleo as amicably as they both shared their sacking bed on the logpile.

One early January evening I saw one of the females stealing along the front of Sylvesturr's pen. Cleo was after his left-overs, but instead of shooting out, as he had done to repel Patra earlier, he was now more discreet. He walked out very slowly, head low, eyes hypnotically fixed on hers, crept up to her and, when their heads were close, made a light '*Phutt*'. She pulled her head back slightly but did not run. For all the world, it seemed he did not want to scare such a lady as Cleo with so crude a gesture as '*PAAAH!*' or a foot stamp. He ate a morsel himself, then trotted back into his den, leaving her to help herself through the fencing.

For the next few nights I went out after dark to see if it was a regular occurrence. Each time I found Sylvesturr prowling round the edges of his pen, which was most unusual. On one mid-January morning his heavy outer door lay flat on the ground; he had clearly kicked it outwards, which seemed foolish, as it made his den draughty.

By this time his coat had grown very thick, so he looked even larger than when I had first taken him from the Zoo. It was also darker and greyer than its former tawny brown, which would give him better camouflage for hunting in the greyer landscape of winter. I secured the door back in place.

I wondered if the deer meat was making him stronger or whether he might be coming into a male oestrus. If some naturalists were right about wildcats having two litters a year, it seemed possible. I had traced an isolated record of a wildcat in Berne Zoo having kittens on March 29; allowing for an average 63 to 69 days' gestation, this placed conception in mid-January. That was under artificial conditions, and I felt it unlikely to happen in the cold winter conditions of the wild.

South-west gales sprang up during the night and heavy hail showers rattled on the tin roof. In the morning I went out to find Sylvesturr's door a full yard away from the den, which was now empty. I searched the rocks and tangled undergrowth round the pen, but there was no sign of him. What on earth had happened? Then I found some of his hairs, far longer and softer than a domestic cat's, on the triangular swing door I had made in the fencing. He had climbed the 5ft fence and, while braced high on the wire, forced his way between the top timber strut and the flat wood lining the swing part of the fencing. On a kink the heavy binding wire that held the door tight had snapped. A man using both hands would have found it hard to force such a gap. What strength he possessed!

Why had he forced his way out now, after being used to confinement all his long adult life, when he had never tried to escape before from the roomy pen? I recalled how he had been searching its perimeter for several nights after dark. He had left half last night's sausage and cat food in his dish. Maybe the sight of the wild woods all around him, now he was used to the territory by sight, had finally aroused his long-suppressed instincts. Or perhaps he had come to like half-raw venison so much he had decided to go in search of more.

I tried to get Moobli to track him, but he had never liked Sylvesturr in the way he regarded the females as his personal property and proved maddeningly obtuse. Every time I said, 'Track the pussy coots,' he put his nose to the ground and tracked the night movements of Cleo and Patra, which kept leading him back to the shed. I checked they were still there, entering carefully in case

51

Sylvesturr was lurking with them, but both were on their sacking bed as usual. Cleo fled into the logs as I entered. I checked the deer carcasses, which had started to decay slightly, but they had not been touched. Moobli could get no scent near the rock cairn where the wildcat had hidden once before. There was too much grass and too many twigs and leaves around the deer to see any tracks, never mind sort out wildcat from fox.

I checked them again by torchlight but could still find no sign. Suddenly, as I stood there in the eerie darkness, the firs and larches soughing in the wind above, I remembered the wildcat tracks in the autumn on the path a mile and a half away to the east. Could his breakout last night have been caused by the presence of another wildcat? If so, and Sylvesturr was now in oestrus, it would probably be a female also in oestrus. I had been out in wild Canadian woods where bears roamed free, but the thought that fierce, intractable Sylvesturr and a mate might now be lurking in the dark near by was more than a little scary. Well, to heck with him, I thought, let him spend the night out. He had come back after escaping before, and would surely do so again when he was really hungry. I put some food in his pen and tied the swing door open, then blocked the females in the woodshed.

Throughout the night and all next day the gales, sleet and rain showers continued. It turned bitterly cold. The food in his pen remained untouched, and I began to worry. Searching carefully, I found some mixed-up scuffs among the mud and spruce needles by a rhododendron bush south-east of the cottage which could have been made by a wildcat. Fortifying the box-cage trap, and oiling the moving parts with butter, I carried it down and set it with strong-smelling venison between the bush and the spruce glade. Again I shut the females in the shed so that they could not take the bait.

I was woken next morning by the cronking of ravens. Four were perched in trees in the west wood, where they had found the deer carcasses. I went out and saw that the trapdoor was down. The meat had gone and the trap was empty. There were no hairs on the bottom of the door. Sometimes, if I set the trip nail too far into its hold in the trapdoor, the mousetrap spring would go off but would not be strong enough to pull the nail out. It was always a delicate operation. Perhaps Sylvesturr had managed to get the meat out before the door fell, and after being loosened by his vibrations, it had dropped later in the wind. I checked the deer again. Besides the raven peckings, they had been well chewed. Moobli followed fox scent for some yards – shown by his occasional leg cocking on tufts – but did not seem able to find any cat scent at all. I reset the trap.

By the fifth day, the new meat in the trap remained untouched and I began to lose hope. After the females had spent a daytime spell in the fox run, I blocked them in the shed overnight, moved the trap nearer to Sylvesturr's pen and put sausage meat in the pen itself. For two more cold and rainy days I did this, hope slightly restored on one occasion when I found some of the meat in the pen had gone. Of course it could have been chewed by hungry shrews or taken by birds. I was sure no large wild animal would actually climb into the pen.

I was thoroughly depressed. Sylvesturr had been gone for eight days and nights. A cat unused to catching his own wild prey, and the dearth of prey in the height of winter, suggested I had probably lost him. I had let the Zoo down; but even worse, I had let Sylvesturr himself down. That night, wearing gloves soaked in boiled spruce needle juice (a trick I had learned in Canada for reducing human scent), I put in fresh venison and set the trap as delicately as I knew how.

Apart from the occasional trek, I had been forced for weeks now to spend the few daylight hours (it was dark before 10 a.m. and after 3.30 p.m.) working indoors on my book, racing against time to get it finished by the due date in March. My only heating was the wood fire and an old paraffin stove. Fumes from the stove and smoke blown back down the chimney were bad for the lungs, and the shimmering light from the paraffin lamp did nothing for my eyesight.

January 18 dawned calm with cold clear blue sky, the first rainless day for over two weeks. I found the trapdoor down, and hurried round to the front. There he was! He saw me coming and raged up and down with ferocious snarls and spits, giving those mad sideways glares as he looked for ways to get out. He leaped up, as loose hairs showed he had repeatedly done, at the top of the netting where he had escaped before, but I had now sewn it all up with stout wire.

There was a little blood on the wooden floor of the box portion. At first I thought it had come from the raw venison, but as I got close and he slammed down his huge foot and '*PAAAH!*'d at me, I was terrified to see a thin trickle of blood coming from his nostrils. Had some sharp deer bone cut the sides of his throat? He was not choking. Perhaps it was only blood from recently eaten meat, coughed up in the act of spitting. He was wet through and had clearly lost a good deal of weight, but he was still full of life and all his old ferocity.

I struggled to carry him up to the pen. Although his den was still dry, I renewed all the hay and bracken. I heard a strange whimper and a watery sneeze. Now there was more blood coming from Sylvesturr's nose. There was something terribly wrong and my heart sank, for this was no mere nose-bleed. He had clearly developed pneumonia, or at the very least inflamed lungs, from being out in the cold and wet for so long without proper food.

I thought only briefly of the inland vet, who did not even have a large dog muzzle. I doubted the ailing wildcat would have survived the boat journeys, the long jolting 88-mile return drive, the complicated anaesthetic operations necessary to examine or treat such a fierce creature. No, my only hope was to try and nurse him through it, in a heated room in my cottage.

I raced indoors and spread newspapers out on the spare bedroom table, put in a paraffin heater, and set the box-cage with its hissing, flaring bundle of gold-eyed hatred on to 2in.-square blocks so I could extract his droppings without disturbing him too much. There was no time for fear. I gathered an armful of dry hay, opened the trapdoor, foiled his furious attack with a blunt hazel stick and pushed the hay in with it. Draping a huge beach towel over the cage so that he would have some darkness, and also as a shield so he could not see what I was up to, I managed to fix his drinking bowl to the netting with wire to prevent it from tipping over.

I found some blue aureomycin, a broad-spectrum antibiotic, and some mild penicillin tablets, both of which I could sprinkle in light doses on his food. When I went in to feed him at night the blood had stopped, but he arched up at full stretch, spitting, and it began to flow again. Yet he pounced on the meat, eating avidly, and drinking the milk as if he had drunk nothing at all during the whole eight days in which he had been free. I left him alone and prayed that he would live.

Next morning he was lying at full stretch on his side. At first I thought he was dead, for I had never known him to do that before, but as I put my head round the edge of the towel he shot to his feet, slammed down his foot and spat. Then he coughed, sneezed, and more blood came from his nose. It was awful to see. I went out quickly, knowing I would have to leave him alone as much as possible to prevent exciting him.

It was hard to get down to any work that day, for I felt sick, sad and terribly guilty. I could blame no one but myself for not ensuring his pen was escape-proof. Whether another wildcat had come around, inducing him to get out, I would never know. He had clearly found nowhere snug and dry while free, and the rain and wind together had caused constant loss of heat. A cat always knows instinctively how to catch small prey, but inexperienced after his years in zoos, and with so little prey abroad in winter, he had been in real trouble.

The fight to nurse Sylvesturr through the first crisis, until the blood stopped completely, took a full five days. At times he was clearly battling for life. At the end of the second day he was so weak he could not get up, and I felt the end was near. He lay on his stomach, his back legs, thighs inwards, stretched out towards the window. His left foreleg was splayed out at right angles to his body, while the right was tucked beneath his chin, as if he had collapsed in that position. He still tried to spit when he heard me come in, growling as I pushed the food right up to his mouth. Then he poked his big head weakly over the edge of the dish to eat a few mouthfuls. I sat quietly hidden in the shadows, after shutting the door so that he would think I had gone out. I saw him pull his legs beneath him, one by one, and stagger weakly to his feet. He stood there, swaying, but he could still lap up his milk. With the loss of blood he was very thirsty, but the bowl held over a pint and I did not have to keep going in to fill it.

During his weakest period I quietly extracted his droppings with little sticks through the bottom of the netting as soon as he released them, or he would have fouled himself completely. He seemed to be in a semi-conscious stupor. He whimpered faintly, like a child, and it was poignant to see him try to clean himself with his long tongue. As I sat beside him, I found myself willing him on. Live, live, *live*, I breathed silently. I felt strangely moved by his courage.

Slowly he began to respond, knowing after the third day, I think, that I was really trying to get him through. This magnificent, unchangeable creature, so inviolate in his pride that he would rather die than submit, once so fierce he would have tackled anything, man or beast, that challenged him, was now reduced to total dependence on a human being. In some ways I saw myself in this old cat and, strangely, he was teaching me a lesson too – to learn to love that which hated me, a lesson we must perhaps all learn if rare wild creatures and the last wild beautiful places of this earth are to survive. I had never felt any strong emotions towards him before; now I found myself loving him. It became extremely important to me to make sure he lived and that his ultimate freedom would not come too late, that he should fulfil his wild destiny next summer, whether he mated with one of the females or not.

Some strangely rewarding experiences came at this time. When I went in on the third evening he did not spit but just looked at me quietly. I had found a way of talking to him that seemed to soothe him, calm him down, and as he lay on his side he actually let me stroke his long soft hair several times without protest. Taking advantage of one such moment, I measured him with a ruler outside the cage. To my surprise he was 3ft 6½ins long, including his tail. He was not quite a foot longer than the females, but he was more heavily built, more like a small puma than a cat.

On the fourth day an extraordinary thing happened. Patra stationed herself on the window ledge outside, a mere two feet from his box-cage, and gazed in at him for at least an hour with a look that could only be described as adoration. He seemed to take little notice of her, however, but in the evening he was back on his feet and eating hungrily from the selection of mutton, liver, venison, cat food and conditioner and eggs that I now varied in his diet. There was no more blood flow from his nose, just a slight green discharge.

Next day Patra spent the whole morning on the window ledge, and by midday he was staring back at her with rapt attention. On an impulse, I caught her with gloves and brought her into the room, setting her on the inside window ledge, by the light side of his cage. She stayed there and the two gazed at each other with such unwavering intensity that I felt an interloper and quietly left the room. Two hours later neither had moved an inch. Her presence seemed to calm him down even more.

Despite all my ministrations with newspaper and cloths, the bedroom was smelling strongly of tomcat urine. I moved the box-cage on to the workshop bench, from which he could also have a full view of the females' woodshed. Being smaller, the room was easier to heat. To my astonishment, Patra jumped down from the window and followed us like a dog.

I had a sudden thought. Perhaps these long periods of staring at each other meant she was ready to mate? If Sylvesturr's recovery was merely a temporary upturn before a final relapse, maybe I should try to give him a chance to mate right now, if he wanted to, and if she was also ready. He was already old, by wildcat standards and for all I knew his chances of being able to mate could well be running out. The two had been gazing at each other for the best part of two and a half days, and it was surely something more than mere toleration on Syl's part.

At dusk, I decided to take the chance. After feeding both, I fixed his door so the gap was large enough to let her in but not, I hoped, to allow him out. If she chose to go in, maybe it would work. Then dressed in three thick sweaters and, with gauntlets and under gloves, I held Patra near the opening. To my surprise, she looked in at him standing watching us intently, then struggled and clawed to get in. I moved her nearer and she reached out with her claws, dug them in and hauled herself through the opening. I winced, expecting an awful fracas, but nothing of the sort happened. Patra sneaked, very slowly, up close to him. He seemed to take no notice whatever of her. I propped the door up so she could get out if and when she chose, but as I left, Syl by-passed Patra and went on the attack again – at me! Now that he had a companion, it seemed our truce was over. Sylvesturr could never have been so close to a single female cat in his entire adult life yet it had come naturally to him not to attack her. To me that was astonishing. When I peeped in later they were gazing at each other, their noses only inches apart.

In the morning Patra was still with him, although she could have walked out at any time she wished. She was unharmed, but her ears and neck were all wet, as if they had been well chewed. Perhaps there had been an attempt at copulation. She was still gazing at him with half-closed eyes, while he seemed to be glaring at her with his huge eyes wide open. Was it possible that in these long staring sessions he was actually hypnotizing her? At times he came close to hypnotizing me! When I went in and he made his usual '*PAAAH!*', Patra stood up beside him and spat too. When she came out of his cage at night, she seemed oddly shy, big-eyed and wary and would not let me anywhere near her. As she looked round for somewhere to hide, I herded her out through the front door and fed her with Cleo in the woodshed as usual.

Sylvesturr was standing up and peering intently outside when I went into the workshop next morning. Now Cleo was sitting on the window ledge gazing at him with loving eyes. Maybe she felt it was her turn, but she was wilder than Patra and would be hard to get into the house. Although Sylvesturr now seemed back to his ferocious old self again, with only a little phlegm oozing from his left nostril, I felt he would be better left alone for a while. Cleo sat there most of the day and all the following morning; I decided two chances were better than one. I was obsessed with the idea of reproducing such a magnificent beast if possible, and I was by no means sure he *had* mated with Patra successfully.

Again, I would let Cleo choose. When I went out with sweaters, jacket and double gloves, Cleo was surprisingly easy to catch, as if she knew what was happening. I put her on the bench and she remained by the cage all afternoon, gazing at him with inscrutable smiles while he appeared to be staring past her, surveying the outside scene with a lordly unconcern.

At night, after feeding both, I held Cleo near the gap. Like Patra, she clawed to get in, and he neither hissed nor flared at all. But when I checked that the end larch slab was secure, Syl, thinking my hand was coming in, hissed and growled. Cleo growled at me too.

Two hours later Cleo was still inside but the cats were facing opposite ways. I had the odd feeling that while Cleo might have fancied him, his feelings were not reciprocal. Cleo had wild yellow eyes and a thin, muscular body and perhaps Sylvesturr preferred the plumper, floppier figure of Patra. He could have killed either female if he had really wanted to. Perhaps the belief that wildcats are monogamous, are faithful to a single mate for life, was true. This would help to explain their poor reproductive rate and their rarity, for a domestic tomcat will mate with any willing female in heat that it can find. Perhaps it was too early for either Cleo or Patra to be on heat. I looked at both females' rear parts afterwards but saw no evidence of what might be described as penetrative activity!

By 10 p.m. Cleo had left the cage. Although she was sitting on top of its covering towel next morning, I felt sure she had not been inside it again. I put her back in the woodshed.

Now the entire house reeked of tomcat. I reduced the heating to prepare him for life outside again. After three sunny days, I hauled the fox pen down to a windless spot in the L-shaped corner at the back of the cottage, filled the thick wooden box with hay, covered part of the ground with sand and shingle, which had been the kind of flooring he was used to in the Zoo, and transferred Sylvesturr.

It was a difficult operation. After I had pushed the box end of his cage into the run and blocked all holes with wire netting, he simply refused to leave the cage. When I tried to shoo him out with the blunt hazel stick, he bit deep holes in it with a force that would have severed a man's finger. I felt sorry, and would have loved to free him, but it was clear he could not survive in the wild in winter, and he was getting no exercise at all in the box-cage. When he did finally jump out, he ran with a low crouch and mad glares, refused to enter the new den box at the far end and stood on it for a few seconds before running straight back at me. He leaped for the dark patch where the top of the box-cage was still covered with the towel, thinking it was an exit. As I struggled to hold on to the box with tiring arms, he growled and tried to force his way out where the wire netting was stapled to the box, a mere six inches from my face. My own growls deterred him not at all. One staple tore free and he was actually forcing his way out against my hand, towards me. Only when I banged loudly on the box right in front of his nose with my other hand did he finally turn and, seeing its dark entrance at last, leap into the new den box. As I quickly hauled the box-cage out and hastily shut down the pen door and fastened it, I found I was trembling all over.

The fracas, which had unnerved me, did not appear to have bothered him too much, for an hour after dusk he was out again, tucking into a meal of mutton, venison and liver. No wonder he was so strong, I thought, as I watched him from the bedroom window. So he should be, on a protein diet better than my own. At least he was now well and safely outside again.

Despite the disruption of the move outside, Sylvesturr seemed more placid and never again went on the attack when I took him food. Whether he regarded me as a strange superior being who could produce female companions at will, or his feline consciousness told him I had nursed him back to health, I could not know. But he was, if not grateful, at least prepared to tolerate my occasional presence.

Now I tried some experiments with the wildcats. The general belief is they rely mainly on sight when hunting, with hearing second and the ability to scent one of their least important senses. One night, instead of putting meat into the fox pen, I just stood silently with it. After about ten seconds, I saw the white flashes of Sylvesturr's mouth, jaw and neck appear in the dark entrance hole. Wildcats probably evolved these white patches on their otherwise tawny, grey-striped bodies, to help see each other in the dark. As he came further out, I noticed his down-curved whiskers were twitching, his pink nose wrinkling. Clearly, he could smell the meat in the bowl I was holding. I repeated the experiment on other evenings and found he could scent meat from a good 25 yards away.

Later I also conducted trials with the females. With Moobli shut in the house, I walked into the woodshed with their food, held it as they '*mau*'d hungrily on the logpile, then walked a distance away and set the meat down in a small thicket of grass and brambles. Patra always found it. Once I watched her walk round the front of the house, pausing every so often to sniff the air, with one paw upraised like a pointer, then locate the meat hidden in vegetation a full 45 yards away. When hard pressed in winter, wildcats are probably able to scent carrion at fairly large distances. Cleo would not co-operate in the experiments, perhaps because she feared being caught in the open while it was light, but months later she was to surprise me with her scenting powers.

Some accounts say wildcats bury their scats – which are usually twisted and double-ended, joined narrowly in the middle like a dumb-bell, and have tapering tips. Other accounts say they never do so. Sylvesturr had made no effort to bury his droppings on dried bracken or grass; now he always buried them in the sand or gravel of the fox pen. From the bedroom window, twice I saw him standing close beside them and raking a foot-high mound over them with his right paw. The females never buried theirs on earth or short grass, but usually did so on dried bracken, and always did in sand, gravel or snow. Usually all the cats defecated after dark, within an hour or so of eating. Although adult wildcats have no natural enemies in Britain apart from man, this could have been due to hereditary instinct, from the days when bigger predators like wolves and lynx inhabited the country. They would not then be caught napping, so to speak, in broad daylight.

In early February, on one of those superb winter days that seem almost unique to the Scottish Highlands, when the sun shone in a brilliant azure sky, shimmering a silver path across the loch surface, I remade Sylvesturr's den, lining it with larch slabs and insulating it with two sackfuls of dry bracken. I made a big bed of dry hay which he could rake round into a bowl. I no longer felt afraid of him, and when I tacked a plywood sheet over his box hole, he did not even growl, as if he knew he was going home.

When I held the box in the pen he dropped to the ground and, without a single pause to look round, ran straight into his old den. Another example of a good memory.

I also decided it was time to pen all the wildcats up together. The females would surely be coming into full oestrus in the next few weeks, and the sooner they were able to mate with Sylvesturr the better, if neither had done so in the cottage already.

I dragged the fox pen to the west side of his pen, the two making an L-shape. I wanted the females to be with Sylvesturr whenever they chose, and so I made a connecting hole between the two pens, big enough to allow them access to his larger area, but small enough to stop him from getting into theirs. It was fortunate he was such a large specimen. If he objected to their company, they could easily escape from any possible attack or sudden bad mood. Then, with a small square of wood on a long hazel pole, I made a gate that I could operate from outside, so sealing the two pens and the cats from each other when I chose. I filled the den box Sylvesturr had recently been using with hay and set it on some logs at the north end of the females' pen, to keep it from ground damp, and left them all to it while I went on a supply trip in the welcome sunshine.

On my return I pulled aside the gate, lifted Sylvesturr's den door on the pulley, and hid myself behind the bramble tangle south of the pens. Cleo was the first to venture into the male's pen. With upraised paw, her head going up and down as she sniffed the air, she slowly went through the gap and padded straight to his drink and feed dishes, licking up the bits he had left.

As she passed his now-open den, he lifted his head from the hay and stared as if he could not believe his eyes. He blinked once, twice, then over that old curmudgeonly, gloomy face there came a soft expression, a positively tender look, and a patriarchal twitching of the whiskers. I could almost have sworn he smiled.

For the next few days I kept careful watch on their mixings, making sure they were separated at night until they knew each other really well. Cleo usurped the coveted inner position inside the females' den box, in spite of Patra's bigger size, and was the first to find her way back from Sylvesturr's pen. Patra forgot and walked up and down three times before rediscovering the gate hole. It seemed the ferocious male liked both females in his pen for he made no aggressive moves, nor treated either with special favouritism. They were now all far happier. They had over 200 square feet of rocks, bushes, hazel trees, brambles and grass in which to sport around.

I was sure Sylvesturr would not try to escape again. He even looked happier. One morning, Cleo sat for two hours on top of his den but Patra was more brazen. She sunned herself on a rounded rock right in front of Syl's entrance, occasionally looking in at him. He just sat with his eyes peeping above the hay bowl he had made for himself. Apparently no invitations into the inner sanctum were issued.

At night both females came rushing in when I fed Sylvesturr, and promptly, without the slightest protest from him, gobbled up all his food. Far from attacking them, his patriarchal gloomy face again took on a benign look. He actually watched them steal his food and squabble over it without doing a thing to defend it from them! I decided to shut them in their pen until he had finished eating – which was now often near midnight.

In the mornings both Cleo and Patra would be milling about by the small gate, smelling his left-overs. The moment I lifted it, they raced in to polish them off. Thinner Cleo was developing into the more cunning of the two. She was usually the first to reach the food and to slam her foot down or stick a clawless paw straight on to Patra's eyebrow whiskers, to stop her reaching the choicest morsel. Yet on the few occasions Patra got there first, Cleo respected her ownership and turned off at her snarl. Again the wildcats were practising first come, first served.

By February 20 Sylvesturr had gone off his food almost completely. He was taking only the fresh raw meat. I had been told by the Zoo this would probably happen in late February and early March. It seemed to be connected with the onset of male oestrus, just as animals like red deer stags eat little during the rut. I hoped the fact that the females were becoming wilder and hungrier meant they too were coming into oestrus. It made sense, for the females would need to build up reserves if about to start carrying kittens. What worried me was that I never saw Cleo or Patra in the den with him.

By the end of February the first of a thousand daffodils around the cottage were flowering in its lee, shaking their heads wildly, as if wishing they could change their minds when the first three days of sun were interrupted by one of south-west gales and rain. Twining honeysuckle stems were sprouting new velvet green leaves, holding out bright jewelled cups of water, and the first bluebells were pushing up their dark green leaves, like stars amid the patches of sodden winter grass. A roe buck and his doe were now sleeping in the west wood, and a few red deer hinds were using the mossy ledges of the rocky escarpment above the wood as their night-time beds. Two huge eagles flew together over the cottage, their white tail rings and underwing patches showing they were first- or second-year birds, too young to breed this spring. A tribe of bull-finches invaded my garden as I dug over and manured the vegetable patch and trimmed back and mulched the four gooseberry bushes. As they pulled at the new leaf buds on the oak, birch and the two cherry trees, they gave plaintive little '*phui*' calls.

As the sun gained strength, even cranky old Sylvesturr seemed to be feeling the stirrings of spring. I caught him outside the den once, stretched out fully in the sun, his whiskered head tucked between his front paws and his long hind legs extended behind him at full stretch. I was rewarded for my unintentional interruption of his warm siesta by a loud '*PAAAH!*' as he dashed inside again.

If the females were to come into breeding condition at all this year, this was surely the most critical time. So I poked Sylvesturr's food and drink dishes right into his den and closed the door down. I could then leave the gate open all night, for the females were hardly likely to push their way right into his den and steal his food a few inches from his nose. They would thus all be free to make their own arrangements as regards a little lovemaking under the cloak of night without the poor old tom being left half starved.

One afternoon I came out to find Cleo racing round the pens, swiping out at something white flying in front of her. As I came up she knocked it to the ground, but with a loud '*PAAAH!*' (a trick I learned from dealing with Sylvesturr) I scared her off it and she dashed into her den box. It was an oak beauty moth, rare in my part of Scotland, and luckily undamaged. As it failed to recover, I preserved it, and it is now in the collection of the Natural History Museum in London

For weeks now I had been putting off a trip south to do urgent zoological research, buy equipment, visit relatives and try to line up enough writing to pay for a few civilized needs for the next six months. In mid-March, with sparrowhawks, tawny owls and other birds showing nesting activities in the woods, I decided to go – to leave them as well as the cats to settle down for a while without disturbance.

As heavy rains had caused the loch to rise several feet, I hauled the big boat up under the log archway, then fenced off half the woodshed so that Sylvesturr would have the whole rear logpile and some 80 square feet as a warm sheltered home while we were away. I hung up cooked and half-cooked meats, hearts and sterilized meat sausage, and covered large bowls of long-life milk and water with pine sheets, so that he could drink from but not spill them. Then I made a hole in the fencing for the females to get in to him, the same system as with the outdoor pens.,

All I had to do now was to trap Sylvesturr. As I carried the box-cage into his pen, Moobli started bounding up and down, playing. Cleo flared and spat at him, then suddenly shot through the gate and straight into Syl's den! To my surprise he barely blinked at her sudden intrusion, and she crouched down quietly beside him. As soon as I came into view in front of his den and he realized I was actually inside, he reared up '*PAAAH!*' and stamped his right foot, flinging out a small pile of hay. There was definitely a protective air about his action. I climbed out quickly and went to shut Moobli in the cottage.

When I got back Cleo was still in the den, her huge eyes glowing with what I hoped was love. She was gazing up at his profile like a fan suddenly close to a favourite movie star. He too had changed position, so that his shaggy old head was close to hers. I left them for an hour. As dusk was falling I managed to chase Cleo back into the female pen with the blunt hazel stick, where Patra was watching these goings-on with a supercilious smile. Then I baited the trap.

To entice the females into the woodshed, I relied on their sense of smell. Instead of feeding them in the pen, as usual, I set out food and drink in the front part of the shed and left their pen door open. Within half an hour both females were guzzling away in the shed. I shut the pen door to prevent them getting back.

Next day Sylvesturr was safely in the trap. I carried his heavy growling form into the shed, set him up in the rear portion, and left the females' exit hole open. After closing up the cottage, I made a rough trip down the loch and hauled the small boat into the wood at the far end. By midnight Moobli and I were well over the Scottish border.

Wildernesse and the two woods which became the wildcats' first hunting ground, seen below before I built the pens on the west side.

above: The wildcat pens. The smaller kept the females away from Sylvesturr until they knew each other.

below: Teaching the kits to hunt prey by winding a dead rabbit along on a line. They soon saw it as an artificial contrivance.

above: Sylvesturr sometimes anticipated his meal and came out licking his lips.

below: Always gentle to the females, Sylvesturr let them steal his food without protest.

above: When Sylvesturr contracted pneumonia, I nursed him back to health in the heated workshop.

below: Sylvesturr recovering in the windless area behind the cottage. Once back in his den, he allowed Cleo to raid his food bowl again.

In London my anxiety about the wildcats' welfare was only one spur that made me dash about my affairs like a scalded cat. The other was the vastly increased cost of living; so high were hotel charges that I spent three nights sleeping in the Land Rover in the noisy streets, though it was embarrassing trying to dress behind a flimsy curtain as a traffic warden stuck a ticket on my windscreen!

In little more than a week, all business completed, I was on my way back to the wilds.

5 · *We've Done It!*

When I hauled the boat down over the pine roots and set off up the loch, it seemed that the whole of nature was welcoming our return. The north-west gales and snow showers that had greeted our arrival in the darkness were gone. The sun shone bright as a diamond in the kind of aquamarine blue sky one seldom sees in the yellow-pale mists of Highland summers, and the mirror surface of the dark blue waters reflected the snow-capped peaks around us as we slid gently along. Moobli stood proudly in the bow, surveying the scene we had both come to love. Although April was still four days away, and the new leaves were as yet buds on the waterfront trees, it seemed as we covered the six and a half miles in an unhurried hour that we were being given a preview glimpse of spring on its way. A glimpse was all it proved to be, for minutes after we had landed, the sky darkened and we were in the midst of whirling snow.

I hastened to the woodshed. All the cats were fine, though Sylvesturr seemed strangely subdued, as if total isolation from humans had not agreed with him. Perhaps he missed having someone to spit at each day. His milk had gone but the cooked beef flank hanging beneath the woodshed window had not been touched. I had nailed it there hoping he would take exercise to feed from it. A domestic cat and young cougars will leap on to hanging meat and take a few bites while clinging to it with their claws, but apparently this wildcat would not. Perhaps he distrusted it in such an unnatural position.

Maybe an inability to adapt to anything new was one reason why pure wildcats had become rare, whereas domestic cats gone wild or the cunning foxes had learned to adapt to man and to use his food stores, wastes, unhoused poultry and specially reared game birds to their own advantage.

Before doing anything else, I put fresh liver, steak and milk in Sylvesturr's dish, shut the door, and then peeped quietly through the woodshed window. His huge old face glared round his den box hole. When he saw me outlined against the window he snarled and drew back into his box. Immediately Patra sneaked in through the hole and started tucking into his food, followed in a few seconds by Cleo. Sylvesturr made no protest. Maybe they had eaten a good deal of his food. When they had demolished everything, I had to entice them out, shut up the hole, and put out his food and milk again. Within an hour of dusk he had eaten the liver and drunk half a pint of milk.

For the next two days Sylvesturr remained very quiet, just crouching in his box, not flaring when I went in, and still not eating all his food. Yet he was not thin, and his few droppings seemed quite firm and normal. He had been lonely, perhaps.

Despite the snow showers, Cleo and Patra were spending little time in the woodshed now. With the threat of being caught out in the open removed while we were away, they had clearly been increasing the range of their foragings. Apart from raiding Sylvesturr's food stores, they had possibly spent almost no time at all with him. Cooped up in the silent woodshed, he had lacked all stimulation and exercise, for he certainly had not the sense to take exercise for its own sake. It was just as if he was in some state of depression. Somehow, he had to be stimulated into activity again, even if it meant the stimulation of anger.

I fitted pine sheet over his entrance and put him back in the box-cage in the slightly heated workshop, where I visited him several times a day, feeding him titbits of best food. After three days, tomcat fight games alternating with the kind of soothing sounds I had made to him when he was ill, he was his old ferocious self once more. Again he launched the furious frontal display, stamped his foot and '*PAAAH!*'d, his bright red tongue curling contemptuously inwards as he glared with a challenging look. It was odd to reflect that the ferocity which once had seemed frightening was now actually endearing to his reluctant jailer.

I wondered where Cleo and Patra were going all the time. When, on the fifth day after my return, they had not returned for their previous night's food, I took it away and set Moobli to track them. He hurried several times round the cottage, zig-zagged over the front pasture, then took off for the west wood, but ran out of scent. Hoping they were now there, I shut him indoors and went to sit on a mossy rock below a broken old rowan tree, leeward of the wood and the north-west winds, so that the wildcats would not get my scent and might show themselves.

It sounds easy, just sitting down for an hour or two waiting for things to happen, but it requires a good deal of patience in the cold winter wind when you feel certain after half an hour that nothing will happen. You must force yourself to stay motionless until you feel you have turned to rock yourself. After about an hour, my hands and feet numb with cold, I saw a sudden movement. Patra emerged from a weed and grass thicket and leaped on to the trunk of a large fallen silver fir which was still in full leaf. Half hidden by the foliage she crept upwards, then made a quick bound on to the moss and heather that covered the side of a 5ft roots tangle at the base of another fallen tree. Immediately a small brown blur shot out past her. As it perched a few yards away on a spray of the fir, making loud ticking alarm notes, I saw it was a robin. For a moment Patra clung there, claws embedded in the moss and heather. She looked around foolishly, then sprang back on to the fir trunk, jumped down again and vanished into the undergrowth.

I went to the upended roots. There was the robin's nest where Patra had landed, with one white and red-brown blotched egg in it. The robin was laying her first clutch, and now Patra knew where the nest was, she would undoubtedly return.

I had feared this might happen in the spring. Although there was an abundance of robins in my woods that year – they had been hotly disputing territories for several weeks – I did not want any of the wildcats preying on nesting birds. The time had come to put the cats back in their pens. Besides, I did not want to keep the females and Sylvesturr apart for too long if there was to be any hope of mating them this year. Some naturalists believe wildcats have a breeding period in May, so the sooner I had them back in the runs the better.

That night I put the females' food in their pen and blocked up the woodshed entrance. An hour or so later, having located the food by scent, both cats were inside and I let down the door.

Three days later I moved Sylvesturr on to the front grass in the warm sunshine while I prepared the den for his return to the outdoors. As I put down the cage the bottom of the trapdoor caught on my knee and Sylvesturr immediately shot at the slight gap, growling loudly as he tried to heave his way out. I had a hard task forcing his feet back without having my gauntlets torn to shreds by his powerful inch-long claws. I struggled to hold the cage up to the pen door and again Sylvesturr dropped out with a hiss and padded straight into his den without looking round.

'You can go free in the summer, if you really want,' I said, 'but first you have a duty to perform, you ungrateful old sod!'

I noticed he had small, half-naked patches between his rear thighs and stomach, and that he had left some buff hairs around the box-cage. He had started a spring moult.

Abruptly the weather changed again, as it often does in the Highland spring. Suddenly we were plunged back into the depths of winter as north-west gales ripped over the mountains and sent the corrugated iron sheets on the spare timber flying, one wafting past the window and landing at the edge of the east wood. Then came the snow blizzards, so thick at times that I could not see the loch shore at all from my study window. After two days of this, with drifts piled three feet high, I decided to forget all about mating him and put Sylvesturr back in the woodshed with a heater. At least that would also provide me with a place to dry out my washing!

This time Sylvesturr refused to go for the meat in the trap. When he had not eaten in 24 hours, I decided in desperation that the only way to get him back to the shed was to haul him out bodily. I wrapped up in an old jacket, three sweaters, and three pairs of gloves, and with a piece of wire netting resting on my arms, to foil any possible damage to my face, I screwed up my courage, lifted up the wooden door and thrust in a sack, hoping I could tangle him up in it. I wanted to hold him, just once; if I held him tight by his neck scruff would he accept it and go limp? I expected him to attack immediately, but although he growled, spat horribly and slashed out with his great claws, he retreated as far back into the den as he could, just beyond my reach. I tried to drag him out when his claws were sunk deep into the sacking but he always let go at the last moment, pulling his feet, with claws drawn in, away from my grasp. He fought off all my attempts to get him out of his den. At last, with the sun coming out again and melting the snow, I thought he had better stay in it after all. I just hoped the weather would continue to improve. He certainly seemed in fine spitting shape after the long tussle. Occasional excitement seemed to do him more good than harm, as if it were an antidote to long hours of sitting down.

'Syl, old boy,' I said as I retired defeated. 'You're on your own.'

That night, when I took him his food, he came out for the first time since the autumn and ate part of it in front of me, glaring and growling as he chewed. What a baffling creature he was.

Later I went out in the dark with a torch and gained a clue as to why he wanted so much to remain where he was. In the bright beam I saw what looked like Patra's big tawny backside blocking up his entrance hole. Cleo's was blocking the female's den box. If they were not courting then Patra was just helping herself to the remains of his food behind the door, but at least one male at Wildernesse was having female company.

On a briefly sunny morning in mid-April I saw what seemed to be an example of wildcat mating behaviour. Patra walked into Syl's pen, peered in at him as he lay in his den, then plumped on her left haunch right outside his door, virtually blocking it. Slowly she lifted her right rear leg, as if capriciously exposing her soft seductive curving furry thighs where the grey stripes faded into the delicious buff and tan of her underbelly, and started to lick. If that wasn't calculated to turn him on, heaven knows what it was! Sylvesturr merely watched her with interest, deep in his raked hay bowl, his eyes peeping just above the rim with the silly soft look he sometimes wore when the females were near him, but he did not move.

By this time the woods were carpeted with primroses lifting their bright yellow faces to the occasional sun. Bluebell spikes were pushing up too, taking advantage of the light before the budding leaves on the trees made the woods dark. Both flowers added a decorative touch to the wildcat pens. I counted 973 daffodils and 58 narcissi around the cottage, hanging their heads bleakly in the snow showers.

Towards the end of April, on the first sunny day after five of sleet and rain, big black slugs began emerging from hibernation and converging on carrion, fungi or plant food which they scented with their moist tentacles from a few yards away. Sylvesturr's food bowl proved to be specially attractive to slugs and, on the first day they were out, I removed five as they slid towards his meat. On the next night I discovered that Sylvesturr had raked a great mound of twigs, leaves and earth over his bowl, and he continued to do that every night throughout the summer. It was an extraordinary example of inherited instinct for he could not have seen a slug before in his adult life. Like cougars, wildcats protect their food kills in this way, not only from slugs but also from ravens, crows and other predators who would scent or see it. The females began to do the same, but not so often because they usually ate most of their food as soon as it was put down. Greedy Patra often sneaked in to take some of Sylvesturr's as well. I just hoped that under cover of darkness he was receiving other favours in return!

On May 19 I went out early to the wildcats and found I had forgotten to reopen the gate between the pens, which I usually set temporarily in place each night so that Sylvesturr could eat his food before it was stolen. As I approached, Patra ran from the gate back towards her den box, only to be repulsed by Cleo who snarled and clawed at her from the entrance. Patra ran frantically round the pen. As soon as I opened the gate, she shot straight into Sylvesturr's den. It was the first time I had seen any of the cats actually fighting. Cleo seemed to be banishing Patra from their den box, and I wondered if that was why Patra was now so often in Sylvesturr's pen. On the other hand, she was actively seeking his company, some of the time at least, actually inside his den.

It certainly seemed as if Patra was in oestrus because her vagina looked enlarged and she behaved very kittenishly before him, rolling on her back, sniffing bluebells and playing with loose leaves. Sylvesturr merely put up with her behaviour, as if not wanting to hurt her feelings by any show of disapproval. When Cleo came out of the den box I noticed she seemed fatter than usual, probably because she had caught a vole or two, which she sometimes did in the pens, or because she had eaten some of Patra's share of last night's meal.

Later, after planting all my vegetable seeds, I saw Patra catch a short-tailed vole which came out of a small hole a mere foot away from Sylvesturr's door. I had noticed the hole a few days earlier but had doubted any vole would have the nerve to make its home in a wildcat pen. Sylvesturr, apparently, had not bothered it. This one had now paid with its life, and Patra ran with it, like a small parcel in her jaws, through the gate and right up to where Cleo was sitting on top of their den box. There she dropped it and ran straight back into Syl's pen.

In view of Cleo's recent belligerence towards Patra (for she was keeping her out of their pen most of the day) it was the oddest incident I had yet witnessed with the wildcats. Cleo dropped down with a growl and ate the vole head-first. Was Patra actually trying to placate Cleo in some way? At dusk something just as strange occurred. When I took out their food, Cleo first drove Patra away from it with a sharp spit, then came to eat it without her normal hesitation in my presence. For only the second time she let me stroke her through the fencing as she ate. She walked as if her feet hurt, and still looked swollen. I wondered if she was ill, or even had a tumour in her stomach. Was she perhaps being more friendly towards me now because Patra had made a conquest of Sylvesturr? Maybe she was driving Patra through into Syl's pen out of jealousy after he had finally chosen the plumper cat's company? It was all most odd, and I could see no sense in all this strange behaviour.

On May 25 (my birthday) I returned from a trek to see Cleo once again drive Patra from the females' pen with great ferocity. I decided to put the small den box in Sylvesturr's pen for Patra's use (the old tom would not tolerate her in his den *all* the time, I felt) and to give Cleo a new den of her own. Then I sealed the two pens off. I could not let the females go free until the nesting birds had all reared their young, though I was tempted to take the belligerent Cleo some miles up the loch. Luckily my father had given me a superbly made pet box on my last visit. Lovingly fashioned by an old Sussex craftsman, it had a hinged front and top, and I insulated it with rubber sheeting and set it on the logs under the roof that covered one end of the females' pen.

I was sure then that Cleo was ill; her stomach was more swollen and white fluid seeped from her rear. She had eaten almost nothing of last night's meal. Yet she did not look ill. Her eyes were bright, her fur in good condition, and she seemed in good shape. As I put the new box in, Patra started to make an awful squawking sound in Sylvesturr's pen as if she were choking. Then she regurgitated a whole vole skeleton and fur on to the bracken on top of Syl's den. I wondered if she too were ill, or if it was part of wildcat courtship ritual, a sort of declaring herself on his territory.

In the evening I stole out very quietly at dusk to see if Cleo had eaten her food. To my surprise both she and Patra were in Sylvesturr's pen, though several yards apart. I must have knocked the gate open as I left after installing the new den box. Sylvesturr's head soon appeared through his door hole. He looked furtively to left and right, came out very slowly, then walked up to Cleo and sniffed her. She did not retreat but lifted her nose to his. They appeared to be kissing. Their mouths were twisted sideways and they seemed to be biting gently at each other's tongues. After a few seconds of this, they stopped and pulled back a few inches. Then both started licking their chops. Although he had not seen me, Sylvesturr seemed to sense my presence and went back into his den, moving like a ghost in the twilight. What on earth was going on?

Next morning Cleo was once again in Syl's pen, as was Patra, but when I got nearer Cleo ran back through the gate and into her new den box. I noticed she looked somewhat thinner. As I left to go down to the boat for a supply trip, I noticed Patra easing herself through the gate. I felt sure that Cleo would drive her out again, but Patra walked up to her den box, made an odd noise in her throat, a sort of turtle dove 'brrrooo' trill, reached in slowly with her right paw, claws well in, and made a gentle movement as if she was giving Cleo inside the box a soft playful swat. Oh well, I thought, it's good the two females seem to be friends again.

For four hours after returning from the supply trip, I noticed Cleo just seemed to be lying asleep in her new den box. When I put in her food and water-milk mix she did not come out at all. By 8 p.m. she had touched neither food nor milk and, feeling worried, I bent down for a closer look. Suddenly I saw one of her legs moving, but it was an odd light tawny colour, unlike Cleo's browny grey, and far more finely striped. Then I saw what looked like a tiny tail. Cleo lay on her side with a blissful expression on her face. Her teats were pink and swollen, with half an inch of thick pink skin around the protruding centres.

Then I saw the little tail move again. Clearly I was not just imagining things, and was eager to discover how many kittens she had. I put on three pairs of gloves, three sweaters and the old thick jacket, feeling I would thus only have to protect my face and eyes, for I was sure she would attack. I crept on all fours under the roof of the pen, expecting a blitzkrieg, but Cleo was just too happy to be angry. Motherhood, far from making her fiercer, seemed finally to have tamed her, for she stayed where she was.

There were two kittens, both exceptionally large, with big feet and claws. They were fully furred, with beautiful chestnut brown and brown-grey stripes and elongated spots on a light buff and tawny background. Each had a big broad head, with ears set low down and eyes tightly closed. One was suckling away for all it was worth, making little squeaky noises. When I went a little too close, Cleo growled a warning, but she still did not move.

I backed out of the pen with thudding heart and let down the hinged door. To relieve my excitement and joy, I performed a stumbling race round the rough front pasture in my wellingtons, yelling, 'We've done it! We've done it! We've bred wildcats!'

The whole area around Wildernesse seemed to be smiling now. The sun had shone continuously for thirteen days and the woods were a patchwork quilt of differing greens. Around the cottage the ground was carpeted with creeping buttercups, and the four-petalled yellow flowers of tormentil lay on their weak stems against other vegetation, while the white stars of stitchwort thrust their heads high. In the marshier places the yellow suns of hawkbit insisted they were no mere dandelions. Almost everywhere blue-bells raised a foot-high canopy of blue like a background canvas to the magnificent riot of huge pink, crimson and lilac flowers that filled the rhododendron bushes.

Later, as with trembling hands I fed Cleo and the other two cats, I realized how foolish and clumsy my attempts to breed them and understand their behaviour had been. To think that Cleo was the wildcat I had least liked. I had even thought of turning her free down the loch, or giving her to a zoo, because of her wildness and bad temper. Sylvesturr, who I believed had tried to mate with Patra in the workshop after his days of freezing unplanned freedom, had clearly preferred the thinner wilder one. Only by chance had they succeeded, it seemed. Even my rare trip out for just over a week had been a blessing for them, for they had been left totally alone and could meet and mate without any human disturbance at all. It was odd, though, that Cleo had been in Syl's enclosure for much of the previous two days, when tom wildcats are reputed to kill kittens. I had noticed this morning she looked thinner when she went through the gate, so she had obviously gone in after having the kits. The oddest thing of all was that, having driven Patra away, Cleo now allowed her to come right up to the den box and give her a playful swat with her right paw. She must have been lying up with her new kits then. It all seemed to go against everything I had read or been told about wildcats.

I went carefully into Cleo's pen next morning, making the soothing sounds she associated with food and friendliness, and spent some time winning her confidence. After a while she let me stroke the kittens. She did not mind me actually picking them up – until they cried out, then she growled and I quickly put them back. They hated being handled and called loudly, not like domestic kittens, but with piercing buzzard-like calls – '*meeeoo! meeeoo!*' – that could have been heard 200 yards away. Then Cleo stood up, stretched herself high with arched back and began making an odd breathy clattering sound in her throat, which was (as I had heard it only once before) probably wildcat for purring.

Both kits were 8½ins long, with 2¾in. front legs and 2¼in. tails. Unlike adult wildcats, which have black feet, their soles were pale pink at one and a half days old. Their eyes were closed, little upward-slanting Chinese slits. As they groped for their mother's teats with bright red mouths, they often fell over on their backs, their feet waving comically in the air. Cleo kept the den spotlessly clean, licking their little vents to induce excretion before they soiled the bedding.

Patra was intensely interested in all that was going on. As I took several photos, she sat up like an otter, dangling her front paws and peering over into Cleo's den from the top of her own box. Whether she was happy at Cleo giving birth, or going all out to secure Sylvesturr's attention now that Cleo was busy, I did not know, but she clowned about in the sun most of the day. She pushed bluebells down and watched them spring up again, hauled them towards her and sniffed them delicately. When I fixed a small plastic pipe to take running water from the kitchen tap into a bowl in the pens, Patra occupied herself with trying to catch the falling drops. Sylvesturr watched with what I felt was silent disapproval. But for the nesting birds, and the thought that Patra might herself be pregnant – she now also seemed fatter than usual, and had after all spent much time with him – I would have turned her free to allow Cleo and Syl sole use of the pens.

Later I heard a slight clonk as I worked at my desk. As I went out I saw Sylvesturr's long tail floating into his den like a disembodied bush snake. One of the 6ft boards I had put along the front fencing had been completely turned over, and of seven black slugs on its underside three had been squashed in the centre, as if he had struck them mighty blows with his paws. Apart from this new revelation of his strength, it seemed astonishing he had worked out that slugs shelter by day in dark damp places near their food source, and that if he turned the board over he would be able to destroy the slimy wretches from which he had to protect his food each night by covering it over. I had not credited him with such intelligence.

By May 29 the kits were not falling about so much. Two days later, their eyes still closed, they gave gentle little high-pitched trills when seeking mama. I picked one up, wondering if I ought to handle them. After a few seconds it opened its crimson mouth wide and squalled with a high piercing '*mau*', or '*maow*', different from the earlier '*meeeoo*' sound.

Sylvesturr took no notice of the kittens' loud calls. Remembering that wildcat toms are supposed often to eat kits, I crawled to the front of the pens to see if he reacted to the sight of it. His expression did not change, but Cleo came after me with a low growl and I quickly made the soothing sounds she knew, hastily held the kit near her and crawled back to her den box with it. She walked close by my hand all the way. Foolishly, I had gone a bit too far, and might well have broken the trust I had built up with her.

With their eyes closed and still unable to walk, two days later the kits began to turn towards any disturbance with open mouths and tried to hiss and flare, but as they had no lung power yet, no sound at all came out. They wrinkled their little pink noses, opened and closed their mouths in what were meant to be ferocious snarls, like those of their father, then usually fell over sideways. Even at the tender age of one week they were prepared to have a go. Cleo spent a great deal of time grooming them all over with her rough tongue, and derived great sensual pleasure from feeling them crawl all over her. She took to looking into my eyes when they were busy with her teats, as if noting my reactions. She was immensely proud of them.

Next day the kits made their first spits, but so weakly that I heard nothing. Still blind and unable to stand, they reared up and spat at my sounds. Then they subsided, resting their heads on the hay in exhaustion with their mouths open as they breathed quickly, still trying to hiss. I lifted the gate to let in Patra, who was pacing up and down the fencing. She walked up to the den box, making a brief 'turtle dove' trill in her throat. Cleo did not drive her away, but let her sister poke her head right inside and look at the kits. Patra made no attempt to touch them and after a minute withdrew.

About an hour later I heard a shrew squealing shrilly and saw

Patra dive below Cleo's box. She missed the shrew and drew back. Straightaway Cleo went right under the box, caught the shrew in the thick grass and bit it to death. Instead of taking it to her kits, or into her box to eat, she trotted into Sylvesturr's pen and dropped it before his scowling face. Then she went back to her box again, on which Patra was sitting calmly as if approving of Cleo's gesture. The two females often caught though seldom ate shrews, but clearly Sylvesturr was partial to them. An hour later it was gone. Perhaps he needed more furred meat than I was able to trap. If so, how would Cleo know that? I was surprised and puzzled by the gift.

Not wanting to take any chances, I drove Patra out of Cleo's pen at dusk and put up the gate again. The kits were now 10¼ins long and their paws measured 1¼ins across. I noticed that after feeding they often lay sleeping against Cleo's warm furry body with their heads upside-down.

On June 3, Cleo greeted me with the same kind of rolling '*brrrooo*' trill that I had occasionally heard Patra make, and she repeated it again when lying in the den box and one of the kits was flopping about in a far corner, unable to find her. I now knew what the call meant: it was both a greeting and a means of self-identification. It could be used to indicate friendliness, when one cat walked towards another, or to call young kits.

Cleo spent most of the morning with her kittens, biting them playfully and turning herself suddenly on her back, as if to keep them groping and searching for her teats. She was still licking their rear ends clean, a practice she continued until they were weaned. I handled them both for a brief period. While I intended to free them later, I felt that constant attention might help to soften their ferocity, just as it had with Cleo and Patra. Although Cleo occasionally trod on the kits as they moved around, she was careful not to put her full weight on them. She had stopped growling when I took her food, though she was once more attacking it fiercely. Patra had long since ceased to growl at food time, unless I moved the bowl.

I noticed Patra had a subdued look, as if she felt that Cleo was the real star of the show and that she herself had failed. Her flirtatious and kittenish behaviour, which Sylvesturr largely ignored, had stopped altogether. Either the mating season was over or the theory that wildcats are monogamous was correct. She was definitely not pregnant.

6 · Raising the Family

As Cleo's kits would soon be walking, I decided to let Patra out of the pens. At dawn she wandered about the house '*mau*'ing loudly, as if she were lonely. She went back to sleeping on their old sacking bed in the woodshed.

On June 6 I found Cleo prowling up and down the fencing, looking bored with being cooped up for so long. I let her out for a run, leaving the door open, and she headed for the west wood. Her kits struggled, scratched and spat audibly as I handled them, as if they knew the danger was greater now they could not hear mama close by.

When Cleo did not return by late afternoon, I was afraid that she might stay out all night. I set Moobli to work – 'Track the pussy coots' – and nose down, he immediately began dodging through the long grass and then into the west wood. I heard the '*tchee-tchee, chirr . . . irrr . . . irrr*' warning notes of great tits and the ticking noises of wrens in the rhododendron bush by the path. It was the sound these birds make when mobbing a cat. Suddenly Moobli burst out of the wood and followed a scent straight into the bush. In a trice he had cornered Cleo under the tangled brown stems. Ears back, mouth open, she growled and spat as I clambered through the foliage towards her; Moobli blocked her escape route. She clawed at my gloves but did not bite. When I seized her by the scruff, she went limp and let me carry her back.

Once in the security of the pens, she was again tame and soon clatter-purring. After eating, she went into her den. She trod – carelessly it seemed – on her kits, whose feet groped helplessly for something to turn them right side up, but they were soon feeding lustily from her full teats.

Sylvesturr surprised me when I took his food, coming out to get it with a loud '*PAAAH!*' and a foot stamp – something he had not done since late autumn when he had been at his hungriest, putting on his winter fat. Perhaps he did so now beccause he had seen me carrying Cleo ignominiously into her pen and did not like to see his mate treated in such a fashion. Or maybe it was to tell me not to try the same thing with him.

Next day the kits' eyes started to open from the inside edges. Instead of being mere slits, they were now triangular, with bright china blue in the open part nearest the nose. They spat and flared as they heard me coming, and their little red tongues curved upwards and inwards at the edges, just like Sylvesturr's. From then on their progress was rapid.

Two days later (June 9) one kit's eyes were completely open, the other's almost so. The vivid bright blue of their irises made a beautiful contrast to their light tawny and grey-striped bodies and legs, but the eyes could not focus at all yet. Their heads were big and square, with ears set low, sticking out sideways with no upward slant, unlike those of domestic kits. Cleo often threw her head back between her kits as if she liked to feel their big feet and claws struggling over her face as they sought her teats. Next day Cleo licked the whitish film from the kits' lower eyelids. One kit was now beginning to focus, its head trembling as it nodded up and down; the other only a few hours behind in development. Their tiny teeth were still semi-transparent. Neither kit could walk properly. They put their rear hocks flat on the ground first, then raised the 'heel' as they moved forward on to the ball of the foot, swaying precariously from side to side as they did so, before collapsing into Cleo's warm fur.

By June 11 both kits' eyes were fully open, rounded and filled with bright china blue. They could make out my looming form for they flared and retreated when I was still outside the pen. They were lovely fat little creatures, over a foot long now. As I picked them up and stroked them, they cried out with even more piercing '*wheeow*'s, more like a whistle than a call. It was almost an exact replica of the calls their mother and aunt had made when I first brought them up the loch. Each time I handled them, Cleo stood up, watching closely, but usually giving her '*brrrooo*' call, which meant she did not mind too much. She was still cleaning their vents and being a marvellous mother.

I noticed that when Cleo was angry with me, the kits too would spit, but if she was clatter-purring, or making her throat trill, they did not. Wildcat kitten psyche would be set early in life by the mother's upbringing, like those of other animals or humans. Being taken so young from his mother could well explain Sylvesturr's mistrustful and angry outlook, for he was thrust early into the artificial concrete zoo environment instead of being brought up like Cleo and Patra, in the natural surroundings in which they were born and in which all their inherited instincts were rooted.

To observe their behaviour more closely, I set up a hide of sacking draped over some hazel hoops, which I could reach from the corner of the cottage without the cats seeing me. Watching from the hide at dusk, I saw Sylvesturr leave his den and walk towards the gate. Instantly Cleo left her box, danced up to him, and with a loud spit, reared herself up as if about to attack. Sylvesturr swiftly pulled his head back an inch and stared in disbelief. Then he turned away and trotted back into his den. It seemed possible that wildcat mothers could repel toms if they wished, for Cleo was considerably smaller than Sylvesturr. But my impression was that he merely wanted to take a look at the kits; there was certainly no belligerence about his investigation.

By June 13 the kits could see objects up to three yards away and were taking more interest in the world outside their box, looking out of the door and trying to focus on distant objects with up and down motions of their heads. As they grew bigger, they disliked being handled even more. When I picked up the larger kit, it called so loudly that Cleo snarled, but with a bewildered air, as if she wanted to rescue it and yet not get too nasty with me. I put it back quickly, and as soon as I did so Cleo broke into her clatter-purr again. Perhaps she was more tame since having the kits because she realized I was the sole food provider and without me she would have had a much harder time bringing up the kits.

By this time Patra had become very subdued in the shed, and for two nights running left half her food. She had a sad, big-eyed look about her. Feeling sorry for her, I put her back in Sylvesturr's pen.

Three days later I brought the kits and Cleo into my study in the den box and set them on the bed. I wanted to try to get the kits at least a little tame before they totally adopted their father's recalcitrant habits. The focusing of their exquisite blue eyes still took time to adjust as they transferred their gaze from one object to another. Every time I went near, they spat and flared, then immediately adopted a bewildered look.

They fed just when the mood took them, and the moment one sleeping kit stirred and touched the other, it too started to struggle to reach a teat. Often they burrowed between Cleo's back legs. When she needed a stretch, she stood up and arched her back, unmindful of the guzzling kits, who dropped off the teats one after the other. Then she lay upside-down again, purring as they struggled back over her body to the nearest part of the milk bar. I noticed how the kits kneaded, pummelled and trod the area round the teats with their big fat paws, to stimulate milk flow.

If one of them crawled too far away, or put its head over the hinged front dropboard of the box, Cleo called it back with the 'brrrooo' trill, and if that failed she called louder with a 'mau', which made them turn and crawl back.

The brief stay in the house seemed to have helped for the kits actually let me chuck them gently under the chin after Cleo responded to my usual calls with a little welcoming trill. The bigger kit took its first faltering steps down the front dropboard on the afternoon of June 17. When it tried to turn round on the sloping surface and started slipping, Cleo 'mau'd and bit its neck scruff very carefully, hauling it back in again. Although still wobbly, three days later the bigger kit scratched an ear with its hind leg for the first time. It also made its first attempt at play. Propped up on its right foreleg, it swatted out gently at Cleo's face with its left paw.

Patra, her good spirits restored, began to steal Sylvesturr's food again, so out of his pen she had to come. An hour later she had caught a vole and eaten all of it except the stomach, which she usually left. I felt she could probably look after herself now without much trouble.

Midsummer day was the first day without clouds or wind for over a week, and as I lay in the sun I had an idea. Although I did not want to domesticate or tame the kits, I hoped later to be able to observe their behaviour in the wild, and it would help if they became used to my presence now outside the house. I went into the pens and brought them all out in the den box, setting it against the cottage wall. As soon as I let down the front dropboard, Cleo leaped clear and ran back into her pen. I had not expected her to leave the kits, and fetched her out again. She stayed for about a minute with the sleeping kits, then sneaked back to the pens once more. She was not acting scared. I thought perhaps she was glad of the chance to have some time to herself, as if she were willing for me to take charge of the kits for a while. Maybe she wanted to visit Sylvesturr.

For the next hour I tried to make friends with the kits. I placed them on the open grass for photos, and soon they were either crawling towards the shade beneath me as I crouched on all fours, or into the thick grasses and buttercups by the cottage wall. Their immediate instinct when in the open was to hide. Once in the undergrowth, they explored it without fear, calling and sniffing the flowers, swatting out at each other from behind grass clumps, and generally having a fine old time. At noon I put them in the box and carried it back to the pens. Cleo was gone. I thought she was probably in the rhododendron bush (as usual, when she was free) and decided to let her enjoy herself for a while.

Towards the end of the afternoon, when she had still not returned, and Moobli was also absent, I called, but there was no response. I went indoors to change into trekking gear to search for them both. I then found Moobli at the front door, soaking wet. I waited until he slipped off again, and followed. He had found Cleo. She had discovered an old natural den in the bank of the burn at the far edge of the east wood, a full 250 yards from the house. Perhaps she was intending to move her kits there, for she was clearly not just hunting. It was too early to release them yet, before they were weaned. Telling Moobli to keep her there, I raced back for the thick gloves.

When I returned Cleo was crouching in the hole, growling, with ears back.

The earth outside had been deeply scratched. Although he liked the females, Moobli had probably thought I wanted him to get her out and had pawed at the entrance while I was away. Cleo would not know he meant her no harm, and as I was not there, his actions had scared her. Her pupils were wide and black and she spat loudly and clawed. I took hold of her neck scruff and hauled her out as she started to kick with her strong back feet. Then she got her claws into the gloves and, twisting her head round, bit deeply through them. I tried to hold on but her teeth went into my hand and her rear claws were drawing blood from my lower arm. I had to let go. She ran straight back and crouched inside growling. She was really worked up now and I was not going to try and catch her by hand again in that mood.

Just before dusk I went back without Moobli but she was nowhere to be found. I knew from working with cougars in Canada that mothers will leave their kits alone for two or three days at a time, but I did not want to risk it with the wildcats. With Moobli playing bloodhound, we went twice round both woods, hoping the noise might drive her back to the pens, but without result. About an hour after dark I went out with a torch. Although I had put her food in its usual place, Cleo was still not back. I then had some awful visions – the kits could be killed by Sylvesturr if they staggered to the edge of the pens looking for their mother, or by gulls or ravens, or by a fox at dawn, or even by a weasel in the den box itself. It was going to be a clear, very cold night. At less than a month old, the kits had had no food all day. I panicked and brought them and their box into the bedroom, put on a paraffin heater and tried to feed them.

It was quite a performance to get warm milk down them from a baby's bottle and a cut-down rubber lamb's teat. They yowled, swallowed some, dribbled it down their chests and over their feet, yowled again, spat, flared and scratched, but never once did they try to bite. Cutely they tried to wash themselves with their tiny tongues, biting at the wet milk between their toes with little nibbles. After some hours I managed to get a mere three tablespoonfuls down each kit. Then I dried them off and covered them with warm cotton wool for the night.

I was just climbing into bed at 2 a.m. when I realized that if Cleo came back at night and found the kits and the den box gone, she might leave for good. I dressed again and put the den box back into the run, made a really deep bowl of dry hay for the kits, then fixed the pen door slightly open – enough for Cleo to squeeze through but not, I hoped, any large fox. I had seen no evidence of weasels in the area. I hoped it would not be too cold, but I had no choice.

Uppermost in my mind as I finally turned in was that Cleo had, without being scared away, left the kits in my care this morning. And her own mother had abandoned her and Patra when they were kits.

I hurried out soon after dawn to see how the kits were. As I reached the pens, Cleo calmly ambled up from the rhododendron bush with a murmured '*brrrooo*' – in complete contrast to the spitting virago of the night before – and walked round the enclosures looking for a way in to her kits. She clearly mistrusted the slightly open door.

I let Cleo in. The kits looked awfully still, lying in the hay nest. I gave a '*mau*' and up they stood and staggered to the box entrance, peering like little old men without their glasses. As soon as mama came into focus, they tried to clamber out to her, but she completely ignored them and began tucking into the food I had left out for her overnight. Clearly no fox had been around for it could have forked the food out with its claws.

Cleo seemed not at all worried about her kits. She had been away on a well-earned break, in which she had no doubt clobbered a vole or two. When she had eaten and drunk her fill, she ambled into the den with a light '*brrrooo*' and sank down among her kits while they went crazily for her teats.

After writing a few letters I went out to find that the kits had climbed out of the den box and were taking their first faltering steps over the pen floor. They wobbled and shook, paused, fell over, but kept trying. Then Cleo decided they had had enough and carried each one back into the box by the neck scruff.

Next morning I found Sylvesturr had not eaten his previous night's meal. He had carried one large piece of meat over to the gate between the pens. There was no other way the meat could have got there, for Patra was now living in the woodshed again. It seemed he had intended it as a gift for Cleo. Perhaps Syl had been concerned at her absence all night. I took the gate down and a few minutes later Cleo eased through, picked up the meat, carried it over to Syl's own food dish and ate it there, right outside his den.

It was really odd behaviour, especially as wildcat mothers are reputed to rear their young well away from the tom so that he could not kill and eat the kits. Twice more I found pieces of Sylvesturr's meat by the gate in the mornings. It certainly seemed to prove that there is some inter-feeding between tom and female, though such behaviour would vary. While the females fought to protect food, he had never once competed with them, or stopped them taking his.

Being nocturnal or crepuscular creatures, wildcats are hard to study in the wild, so it is probable that the wildcat tom gained his bad reputation from rare instances where both tom and female had eaten their own kits in zoos – in noisy artificial confines, with constant human activity around them. If it did happen in the wild, it could be an aberration caused by a scarcity of prey, a strange tom chancing upon kits that were not his own, or by a 'personality' defect in a particular animal. Eight years of wilderness living had taught me that animals (especially my wildcats) are as varied in character as humans. The animal world also has its unnatural spoilers and fools.

Three days later the kits launched their first 'attack'. Instead of visiting them in the morning and picking each one up briefly as usual, I went in the late afternoon. Despite the normal soothing words, which brought the usual '*brrrooo*' response from Cleo, they retreated behind her when my face loomed, and spat and flared. When my hand moved to pick one up, they spat again and both swiped out with their claws. The swats did not seem to be aimed right at the hand but near it. They had no idea yet of pulling the finger on to the bite, a wildcat characteristic. They also growled for the first time, like small high-pitched dynamos, baby versions of their ferocious father. As soon as I showed I was determined and actually picked them up, they went all soft and childlike again, with an odd bewildered look.

The slightly larger kit with the broader face still could not focus its eyes completely, but it was the fiercer of the two. As soon as I put it down it ran and hid beneath the small plank on which I set out the food. Cleo seemed not at all concerned by their tiny attacks on me. She ignored their hissing and spitting, nor was she angry with me in any way. I felt proud that after her wild suspicious youth she seemed to trust me now she had kits, especially as it was the opposite of what I had expected.

Patra now seemed settled in the woodshed and was catching many mice, voles and a few shrews. The ones she left I dropped in to Sylvesturr, who ate them all avidly, even the shrews.

The next two days were spent scything down the bracken in front of the cottage (for the third time that year) and weeding my vegetable garden. I transplanted over 100 young cabbages and, having no hose, watered them in from four bucketfuls of water with a small siphon pipe. It is surprising how far a small amount of water will go if directed to each individual plant. Within four hours their flattened sun-wilted leaves lifted up and began soaring nicely. That evening, as Cleo was eating, the larger kit sniffed the air and staggered near to her, to be immediately repulsed by a growling Cleo. The kit recoiled and looked at its mother with astonishment. As it sat there, broad face perplexed, ears set so low down it looked as if it was wearing a cloth cap, I decided it was surely a male and to call it Freddy.

Wearing gloves, I managed to take a close look at both kits: male and female. The male was now 15 ins long, while the slightly smaller, prettier kit, with rounder eyes and a smaller face, was just under 14½ ins. I called her Mia – after a young girl with a back ailment, who had been writing to me from America ever since I had published two articles about wilderness living in the *Chicago Tribune* magazine two years earlier.

It was now time to transfer Cleo and the kits into the main pen, and to install Sylvesturr temporarily in the woodshed, before I tried the first experimental release of Cleo and the kits into the woods in a few weeks' time. I carried the box-cage trap into his pen and, leaving his food dish empty, baited it with some sheep flank.

Next morning I saw that Sylvesturr had been in the trap. He had bitten through the thick nylon line to the bait, and had forced his way out again between the side netting and the roof, which foolishly I had forgotten to bind with wire. He was now back in his den wearing what seemed a most self-satisfied air. There was no chance he would go into the trap again. Knowing his memory, I was surprised he had gone into it at all. He must have been hungry. I now had no choice but to drive him into it. I opened the trapdoor and held it up with nylon line threaded through the roof fencing with my right hand while I prodded with my left into his den with the blunt hazel stick, around which I had wrapped thick wadding. He immediately turned on the wadding and attacked it, biting and clawing. I was glad it was not my arm in there.

Finally he shot out growling, glared about for somewhere to go, ran into the trap then straight out again before I had time to release the trapdoor. He ran round the edges of the pen like a small cougar. Then he came towards me and spat heartily in my face, set off on another circuit and stopped to look up at the sky. Suddenly he leaped up at the thick wired roof and held his entire weight on the claws of one paw as he looked round for a gap. He had incredible strength, and looked like a large gibbon hanging there, with his long striped tail dangling. Then he walked across the roof by his front claws like an acrobat. I had never seen a cat do anything like it before. His shoulder muscles bulged powerfully as he moved. What extraordinary agility for an old cat! I had noticed before that wild-cats can be at peak form in a split second after days of lying about without exercise. Finally he dropped down and ran into the small den box that had been used by Patra. I transferred him to the woodshed where he had his former half-section, the logpile, a nice big window and lonely Patra for company.

Next day, before renovating Sylvesturr's den for Cleo and the kits, I found Patra to be more than mere company for Sylvesturr. She had caught a large vole and had taken it to him. I saw it lying on his side of the fencing, along with two shrews. For all her faults, Patra had developed into a fine hunter, and was now as good as Cleo had been before having the kits. Whether she was trying to reinstate herself in old Sylvesturr's favour was mere human speculation, but she was sharing her prey with him. Patra was useful at last.

It became obvious that Cleo and the kits were happier in the larger natural den and the whole area of the two pens. Freddy and Mia began to explore the small hazel bushes, the little shady groves beneath the ferns and bracken, the shelter from the archway of brambles, and they stalked each other through the long grass, leaping out clumsily in most inefficient ambush. They often hissed when there was no danger, just if the wind blew a leafy frond. They dived into the semi-circular entrance in the den door when they saw me coming. Often Freddy would poke his nose out again, blinking at me owlishly, his eyesight still not at its best.

Although I gave her all the milk and food she could take, Cleo had become quite thin with the demands of feeding the two large kits. Oddly, while Sylvesturr would crack open and eat eggs, neither Patra nor Cleo would do so unless I broke them first. I once found a chaffinch's eggshell on the shed floor which Patra had brought in. As wildcats climb trees easily, it seems possible that occasionally they do prey on birds' eggs, but perhaps only if rabbit, vole and mouse prey is short.

On July 12 I came back after watching two young sparrowhawk chicks learning to fly in the high tree tops, and set Cleo's food out early. As she stood by the dish eating, Mia came out of the den, saw her tail and stalked it, pouncing on its black tip with both paws. Cleo took little notice as she ate but kept flicking it about airily, just out of Mia's reach as she leaped and tumbled after it.

Two days later there was a thunderstorm and a great deal of rain. I came back after baling both boats and hauling them above the higher loch level to find that Mia had disappeared. I searched the pen but found nothing. I dashed round the area in the rain, but again drew a blank. I then commanded Moobli to track the cats but he just stared at me, and for once, just when I needed him most, did not seem to understand what I wanted. What a time to be obtuse! I forgot myself, yelled at him, shoved his nose to the ground and simulated sniffing. He stared at me as if I was mad – and at that moment I probably was – for what seemed his deliberate refusal to track Mia made me so angry that I clouted him hard. This upset his dignity so much he walked straight into the kitchen and refused to come out. When I had cooled down, I apologized, and at dusk we went out again. With patient encouragement he tried hard to track Mia, but apart from a whiff of Patra in the east wood, we again drew a blank.

On our return to the cat pens, I heard a weak plaintive '*mau*'. Cleo came out of the den and began sniffing the air. Then she walked to the little sandpit I had made for the cats, urinated, squatting on her haunches, then went to the big rocks beside the den. At that moment little Freddy, who had watched all this, went over to the sandpit, sniffed and began to '*mau*' and scrape at the sand. Whether Cleo had actually taught him this or he was just instinctively copying her, I did not know, but it was so comical, that I smiled. Then I heard the faint '*mau*' again, and saw the grass moving at the back of the pen.

There was Mia. She must have squeezed through the fencing and spent the day among the crevices and huge rocks which I had cut into to make the pen in a natural area. She had been too scared during the thunder to make a move. Now that dusk was falling and the thunder had stopped, she wanted her mama. Cleo saw her and moved towards her. Fearing she might just dodge back into the rocks again, I crept behind her and pounced on a suddenly raging, open-mouthed bundle of claws and teeth. She could not bite, for I had her tight by the scruff, but she clawed with surprising strength. After carrying her round to the front I put her through the camera hole in the fencing. Cleo waited, then followed her wobbly gait back to the den with a solicitous maternal air. I looked at my bleeding hand, surprised that she could inflict such damage at barely seven weeks old.

Next day Mia vanished again, but she was back before dusk. Shortly after I fed Cleo, Freddy ran up to her side as she was chewing in the bowl. He sniffed the meat, grabbed a piece in his jaws, growled while holding it still, as if ready to flee with it, then decided it was quite safe and began to eat. Cleo not only allowed this but backed off slightly when Freddy made his high-pitched dynamo growl. Cleo would never have given way to Patra over food, and had never had to back down to courteous old Sylvesturr, yet she had backed off from her own kit at his first attempt to eat, in that way encouraging him. So at 50 days old, Freddy was weaned. I noticed that the bright blue of his eyes was being banished by a light grey, which was working outwards from the pupil in an irregular oval shape. Mia showed no interest in solid food yet.

Cleo, at this time eating almost twice as much as usual, was still hungry after her feed the following evening and walked up and down the fencing with loud '*mau*'s. As I brought her more, both kits came running out, but this time, as Freddy went near, she clobbered him with a clawless paw, bowling him over. Then she carried a piece of meat away and let him have his pick from the rest.

Both kits were now spending part of the day in the rocky crevices behind the fencing. Around 8 p.m. both came running back to Cleo for a suck. '*Mau*', they called as they came, with a responsive '*brrrooo*' from her. Freddy lay upside-down as she stood over him, while Mia fastened on to a rear teat like a deer fawn, down on her front knees with her backside up in the air as her hind legs were bent while still on their toes. They had much bigger jaws and canid teeth (now pure white) than domestic kittens. The soles of the feet, which had been darkening since birth, were now all black and the underside fur of the rear hocks was also turning blackish, like their elders'.

The following afternoon the cats played together. Watched by the kits, Cleo made mock stalks, pouncing on leaves and pieces of grass moving in the breeze. The kits tried to imitate her with their two front paws but fell over to right or left at the rear. Occasionally Freddy grabbed his mother's moving back legs in abortive Rugby tackles, which she bore stoically.

Later, after both kits had ventured again into the rocky crevices behind the pens, Freddy became stuck getting back through the fencing. I hauled him out with both hands, but he immediately turned, scratched hard and sank his canines in so hard they met in the underside of my forefinger. I shoved him back through the camera hole and Cleo immediately seized him by the neck. Stagger-ing, she half dragged and carried him into the den.

I was worried by the kits' apparent desire to leave Cleo and be alone for a while each day, and shut off the rear rocky mound with doubled netting. They were still too young to be out overnight, when a big prowling fox might get them. By next morning Mia had again found a way through. I gave up: Cleo, a good mother, would stop Mia if she felt there was any danger.

When I went to feed Sylvesturr in the woodshed, he came out early, stamped his foot and spat. Most of his side fur and some on his back had moulted, so that his flanks looked pink and half naked as he walked. At first I thought he was eating too much Vitamin A (in the liver) but saw that in places new short paler hair was already sprouting. It seemed he had both a spring and a late summer moult, and the summer coat was lighter than the winter one. It made sense, for it would camouflage him better among all the new growth and increased light of the warmer season.

On July 18, Mia ate her first meat. Cleo actually moved over to make room for her at the bowl. I noticed Mia's eyes were also turning grey. She was about three days behind Freddy in physical development, yet she was the wilder of the two kits, still squeezing to the rocks behind for an hour or two each day.

That day Sylvesturr faced me down in the shed with a loud '*PAAAH!*' As he glared directly into my eyes, growling, fully extended on his front legs, I thought I had learned one secret of his 'attack'. Caught out in the open, he was probably afraid to turn his back on potential danger, because it would make him more vulner-able. Instead, he would launch a full-frontal display of ferocity without actually attacking, just to set you back on your heels and thus gain enough time to make an escape. At the front he had sight, teeth, claws and an awful aspect, but at the back he had none of these, nor could he see so well. Sure enough, when I retreated a few paces, he slid into his box. His 'attack' was therefore based on fear, on defence, and not upon overt aggression – unless he was cornered. I put down his food, and some for Patra, and left.

Next day dawned bright and sunny for the first time in over a week. Cleo and the kits revelled in the morning heat. She seemed to be teaching them to hunt. Wherever she moved, she switched her tail about and the kits dived, jumped, rolled and grabbed at it with their claws or teeth, or pinned it to the ground with both paws and bit at it as though they were holding a mouse down. Recovering slowly from the strain of carrying and suckling the kits, she could easily flick her tail about when feeding, even when lying down and sunning herself, and thus help make her kits faster, stronger and more secure on their feet, without needing to expend energy herself. The jet black blunt tip made a fine target, and hunting Cleo's tail now seemed a regular feature of the daily play. Perhaps this is why wildcats have black tips to their tails.

Despite the tail-twitch training, Cleo slowly became more fierce with the kits at feeding time. She began to growl if they attempted to thrust their heads into the feed bowl. After eating her fill, she would walk away, leaving them to get their own. The kits also began to flare at each other over food. Cleo would not have attacked the kits, of course, but seemed to be teaching them that food was something to be valued, and once reached, kept strictly to oneself.

By now the kits' eyes were almost all grey but before the bright blue disappeared from the outer edges, the lighter yellow-gold colour of their mature eyes was already starting to replace the interim grey.

During the next few days, Mia spent much of her time alone in the rear rocks while Freddy had clearly decided he preferred to stay around his mama. This coincided with what I had learned about cougars in Canada, where young females were far more independent and became skilful hunters quicker than the young males, which often made mistakes when hunting their first big prey, such as deer. At that stage in their lives they preyed more often on easier farm animals. Naturally, this caused an outcry from farmers who wanted the marauding cougars shot, despite their rarity. There is a similar situation in the Highlands where, because of their occasional 'offence' of preying on loose poultry and upon game birds and their young, the wildcat was brought almost to extinction before the First World War. In its pure form it is still rare today. We tend to forget that we have taken over most of these animals' hunting grounds, reducing their natural prey, and thus forcing some animals to prey on stock in order to survive.

After phoning Dr Brambell towards the end of July, I formed my final plan for releasing all the wildcats except Sylvesturr. In the west wood I found a completely dry spot in tangled undergrowth between four large criss-crossed windfall trunks, a few yards south of the cairn of boulders on the east edge of the granite escarpment.

Two of the trunks ended in a five-foot-high, up-ended root cluster which also had sheltered tunnels and a natural chamber beneath it. To make sure it all stayed dry, I erected a sloping sheet of corrugated iron between the trunks, where the undergrowth almost obscured it, and large fronds of dark green bracken hid the open area below. I would put Cleo's box there, and they could choose between this shelter, the area under the roots or the rocky cairn as their future home. Just to the left was a large square rock with a flat top covered in lush green moss. On this I would regularly put out their food and drink each evening. Whenever hunting proved poor, they could always regard the mossy rock as the place for food.

But what was I to do with Patra? She was now idling away her days in the woodshed. She was leaving most of the food I put out for her, so was clearly earning most of her living from the woods.

On recent supply excursions I had noticed a pair of kestrels had moved on to the small green island that was a Highland burial ground, six miles up the loch. Wondering what had attracted them, I wandered over it and was astonished to find a plague of voles. Wherever I looked in the open areas between the azalea, whin and rhododendron bushes, voles were scuttling to and fro like little animated cigar butts in their daytime tunnels in the grass. At first I thought my eyes were playing tricks − zip, zip, zip, the little furry bodies shot here and there through the tangles between the old gravestones. There must have been thousands on the island, and they would certainly be causing damage to the young trees and bushes which helped make it such a picturesque place. The kestrel pair would barely dent such an overcrowded population. Here seemed the ideal place to release Patra, at least for a few weeks. Not only would she keep herself healthy and learn full independence, but also perform a useful community service.

By now the kits were more than two months old, and even Mia was finding it difficult to get through the fencing into the rocks behind. They spent much time stalking moths and flies in front of the den, some of which they ate, and in grooming each other. Freddy could repel Moobli easily when he came sniffing at the pens, with a show of ferocity like a small version of his father. Moobli just whined and looked up at me with hurt eyes. He was, thank heaven, remaining gentle as far as the females and the kits were concerned.

I had arranged to meet some friends, a local estate foreman and his young daughter, and bring them back by boat next day to have a look at Wildernesse and the wildcats. That would have to be the big day, I decided. My friends could not only see my home but also usefully witness Patra's release on the green island and the freeing of Cleo and the kits in the west wood. As I made final adjustments to their future home site, I congratulated myself on how well things seemed to be dove-tailing together. Cleo and the youngsters would have plenty of time to become used to the area, to find the best hunting places before winter, and the kits could grow strong and fast before I finally released old Sylvesturr.

7 · A Taste of Freedom

Freedom day did not run according to plan. To begin with, Mia had escaped again into the rocky mound, but I would have to deal with her later. Wearing gloves, I managed to coax Cleo and Freddy into their old den box, then carried them, growling slightly, to the sheltered spot between the windfalls. I set out food and milk on the large mossy rock which was to be their regular feeding place, and let down their front door. Cleo looked carefully round the new scene, sniffed the air, then lay down casually while Freddy nuzzled into her furry belly for a teat.

After lunch, I tried to put Patra into a thick deep-sided cardboard box, ready to drop her off at the green island but she 'mau'd, bit the gloves, scratched and fought like a fiend. Despite my efforts to hold the lid down, she forced her way out again and ran like a huge hare towards the burn in the east wood.

Later, after I had fed Sylvesturr in the woodshed, Cleo walked up to the pens from the rhododendron bush by the path and 'mau'd. Then, from the rocks behind, out came Mia. I stood well back as she came to the front of the pens 'mau'ing anxiously. Cleo greeted her with a little 'brrrrooo' trill. Mia rubbed nose and whiskers with her mama, then followed her through the undergrowth to the west wood.

Shortly before dusk next evening, Cleo came back to the pens again, and just behind her were both the kits. There was no fencing between us now, to make the kits feel secure. I walked slowly towards them. Cleo showed little fear but Freddy and Mia shot away a few yards and crouched hidden and immobile in the long grass and bracken. They were difficult to see, for their thin dark stripes blended perfectly with the stems of the surrounding foliage.

They now had to regard the west wood and not the pens as home, so I clapped my hands at Cleo, shooing her back to the south edge of the wood. Seeing their mother running off, the kits bounded after her with their tails high. I found Patra back at the woodshed, but she was very wary after yesterday's attempt to take her to the green isle.

An hour later I gave the usual calls and put the food down for the mother and kits on the mossy rock. Cleo came out of the undergrowth a minute or so after I called but the kits kept their distance, though I could hear their little '*mau*'s.

When I went out next day, there was a large wildcat dropping in the middle of the doorstep. Perhaps it was a mark of rejection by Cleo, or of anger by Patra. At dusk, Cleo came to the feeding rock when I went to take a look, but again the kits kept in the undergrowth '*mau*'ing faintly. As I walked back to the house to get their food, Cleo followed a few yards behind, not along the open path but in the undergrowth by its side. She stopped at the rhododendron bush. It was good that she was still associating me with food. When I came back with it, she followed again but would not let me touch her now she was out of the pens. She jumped on to the rock when I was a few yards away and began to eat, while the kits called, still keeping out of sight.

Towards midnight, I crept down the edge of the wood from the north and waited in almost complete darkness. Before long the wildcats began calling to each other. It was an oddly thin call that a human could easily have mistaken for a wind sound, a high-pitched, drawn out '*awrooori*'. It was a sound that carried far, but it was hard to tell exactly where it came from. I heard this strange call many times later and realized it was a special wildcat sound, made so that a family could keep in touch yet confuse any would-be predators.

For the whole of August and in early September I kept close watch on the movements of the wildcats while still allowing them complete freedom. Moobli looked forward to the days when we went out to track them by scent. As soon as he located any of the cats in the undergrowth, they immediately shot up the nearest tree, where I could more easily check their condition. By noting exactly where he found them, and when, I could work out the rough pattern of their movements and their hunting areas, which became wider with each passing week. Without Moobli the wildcat release project would have foundered, for in such woods and dense under-growth, including the six-foot-high bracken forests on the north hill, contact with the kits could easily have been lost.

Moobli got a good scent along the rocky shore on August 3 and shot off 70 yards over big rocks obscured by bracken and started whining. Patra was up a tree near the loch shore. We left her, tracked all through the east wood along the foot of north hill and all through the north end of the west wood without finding any scent. Cleo and the kits were not in the den box but Moobli found Cleo and Freddy in a tangle of thick bracken and fallen tree branches that I had piled up during the winter on the wood's eastern edge. Cleo shot 15 feet up a larch tree, while Freddy scrambled to the top of a seven-foot cluster of fallen tree roots where he perched spitting loudly. He seemed in fine shape. Of Mia there was no sign.

With Moobli in the house, Cleo came to my calls at feeding time as dusk fell. Freddy came skulking along under the two fallen larches and, for the first time in my sight, sprang up to join his mother feeding on the rock. Back at the cottage later that evening, Moobli whined at the front door and I darted out to find Mia under some spare hay, which I had piled in the open porch to keep dry, and Patra fleeing into the dark. As Moobli sniffed closer, Mia spat and swiped out, and he narrowly missed losing part of his nose. Wilder now, she looked fat and healthy, her tail as wide and bushy as a flue brush. She was easy to hold at bay with a hissing paraffin lamp because she could not see past it into the dark. But we left her, happy to know that she too was still all right.

The next day was sultry and hot. I cut a quarter acre of second crop hay before the irritating hordes of midges put a stop to the work. Then I spread armfuls of loose green bracken over Sylves-turr's main den, preparatory to putting him back in the pens. The winter frosts and snows, the spring and summer winds and rains, and sexton beetles working away at Sylvesturr's old dung, had reduced the original ten armfuls to a few handfuls of dust.

Tracking round after the cats before lunch, Moobli put Patra up an old ash tree on the far side of the burn, well beyond the east wood. It was the first time we had found any of the cats across the burn and, as she was seldom in the woodshed now, it seemed she

above: On May 25 Cleo gave birth to two fine kits, Freddy and Mia, seen here at six days old.

below: At eleven days old, their eyes not fully open, Mia and Freddy tried to hiss and spit at human disturbance.

above: Cleo with Mia and Freddy, now over three weeks old, in their den box.

below: At one month old and enjoying their first outing, exploring the sunny world of grass and flowers.

above: Freddy and Mia flared in their den at my looming human form. They bit if handled.

below: Cleo with the kits on July 22.

I set free the wildcat family at the end of July and used Moobli to track them, putting them up trees so I could check their condition. I fed them on a mossy boulder.

was going wild easily. Maybe I would not need to put her on the green island after all.

While walking along the shore directly below the cottage in the late afternoon, Moobli began an anguished whining up ahead. He had Cleo at bay in a natural blind burrow that went deep into the bank under the front fence. She knew well enough that he could not get in and so just lay there, ears back and growling. I called him away. Two hundred yards further on, at the mouth of the burn, Moobli got another strong scent. He ran through the bracken, and up a tiny fir tree shot Mia. The odd thing was that Patra was with her, but she bounded away westwards towards the temporary refuge which Cleo had found under the fallen tree branches. Mia was perched with her front and rear feet about 18 inches apart straddling the top twig-like branches – a perfect picture. I ran back to the cottage for the camera. I had to change lenses and put in a new film, but when I got back Mia was still there and I got a good shot.

She stayed in the tree for half an hour. It was clear that, though adult wildcats take to trees, the young inexperienced kits go up the first tree stump or root cluster they can find, even if it is small and unsuitable.

That evening Cleo came alone to my call at feed time in the west wood and there was no sight or sound of the two kits. She was very hungry, springing on to the rock as soon as I put out the food. I saw she was still very thin, though her milk glands were full, so she was obviously still feeding the kits.

A possibility then dawned on me. Maybe Patra had assumed some maternal duties and was helping to train the kits to hunt and forage – at least during the daytime. In this way Cleo would be left to get the best of my free food and rebuild her energy and strength. This was certainly in line with Percy Dewar's observation of cougars in Canada, where he had found that sister cats would run together for up to two years, and that the unmated sister would sometimes help with the kits on hunting expeditions. That wildcats might also follow this behaviour was interesting.

The thick bracken jungle behind the house had become the favourite pre-dawn hunting area for the kits, and the most eerie experience I ever had with them occurred there.

After hearing both kits 'awroori'ing in the west wood on the morning of August 5, I relined Sylvesturr's old den with new hay and, having boarded him up in his box, transferred him back to the pens. Once again, after the usual growls, he dropped to the ground and with perfect memory, head down, padded off straight into the den like a furry tank. Two days later Moobli ran through the bracken on a strong scent line, then abruptly shot a few feet backwards. He had cornered Freddy far from any tree, and what a packet of ferocity the kitten had now become! Back on his haunches, eyes glaring, ears flat, tail as thick as a bottle, he spat and swiped out with claws so far extended that his paws looked like round black metal plates filled with sharp scimitars. As the looming threat of Moobli kept him there, I decided to try and measure him and get a good close-up photograph.

I took off my jacket, knelt on its edges, my elbows holding down the sides, and threw it tightly over the hissing bundle. There was no sound, nor any struggle. He just lay crouching underneath. Bit by bit I peeled back the coat, ready to grab his neck scruff with my gloved hand. There was nothing there. The wildcat kitten had vanished. It was as if a magician had performed a disappearing trick. I dug into the soft ground with my fingers. Nothing. Even Moobli was still staring at the spot. The comical expression on his face must have been nothing to the one on mine.

We had heard nothing, felt nothing, seen no movement nor one stem of bracken quiver. That young wildcat, a tangle of tendons and lithe sinew, had shot away faster than the dog's eyes or mine had been able to follow. It was one of the most uncanny experiences of my life.

A quarter of an hour later, as we worked our way through the bracken to the north-east corner of the west wood, we encountered not Freddy but Mia. She ran up a small willow tree, where I photographed her several times. As we turned to leave, I saw both Freddy and Patra sneaking along the level trunk of the huge fallen silver fir that lay along the top of the rock escarpment in the wood. I was now certain that Patra had taken over the training of the kits, at least some of the time. But where was Cleo?

We found out when we returned home. There she was in the workshop at the back (the door of which I had left open) helping herself to Moobli's sterilized meat sausages. It was the first time she had returned to the workshop since her own kittenhood. She had two sheep ticks behind her right ear and looked run down.

What an odd reversal of roles! When young, Cleo had always been the wild one, the expert explorative hunter. Surely this was one reason why Sylvesturr had chosen her. Now Patra, strong through not having kits to feed, had become the mighty hunter and Cleo was allowing her to run with the kits and help teach them to hunt. To think that I had intended to banish Patra to the green isle a week or two ago. She was certainly earning her keep now.

In the heat of the afternoon I crept quietly down to the bottom of the west wood with binoculars. Cleo was lying in the den box. Both kits, now almost as large as their mother, were suckling from her teats. There was no sign of Patra. What an odd lot they were, I thought. Only Cleo came to the feeding rock at dusk, but I saw Patra running through the wood with one of the kits behind her.

Later, as I cooked supper, Moobli whined at the front door. Instead of letting him out I went into the dark study and peered through the window. Mia was sniffing a small dark object on the ground beside the log porch. As I watched, the object jumped forward a few inches – *flub*. She poked out a tentative paw. Again it jumped, weakly, heavily – *flub*. It was one of the two toads that had moved in to hunt insects in the hay. She sniffed it again, and this time it jumped towards her. Immediately she shot backwards, looked at it again fearfully, then ran away towards the west wood. Mia was interested in frogs but this fat old toad, with its dry, warty, poisonous skin, which had no fear, was clearly something to be left alone.

Next morning I turned my hay crop in blazing sunshine, laid out some edible toadstools to dry, and went to post some urgent mail. As I boated home under gathering clouds, a loud thunderstorm broke out overhead and small spikes of lightning struck the rock faces of the higher mountain ridges. I hurried to gather my hay before the deluge, but the storm luckily missed Wildernesse, while three miles to the west the clouds dragged dark grey skirts of rain across the loch. At dusk, both kits followed Cleo when she came to my calls and stopped six yards away as she leaped up to feed. When I backed away, Freddy also jumped up, and was followed by Mia, who first sneaked round to the rear of the rock. All the cats growled as they ate. Freddy swatted Mia for coming too close to his piece of meat. It was the first time I had seen all three on the rock together, a small moment of triumph.

After leaving them alone for three days, we tracked the wildcats again on August 10. Moobli put Freddy up a tree near the den box in the west wood. At feed time Cleo came to the rock, followed closely by Freddy. After feeding, she went into the den box while her son hid in the natural root tangle chamber below.

My practice each morning the sun shone was to pull Sylvesturr's door up for an hour, to warm up his den. Each time I did this, he built a barricade from his hay bed and hid behind it, his glowering golden eyes just peeping over the top. Whereas we often found the kits and young females out hunting by day, Sylvesturr seldom came out until evening and certainly never ate until it was almost dark. It seemed to me possible that young kits hunt first by daylight, and that nocturnal hunting is something they have to learn as they grow older, taking advantage of the ability to see in almost total darkness.

Two days later Mia ran nearly 200 yards through the undergrowth and scooted up a small fir from which she could have been shaken by hand. Patra, who was with her, shot along the banks of the burn and disappeared. Moobli was slow at sighting the cats because he was low in the bracken himself, but he could run nose-high on a fresh scent.

Shortly after that I collected with my mail a note from Dr Michael Brambell of London Zoo, whom I had asked to visit me on his next holiday in the area. He and his wife Patricia and their two young sons would be at a small pier at noon in four days' time. I was delighted to have the chance of showing them not only that old Sylvesturr was thriving, but that he was indeed the father of two lovely kittens.

No sooner was the visit arranged than the kits disappeared. In dull drizzle we tracked all round the north hills and the west wood and along the shore without any sign of the cats. I felt a little worried. I took Moobli to the north edge of the east wood. He picked up some scent near the waterfall, then we scrambled south along the banks of the burn. Twice he lost the scent, stumbling through the rushing burn as I crossed on a creaking dead larch. Then he went back across the burn lower down as I negotiated the treacherously slippery trunk of a fallen beech to follow him. Suddenly a buzzard, perched low on a stunted beech tree near the shore, shot away through the wood, flying with curved back wings like a huge hawk. My heart jumped. A buzzard's eyesight is eight times better than a man's. What was it doing perched so low in a wood? Maybe it had spotted something dead – like a wildcat kitten – and the dense bracken had prevented the scent of the corpse reaching Moobli.

We ran over, but found nothing. Then Moobli picked up a strong scent and dived under the shore fence. As I caught up, both kits shot up two alder trees. I climbed up close to Freddy. He looked really mad and evil, ears back and down, and snarling. I took two photos and was about to get down when Freddy walked down the branch towards me, then leaped – all four limbs extended, claws out, like a sky-diver trying to control his fall – and almost glided the 16 feet down to the ground. He landed with an audible plop on a flat rock, as if all the air had been forced out of his lungs. I felt sure he was badly winded, if not worse, but he bounced immediately and high-tailed it into the east wood, heading for the beech tree which bridged the burn.

It was an astonishing escape. His slanting air flight must have been a good 20 feet and reminded me of the flying squirrels I had often seen in Canada. As soon as Freddy had landed, Mia scrambled backwards down her tree five feet away and scampered north-west through the bracken. As she reached the top of the rocky bank, Patra sprang out of hiding and went with her.

As I wanted to determine whether both kits or just Mia were really running with Patra, we went out again in the late afternoon. We quickly put Patra up by the rhododendron bush south-east of the cottage. I held Moobli back and watched her run. She headed south-west to the gate and shore, then turned left and was lost to sight. I let Moobli go after a minute and he sped away, tracking nose-high, following her route exactly where she had doubled back from the gate 250 yards along the bracken-filled shore. When I reached him, Moobli was showing great interest in the root tangle of an old stump on the edge of the secondary burn mouth. From the snarls and spits that erupted when Moobli put his nose down, I reckoned that Patra and at least one kit were in there. So this was Patra's den. It explained why we had so often found her and Mia in the vicinity, and today Freddy too. Cleo's den was still the den box, or else the near-by roots chamber in the west wood.

It seemed finally to establish that the kits (but more often Mia than Freddy) ran with Patra during the day yet returned to their mother at night for the dusk feed, and for her milk feed during darkness. Patra, if not a surrogate mother, had become a real working aunt. Once the wilder of the two, Cleo had less chance to develop fully as a summer hunter while rearing and being penned up with her kits earlier. She had been happy to allow Patra to take over daytime training duties.

After torrential rain and south-west gales for some 20 hours, there was no sign of any of the wildcats in the wood at feed time. I found them all in the woodshed! While they did not mind light rain, they disliked strong winds, and, possibly, the noise and danger of falling branches. Neither kit had been in the shed before, so obviously the two adults had brought them there. Although I wanted them to stay in the wild area of the west wood, I took pity on them that night. As I went in with a second supply of food, Freddy flared from his new bed in the hay box that the females had spurned as kits, Cleo was high on the rear logpile, Mia had squirmed along the log crevices until she was almost out of sight, while Patra sat on their old bed with half-closed eyes.

The gales had abated in the morning but a steady drizzle was falling. All the cats were still in the shed. By nightfall Patra and the kits had gone, leaving Cleo behind on the bed. I walked down to the feed rock, and she followed me, suddenly emerging from beneath the windfall trunks.

On August 22 I met Michael and Patricia Brambell and their two boys at the little old pier and brought them back by boat. Sylvesturr should have won an Oscar for his performance that day. Confronted by this new mass of humanity, he flung a whole pile of hay outwards as I raised his door. He '*PAAAH!*'d louder than ever as he braced up on his powerful front legs and easily stared us all down. The Brambells were delighted to see him alive and in such good shape.

'He hasn't got any nicer, has he?' Michael remarked. 'I thought you'd have had him eating out of your hand by now.'

We put Moobli to work after lunch. As we tracked round both woods in the drizzling rain, he suddenly put his huge black nose low and took off along the shore of the south-east land spit. Twenty yards from Patra's den he bounded into thick bracken, and up a hazel tree shot Freddy. He growled, then spat, superbly on cue, a perfect replica of his crusty old father. At this fine moment of proof for Dr Brambell that the whole experiment had been a success, I resolved to track the cats for only two more weeks. Although I would still set out food for them after that, I would leave them to revert naturally to the wild.

Two hours after boating the Brambells back to the pier, I took the night's meat and milk down to the west wood. Cleo came running through the undergrowth, and ten yards behind her Freddy sneaked along. As I left, Mia also headed towards the rock to join the others. Patra was nowhere to be seen.

When I reached the cottage I knew why. She was in the kitchen with Moobli, eating at his huge bowl. It was another example of the duplicity of the wildcat mind. All the cats were afraid of Moobli in the open, but Patra knew from kittenhood that he was harmless in the house. As she ate his left-overs, Moobli sat smiling at a distance, looking as proud as if he had herded her indoors just for me, his tail wagging like a great hairy flag.

Over the next week our trackings established that both kits had gone back to Cleo in the west wood. They were using the dry chamber beneath the root tangle as their main den, and Patra's duties as a hard-working aunt were over. Cleo was now restored to her former lithe sleekness. Towards the end of August Patra began coming to the rock for the dusk feed and to compete with the kits and Cleo for the free food.

On August 28 Cleo and Patra spent most of the day in the under-growth near Sylvesturr's pen, leaving both kits alone in the west wood. Moobli started Mia up an old larch snag from a small clearing in the bracken. She had been feeding from a wood pigeon, a small flock of which had colonized the wooded loch shores that summer. Only the wings, tail and green gizzard with gravel teeth in it had been left. One of the wings and some breast meat had been carried a few yards away, probably by Freddy.

At dusk, Cleo and Patra followed me through the side under-growth down to the rock. As I kept calling, both kits emerged from the fallen trunks and leaped on to the mossy surface, squabbling over food. Freddy swiped at Cleo, who backed off from her son and took another piece of meat two feet away. Then Patra growled and swatted out at Freddy. When I saw that, I decided it was time for Patra to go free. I did not want her upsetting the new fine balance between mother and kits, for Cleo was still giving them milk. It would be better to let Patra go while it was still summertime.

I found Patra asleep in the porch hay next morning and enticed her into the kitchen with meat, but as soon as she had eaten it, she sensed something odd was occurring and began 'mau'ing and sneaking round the floor for some way out. I drove her into the dark of the small den box, then took her to the island.

She hated the boat journey, growling and thrusting her big claws through the ventilation holes in the box. As I saw them I appreciated what a big, tough cat she was, and how lucky I had been to handle her occasionally without gloves – though of course not in this mood. As soon as I put the box down on the lush green grass below thick azalea and whin bushes, she ran out, paused to look back, then vanished into the shrubbery. As I watched her go, I decided I would try to pick her up again before winter.

On my way back from fetching mail, I stopped at the same spot on the island and called with imitation '*mau*'s and within two minutes she emerged from the bushes. She looked lonely on the shore. I put down a whole 15oz sausage for her. She came down cautiously, grabbed it and carried it off dangling like a plastic-covered rabbit from each side of her jaws.

At dawn next day I saw Cleo and both kits troop past below my window. Freddy and Mia looked like two beautiful little cheetahs with their lithe long striped legs, such an accentuated wildcat feature in kittenhood. Every so often Cleo peered up over the grass like a weasel, and the kits paused too, looking nervously about them. They went down into the pasture, skirted the spruce glade and passed on through the east wood towards the burn.

In the afternoon, as I was photographing a red squirrel on a larch trunk, Moobli started yiping after putting Mia up a tree on the far side of the swollen burn. Cleo and the kits must have crossed over one of the two fallen trunks. I made the usual soothing sounds, and left her again. This was the family's first crossing of the burn and it was obvious they were now wandering further afield.

The problem now was how and when to release Sylvesturr. Although I felt he might go for the kits when they were all ranging the same area, I also had several reasons for optimism. For one thing, they were just about big enough to look after themselves and could certainly scoot up trees faster than his big bulk would allow. Besides, he had never shown any belligerence towards them or either of the two females. I had also found the first fox scats in the west wood since last winter, and there wasn't a fox in the world that would face up to Sylvesturr's devastating ferocity.

By early September both kits were ranging away from Cleo during the day and seemed to have set up their own daytime head-quarters amid the thick foliage and bracken beneath the large silver fir that lay across the rocky escarpment, but each night they came to my feed calls, a few yards behind Cleo. Afterwards they seemed to spend time with her in the roots chamber near the rock, suckling

104

milk. One afternoon I saw them leap from the bird table and hare off into the east wood. When I went to feed them, I heard their faint '*awroori*' calls coming nearer and nearer but I could not see them until they were only a few yards away. Somehow they had covered the whole distance between east and west wood under cover. The ventriloquial quality of their calls made their exact positions impossible to determine.

I noticed Mia was becoming even more wary, and would not jump on to the feed rock until I was many yards away. She would swiftly seize a piece of meat and jump below the fallen trunks to eat it. By contrast, Sylvesturr was now advancing out of his den for food each evening. He was in magnificent shape and I decided the time had come to let him go. I would set him free while Moobli and I were away, so that he could acclimatize to the whole area in peace.

A great problem when releasing animals into the wild is that one can so easily upset the balance for other wildlife in the area, especially where predators are involved. Hence I intended to check the isle at regular intervals, to make sure that Patra and the kestrels could co-exist without either destroying all the wild prey or taking so much as to affect each other's survival.

On September 5 I boated up the loch to buy cats' meat. My Highland butcher asked me if I had any use for 10lbs of hearts that had become unfrozen. On the way back I pulled the boat in to the eastern shore of the green island and made the usual feed calls. To my surprise I heard Patra '*mau*' in return, the calls coming nearer until she emerged from some thick brambles. She looked carefully about, half ran until a few yards away, then became scared and skulked in the thick grass. I kept '*mau*'ing, broke two eggs for her, and she overcame her fears and came down to eat them. She was fat and in fine shape. As I left, I threw one of the hearts into the deep grass as a treat.

Next day I cruised the woods for a good place to release Sylvesturr. At the top of the west wood, near its north-east edge, I found a huge inward-curving stump and roots cluster that was heavily screened with long bracken and had thick heather sprouting from the top. It faced south and the area below was dry with powdered dust. It was nearly 150 yards above the area where Cleo and the kits had their den, with a marsh, many tangled windfalls and the rocky escarpment between them. It was the ideal place. I hung cooked and half-cooked beef ribs, liver and flank in strategic positions. Sylvesturr would have to go a yard to get three hearts tied to a fallen log and three yards to reach four more and some ribs nailed to a tree. I distributed other fresh meats and sausages in the thick bracken. Near by, where the den box was going to be, I set a large plastic bowl with seven pints of long-life milk and water. I made the same provision around Cleo's den.

The moment for Sylvesturr's freedom had come. I set the den box in his run and after driving him out with a broom, when he once again performed his one-handed gibbon act on the pen roof, he dashed into it. I wedged a pine sheet over the entrance. I managed to carry box, broom and now silent Sylvesturr through the tangled undergrowth and over fallen logs to his new home in the wood. I wondered if wildcats were psychic, for they seem to sense when something momentous in their lives is about to occur.

I had never had a confrontation with Sylvesturr in the open, and my heart thumped when at last the moment came. To forestall any possible attack, I lay over the heather on the stump, well above his box, and prised the pine sheet free with the broom handle.

I saw his great head emerge slowly, take one glaring look this way, one glare that, both slow and terrifying, his golden eyes like great black-centred orbs. Then he shrank back again into the box. He always took a careful look at anywhere strange before making any move. I knew then he would not leave the box before dark.

As I walked back to the cottage I felt bereft. I loved Sylvesturr. I respected his pride, his courage, his refusal to compromise. I would not sentence him to another winter of imprisonment. Although he was nearing his old age, I was happy to give him a natural home, to have shown him the long-forgotten wilds of his childhood, to have provided him with a choice of mates from one of which he had produced two magnificent kittens. He had never shown me any love or even liking – it was just not in his make-up. Plucked from his wild heritage as a kitten, and jailed by man for all his long life, his motivation sprang from fear and distrust.

Before pulling out on a trip south next day, I checked Sylvesturr's box, approaching with caution in case he attacked. He had gone, so had two hearts, but the milk appeared untouched. I decided not to track him. His life was his own now. Knowing his memory, I would put food out for him in the same place on my return.

As I boated up the loch in mist and rain with Moobli, I felt I had done my best for all the wildcats.

8 · Death in the Afternoon

Eight days later we returned to my old small upturned boat in the woods and the fury of a Force 9 south-west gale. Heavy showers of rain hissed into the foaming crests of the deep-troughed waves that were marching up the loch. I laid a pathway of broken branches across the gravelly shore, overturned my boat, hauled it down to the water's edge and set it to ride just off the rocks on a small anchor. It would be a rough trip, but I was used to the loch in the storms of icy winter. My 20 h.p. outboard should be equal to the task. I was anxious to get home to check the wildcats.

As I set off, I hit the main run of the waves, and the hissing rain made vision difficult. There could be no question of stopping at the green island to check on Patra. I made continual adjustments to the throttle, accelerating sufficiently up the broad slope of the rolling waves to avoid being swamped by those following, then throttling back when slide-racing down the far sides so that the bow did not plough into the bottom of the next wave, thus turning boat, dog, gear and self into an unwilling submarine. All the time the boat had to be kept under power, slightly faster than the waves, for to have veered sideways would have meant being instantly swamped. While Moobli and I could probably have made it to shore, I doubted if I could do so with my only valuable possession – the heavy briefcase of photos and notes I had amassed during my Highland years.

After reaching home safely, I went into the west wood and made the usual feeding time calls. Cleo came, followed by the huge Freddy with stealthy lion-like walk. I then checked Sylvesturr's den box. There was no sign of the old boy. All the hearts, liver, mutton and most of the milk had gone, but a cooked beef flank still hung untouched on the curved stump and some of the sterilized sausages were still intact. Eight days mean little to wildcats, or even to domestic cats, which are far better left with food on their own familiar territory than being transported around in cages or left with strangers during the temporary absence of their owners.

There were no fox scats anywhere next day when we went tracking. Moobli found no scents until we reached the roots chamber near the feed rock. He sniffed and whined, but though I could not hear any growls, I presumed one of the cats was down there, probably Mia, for when we returned we found Cleo and Freddy had spend the night in the woodshed!

At dusk Cleo came to the feed calls again, walking near my feet like a dog. Freddy also came down, sliding along furtively through the herbage like a small wolf. I did not see Mia but could hear what I thought were faint '*mau*'s from the fallen trunks about thirty yards away. I wondered if Sylvesturr had left the area. I was fairly sure he was not dead because Moobli would have scented his carcass easily, even down a hole.

Apart from the two woods around the cottage, another wood, over two miles long, with plenty of open grassy patches, rocky cairns, small burns and old hollow stumps, began a mile to the west. I felt he could well be there. He was powerful and in fine shape when I had released him. As the days went by, I had a nagging wish to see him again, to know he was all right. I was in fact missing his harsh, proud old face.

Over the next three days Cleo and Freddy alternated between the west wood and the shed, both coming to the dusk feeds. Freddy began jumping on the rock at the same time as his mother, so both were feeding while I was near. He was still trying to suck milk from Cleo, and as he nuzzled beneath her in the shed, he once lifted her back feet right off the ground. He was now longer and more burly than his mother. As far as I could tell, he got no suck at all, but Cleo seemed to enjoy her huge kit's caresses, and turned over on her back twice as he pushed and probed. I was now worried about Mia, whom I had not seen at all. Maybe she had left, perhaps with Sylvesturr? It made sense that she might be the first to leave. She had always been the wildest, escaping from the pens long before Freddy showed any desire to go. The odd thing was that the new meat I left near Sylvesturr's den box and release point remained untouched. There did not seem much point in setting the trap for her.

By September 23, after four days of incessant gales and the first hailstorm of the coming winter, it seemed certain that Cleo and Freddy were going to make the woodshed their main quarters. Much as I wanted them to go wild, I had not the heart to drive them away. I would have to put out sand and gravel as litter, and took advantage of a calm sunny spell in late afternoon to collect some from a beach one and a half miles away to the west. While Moobli ran along the loch shore, I rowed there with shovel and some heavy duty plastic sacks. As I was filling the sacks, he disappeared. I whistled, but there was no response. Darn him, had he gone after some deer? I walked to the end of the beach and climbed up the high bank covered with bracken and scrubby birch and alder trees, where he came running back with an odd look, whined, and took off again into the bracken, but not on any trail. I followed.

Mia lay in a puddle below the tangled roots of a fallen birch. Blow-fly maggots writhed under the skin of the carcass which gave off a putrid stench, and the half-open eyes were sunken and opaque. I could not pick it up for it would have fallen to pieces. I felt awful as I stood by the shattered birch in that bleak inhospitable place, feeling I had failed. Perhaps neither Cleo nor Freddy had let her feed from all the meats I had left, yet there had been enough for ten cats for a fortnight, and there was much still left on our return. Had she run foul of a fox, a big otter, or even Sylvesturr himself? I poked the remains about but there was no sign of external injury. The fur looked darker than hers had been.

I went home in a black mood, perplexed. The carcass seemed too decomposed for less than two weeks' exposure. Then I remembered Patra on the green island. She could have swum the 250 yards to the mainland, trying to reach her old home. Weakened by the swim, losing heat from being wet on the long rough journey along the shore, perhaps hungry, she could then have fallen prey to something. The thought only increased my misery. I would now have to check Patra's presence on the green island; if she was there, the remains had to be Mia's.

That evening, as I prepared the cats' meal in my workshop, I saw Freddy emerge from the bracken with a vole in his jaws and take it into the shed. When I went in, he was curled up in the old hay box and Cleo was eating the vole. He had clearly brought it for her. It seemed odd that a kit should hunt for its mother, yet he was a tom, and the incident lent more credence to the possibility that toms do occasionally feed females. I fed them in the shed, weakening from my earlier resolve because I did not want to lose Freddy as it seemed I had Mia.

Over the next few days I saw Freddy bringing three more voles to the woodshed. He was now hunting entirely alone while Cleo lazed in the shed most of the day. The meat left untouched in the west wood while I was away suddenly disappeared. Perhaps at least Sylvesturr was still alive.

I pulled into the green island on my return from a supply trip. My heart sank when I saw the sausage lying intact on the shore where I had left it a week earlier. But next morning the meat in the west wood had again gone from where I left more of it. There was a large four-toed wildcat footprint in a small patch of mud near by. It was too big for Freddy. My hopes rose. That night I set the box-cage trap on the spot with a sheep's heart. At dusk on October 1 the door was down but the trap contained Cleo. She had smelled the meat on the west breeze from 250 yards, yet more evidence of wildcats' scenting ability.

I would have to pen up Cleo and Freddy again while I tried to trap Sylvesturr. I baited the pens, set in food and milk, and when once they were inside, I ran out and slammed down the swing door. Now they were safely out of the way I could set the trap with impunity.

Next morning the trap was unsprung but the meat bait had gone. The thick nylon trigger line had been neatly chewed through. No fox would enter such a trap, at least not unless it was desperate from starvation in the harsh depths of winter. It could only be Sylvesturr, his perfect memory enabling him to chew the bait free and get away with it without setting off the trap. In great excitement, wearing plastic gloves which I dipped in boiled spruce needle juice to reduce the man scent, I set the trap again with all the cunning I could muster. This time I tied the bait on with plastic-wrapped wire fishing trace. He would not chew through that in a hurry.

The south-west gales sprang up again overnight, and when I saw the trapdoor down after breakfast, I felt sure it had just been blown loose. As I crept round in my usual half circle, I saw that the mousetrap spring had gone off. A cat was crouching in the box part. I ran up. It was Mia! She was bigger than before, and as I drew near she became a raging monster, with her tail almost three inches thick. She flared and spat like a huge firework, and closed and opened her eyes slowly as she glared round for a way of escape. She dashed at the thick wire netting, looking to the left and to the right, then straight at us, hitting the netting as if she were blind or thought a mad rush would force her through it.

Beside myself with delight, I raced back to the cottage for my camera to record the victory, fell over in the small burn after catching my boot in the rusty traces of some old fencing, and grazed my palms on its stony bed. Feeling no pain, I shot indoors, feverishly changed the lens, and ran back. I took three shots as Mia crouched in the box, her face full of hate and ferocity. It was certainly Mia, the same light tawny fur that Freddy still had, and the yellow-gold eyes with black pupils. Her spit was not as strong as Sylvesturr's but this was his daughter all right. What was I to do with her? Put her in the pens with Cleo and Freddy? Would they still get along? They had been apart for a long time now. Well, I would try it for a few days anyway, using the gate if necessary.

I chased Freddy, who suddenly became block-headed and started spitting, out of the small pen and into the main one and shut the gate. After cleaning out their old den box, I filled it with dry hay and set it back on its old logs in the small pen corner. Then, with Moobli in the house, I went back to the wood with thick gloves to carry Mia and the trap up to the pens.

She had gone. The wire netting on the roof, where I had sewn up the edges with wire, had been chewed through in three places and through that hole, barely four inches in diameter, she had forced her way, leaving behind some scraps of fur. Although Moobli tracked her for a while, her scent petered out on a wet rockface north-west of the wood. He lost interest and started playing with sticks.

I would probably never see her again and felt sad. Yet I also felt an enormous relief. She was alive and in superb condition, and as she had always been the wilder one, it was right she should stay free.

I had never found any evidence of wildcats in the long wood to the west, but I decided to go there and make a long search. On the way I checked the west wood again and found some typical wildcat droppings. They seemed too large to have been made by Mia. Reaching the long wood, we searched in ever-increasing spirals out-

wards from the carcass. Within an hour we had found wildcat droppings on a grassy patch between the browning bracken. They were
as large as those in the west wood.

Surely they were Sylvesturr's? Hating man as he did, it seemed
likely that he had now made his home in this long wood, yet was
returning occasionally to his old home for the meat I put out. When
I checked my diaries, I found that meat (including the trap bait) had
been taken every seven days. It was possible he was traversing over
a mile of loch shore each week, the largest section of it open, boggy,
tussocky ground. If only I could trap him, know for sure he was
really still alive.

Autumn came to Wildernesse. The leaves of the ash trees, following
the earlier alders, were turning yellow and falling. The bats in my
roof were flying every dusk, feeding on the last flying insects to put
on fat for their winter hibernation. On October 11 the first heavy
winds came, scattering the nuts, rowan berries and tree seeds. At
night now the woods were filled with eerie hootings as the tawny
owls re-established their territories and the year's young looked for
their own areas. As the air grew colder, red deer hinds came down
from the hills to shelter in the warmer glades.

Cleo and Freddy were both happy in the pens. If I let them go for
a day or two, they always returned at dusk to be fed. Freddy now
greeted me with '*mau*'s and odd spits and flares when I came with
the meat, reaching through the fencing to swat out at the bowl.
Competing with Cleo, he soon learned that the springy sterilized
meat sausage would bounce when it hit the ground after I poked it
down through the roof. He watched the operation carefully, timed
his run to catch the sausage in the air after the first bounce, seized it
with a growl and dashed a yard or two away to eat it in the herbage.

Cleo would swat Freddy for trying to suckle her empty teats. She
swatted him so hard he stumbled. It was more a displacement
activity on his part than a serious attempt to get milk, as if he were
seeking reassurance. When he tried to stalk her twitching black tail
tip, she shot a paw out at him. Once she even did it when he was
only staring at her tail, as if about to pounce.

That week the winds switched to the south-west, bringing heavy
rain. Winter was coming and it was time to plant new trees.

On October 24 we fought our way down the loch and drove 320

miles to a forestry nursery at Fochabers near the east coast to fetch 150 young trees – spruce, sweet chestnut, Canadian hemlock, Douglas fir and oak. Along with those already established, these trees would help make the woods as varied a wildlife habitat as possible, for it is the well balanced woods, with a variety of broadleaf trees among the conifers, which are the best for birds and animals. On the way, I called to Patra at the green island, but again there was no response.

When I cruised the west wood next day for the best sites for my new trees, I found two huge wildcat scats and one large footprint which I was sure could be only Sylvesturr's. I hauled the trap from where I had been setting it without success by his release point, determined to try once more before winter. I set it near the print, using bloody, strong-smelling raw venison from a dead deer calf we had found near the burn in the east wood. Around the trap I scattered a few pieces of meat sausage.

Checking the trap that evening, I found it unsprung, but all the sausage pieces outside it had gone. Well, mice or shrews perhaps could have eaten them, possibly Mia, though I doubted she would return. I threw more loose meat inside the trap, feeling I was probably wasting my time, and went indoors.

As I peered round the side of the box shortly after noon next day, there was a loud '*PAAAH!*' It was like a small bomb going off, with debris flying in all directions. *Sylvesturr was there!* The sudden unexpected blast of his spit and the noise of his big foot thumping on the wood was enough to throw me backwards. I felt as if I were in a dream. Driving the whining Moobli back and away, I turned round again, heart beating like a trip hammer. The ferocious old devil was caged there at last, braced up on his two powerful front legs, his head touching the top of the 2ft 4in. high netting.

'*PAAAH!*' again, with a sideways whack this time, his huge horn-coloured claws sticking through the mesh. He held his ground, not retreating into the wooden box part, but glaring up at me. He was a terrifying sight. Hell, was I glad to see the lovely proud old fool, the big tough old warrior whose unchanging character and cussed independence had made him resist for over ten years the attempts of a succession of human experts to tame him, to have him show just one moment of gratitude, or even compromise, which characterizes most of our human lives. It simply wasn't in him. He was now, even now, after 52 days of freedom in this harsh wild landscape, as wild and tough and resolute as on the day when he had been found and taken from this land.

'Sylvesturr,' I said slowly and softly, bending down to take a closer look.

To my surprise, he did not spit again, though he flared and hissed, looked sideways with that slow series of glares, his eyes twitching from object to object. Then he walked slowly, growling, into the wooden box. Had he been there all night? He did not rage about, as I expected, like Mia had, but crouched low. The box was splashed with the raw meat, for he must have turned to run after grabbing it, only to meet the fallen trapdoor. He crouched down, shifting slightly from foot to foot. Then for a few moments, he cast his eyes down at the ground as if I was no longer there. A sad look of defeat, of self-disgust at being caught again, at the realization this was the end of his late-earned freedom, came over his long-whiskered old face. Written there again was all the gloom, the despair of ten years of solitary confinement, of endless prison days, which had formed the principal cast of his countenance. It was heart-rending.

I checked the netting was secure, pushed the trip nail through the staples so the trapdoor could not be opened from inside, and went back to the cottage to think.

He was in first-class condition, his fur thicker than I had ever seen it. To imprison him again would not be a victory but total defeat. This cat had proved he could make it on his own, despite his age. If he lived only one year more in the wild, it was better than five in jail. He had well earned the right to be in his natural element, to take whatever this Scottish wilderness, his heritage, could now give him. I put on the sweaters, double trousers and thick gloves in case he attacked. Then, with a square of heavy fish netting held before me, I went back and removed the nail, lifting the door right out of its runners.

There was a pause. Then Syl came straight out, leaped to the top of a rocky, mossy ridge in three bounds, stopped, turned back briefly, as if for one last glance, then disappeared into a thicket. There was no attack, no need for the netting. I whispered softly: 'Goodbye, old fellow.' I sat down on the box for a minute or two to collect myself before carrying the trap back to the house. There would be no need to use it again. Sylvesturr and Mia, after I had long thought them dead, were alive and free. The rest was up to them. Only Patra, it seemed, had lost out, and it was no one's fault but mine.

9 · Not Too Bad a Thing

In early November, as the first skeins of white-front geese began to fly in from the Arctic to winter among the small flocks of greylags at the far end of the loch, I decided to make one last attempt to find Patra.

It was a dull, misty and totally windless day when I landed the boat gently, stern first, on the grassy shore of the island. I walked up the hill between the gravestones, giving the usual feed calls. Hearing nothing, I turned back. Then I heard an answering 'mau', very faint. I stood still, kept calling, and slowly the sounds came nearer. Suddenly out from the thick azalea bushes stepped Patra. She looked the same as before, plump and well fed. She began walking to and fro without approaching me. I went to the boat, ripped open a meat sausage and gently threw her a small piece. Very gingerly, looking all about her, she came down, took it and ran into the undergrowth. Again I stayed still and she watched me drop a piece near my feet. Out she came again, 'mau'ing and walking up and down looking at the meat. When finally she came close I picked her up with the gloves, expecting an explosion, but she neither spat nor struggled, as if she was glad to see us both, for Moobli was staring with intense interest from the boat where I had told him to stay.

I put her loose into the boat and started the engine. We were eight yards offshore when she ran round the boat, leaped over the stern with all four feet splayed out, swam to the beach, shook herself and ran into the bushes. Whether she jumped off because she was scared of the boat or really liked the island, I was not sure, but it was wonderful to know she was still alive after all. The carcass, then, was that of another cat altogether. It was unlikely to be a domestic animal for my nearest neighbours, 6½ miles away, told me they had not lost a cat.

I picked up the skeleton on the way home and have kept it to this day. I never solved its mystery.

Five days later a local tradesmen told me he had been with a grave party to the island when they heard odd mewing noises. One of them had glimpsed a large grey-brown cat in the bushes. Apart from earning her own keep, Patra had been performing a useful community service, and it would not have bothered me to know a wildcat was hunting a living round my own or a relative's grave. Others, I realized, might not share this view. I had intended to fetch Patra back before winter, so I put in again at the island and called out loudly. It was almost as if she had heard the familiar engine coming and had waited for me, for she materialized out of the bushes almost immediately and she came down for the meat in my hand.

I caught her easily with the gloves. This time I held her on the seat next to me until the boat was well off shore. She then walked all round, '*mau*'ing noisily, the semi-cabin acting like an echo chamber. Then she stood on the centre seat next to me as I controlled the wheel, put her front paws on the little roof and peered all about her like an otter. She was still playing the clown. I caught her before the boat landed. Leaving it to bump up and down in the light waves, I ran up the path and put her in the pen with the others. After hauling up the boat and carrying up the supplies, I went to feed the wildcats.

Cleo and Patra were having a fine reunion, walking round each other and banging their heads together like a pair of rams. Freddy seemed quite left out of things. As I pushed meat through the roof, I found he had learned a new trick. He stood on his hind legs, as often Patra had done, and leaped up like a kangaroo to the wire mesh above, to which he clung while he grabbed the meat in his jaws before dropping down with it. A full five-foot leap from the standing position, just from his back feet alone, seemed nothing at all to him.

Next day, when Freddy walked towards Patra, his old hunting teacher, to bang his head against her in friendship, Patra growled and clouted him with both paws. He went to Cleo, who did the

116

same. At feed time, however, Freddy was the quickest and most powerful, and he drove Patra off, more by his heedless rush at the meat than in an attack.

I let them all run free on fine days and they came back to the pens at dusk for food. I also set meat out in the old trap spot in the west wood. It still vanished every six or seven days. As this regular date came up, I shut the three in the pens until the meat had gone. Large droppings showed that Sylvesturr was almost certainly the taker.

The other cats ranged widely on their free days. Cleo and Freddy had long ago learned not to raid the bird table, having fled after being greeted often by a violently thrust open window, clapped hands and a spit louder than Syl's! Patra, more persistent, was soon wise to this old trick. Fortunately the birds came to the food I set out mainly in the worst weather, when the cats were in the pens.

There were moments of comedy. Once Patra and Cleo were drinking from the milk bowl when Freddy, who had already had his turn, heard their lapping noises and decided he would swig some more. He marched in, gave Patra a swift sideways butt with his big head, knocking her right off balance, and started drinking. When he tried this with Cleo, she gave him a thump, just to let him know who was the real boss.

Patra started raiding the house for extra food whenever I was closeted in my study, for unless gales were blowing I usually left a door open for Moobli to go in and out. I would go into the kitchen and find her on the sink, where I kept their nightly sausage. She would snarl defiantly until clapped hands and human growls drove her out again. Patra, it was now obvious, lived mainly for her stomach. She would eat twice as much as the other cats, until her gut swelled like a balloon.

By the end of November the first snow blizzards arrived and suddenly the mountains took on the appearance of vast ice cakes topped with white sugar. Yet the Highland mountains can be savage in winter, soon reducing a man to size.

It was on December 4 that violence first occurred among the cats. At feeding time, Freddy suddenly seized Patra by the side of the throat and dragged her away screeching after both had gone for the same piece of meat. He left her a yard away and went back for it. Next day all were amicable again, but both Cleo and Patra began to give their burly six-month-old son and nephew a wide berth in the scramble at feed time. Just in case Freddy was turning nasty, or it

117

was the natural time for him to leave his mother, I now let the cats run free some nights too. When Freddy stayed away for two nights and three days, however, I became worried. I was sure Cleo and Patra were safe from Sylvesturr, but it was likely that the two toms would fight, and I wanted neither of them hurt.

At dusk on the third day, after feeding the females in the pens, I set a steaming pan of meat on the bird table after all the birds had gone to roost, so that its smell would waft round the estate. Within a quarter of an hour, as I watched from the study, Freddy emerged like a grey ghost from the direction of the west wood. He had scented the meat from over 250 yards away. He crept up to the bird table, head raised, sniffing, and stood on his hind legs. He was about to perform his kangaroo leap but was forestalled when I went out to put the meat into the pens. He was very hungry, and for once stood his ground, like Sylvesturr, and flared and made passing swipes at my shooing hands as I walked along. When I put the meat into the small pen he shot inside.

Generally, the new system of alternate daytime freedom and being in the pens seemed to be working splendidly. One afternoon I was greeted on my return from a supply trip by all three wildcats running down close to the path. Freddy flared, ran away a few steps, ran back and spat with ferocious expression, then made off again. He clearly wanted food but not the company! He began to spend more time alone in the woods.

On wet days Cleo and Patra holed up in the woodshed on their old logpile bed. One morning I watched Patra sneak along past dozing Moobli. He scented her and got up, but she made a quick feint to the left, put him off balance and swerved round the porch. When I went into the kitchen she had the open butterpack on the floor. She always stole things, and was becoming a nuisance. She knew she was not welcome in the house. I left food for the wildcats in the woodshed on New Year's Eve and went off into the woods to spend two nights out in the open – cooking on campfires and sleeping in the fresh air – a yearly habit of spiritual renewal. When I returned on the afternoon of January 2, there was no sign of Patra. The other two were still around the woodshed. She failed to appear over the next few days. This was odd, as she had always been the most fearless of the wildcats. I wondered if Freddy had driven her away.

After stalking a small herd of hinds and a young six-pointer stag in falling snow three weeks later, Moobli picked up a strong cat scent in the west wood and within minutes led me to a sheltered mud patch where there were two large four-toed prints and near by a huge double wildcat dropping – almost certainly Sylvesturr's. Excited that he was still about, I put some meat down that evening and fed Cleo and Freddy a large meal, hoping that would deter them from venturing into the west wood. The missing Patra could find it if she was in the area.

When we went to the wood next morning all the meat had disappeared, but Moobli could not find any scent. We zig-zagged up and down westwards. Suddenly, in an open patch amid the big tussocks on the wood's far edge, there were Sylvesturr's tracks in the snow, heading out of the wood. Try as we did, we could find no tracks leading in. He had probably come in higher up, where the trees were thicker, and had found it easy to avoid the snow patches. My theory that he was now quartered in the long wood a mile to the west was probably right.

We went out again in the afternoon and walked a good half-mile into the long wood. There we found Sylvesturr's fresh tracks in snow that covered the tops of some large fallen trunks. They were firm, and his strides were well apart. I felt sure he was still in good health. Again the snow was too patchy and the ground too wet to track him to any den, either by sight or Moobli's scent.

By timing the disappearance of meat, and finding his tracks and scats, I established during the next few weeks that Sylvesturr was indeed patrolling a distance of at least one and a half miles, and was reaching the west wood roughly once every seven nights. It was interesting that he would cover the boggy terrain which was almost totally open. He clearly did not live in just one den and operate from there. Wandering about his territory, he used various day dens, from which he hunted by night. We found one a few days later. Three rock slabs formed a small natural chamber, from the edge of which grew a stout dwarf birch tree. Beneath was a perfect dry oval bowl of mosses and grasses, just like Syl had often made from the hay in his den in the pens.

By now Freddy had become shyer. On free days he refused to come at dusk to my food calls at the woodshed, though he certainly heard them. One late afternoon I banged the dishes together, called as usual, and waited in the trees east of the shed. I saw him emerge from the west wood, sneak along a low natural ditch with small pools of water in it, then leap on to the rocks of an old ruined wall, where he waited, peeping through a hole between the rocks to see if I had gone. Once he was in the shed, I took Moobli over to where I had seen him running along, but he could find no scent. I remembered how cougars in Canada, when tracked by hounds, often ran over wet swampy ground where the water de-scented their feet. The hounds wasted minutes on the other side trying to pick up the scent again, by which time the cougar was much further away. This was probably why Moobli could so rarely track Sylvesturr. It was interesting that wildcats would obscure their scent in the same way.

When Patra did not return after two weeks, I became seriously worried. I wanted her to go free, but I also wanted to know she had not met with an accident. After finding smaller tracks in the snow near her old east wood den, I set the trap there for her. Next morning Freddy was in it, raging about and hurling himself at the netting, just as Mia had done. He was covering a lot of ground now. To keep them out of the way while I tried to catch Patra, I carried Freddy into the pens and later also enticed Cleo in with food. For two days the trap remained unsprung.

While returning from a supply trip in late January, Moobli suddenly became agitated, sniffing and looking from the boat at the shore. I thought he just wanted to go for his usual run: because it was raining heavily I had decided to make it shorter that day. As soon as I let him ashore, he was greeted by a wildcat coming out of the dead bracken. It was Patra – a full two and a half miles from home. Moobli just stood there, as huge as a small donkey, while she walked all round him. She immediately fled when I stepped ashore. I managed to entice her back with meat and the usual calls, and put her into the boat. She was certainly glad to see us. What a noise she put up, walking round and round inside the semi-cabin, which rang with her loud cries of '*mau*' as we took her home again.

I put her into the pens. The other two appeared to accept her but there was no friendly head-banging reunion between her and Cleo this time. On the following nights Cleo and Freddy slept together in the main den while Patra seemed banished to the small den box in the smaller pen. Freddy had become furtive and extremely shy in the open, and fierce if cornered, but was quite tame in the pens, where he walked about happily with the other cats.

One gloriously sunny day in early February, I let them all free again for a run in the wild. At dusk Cleo came home with a vole and took it into the pens to eat. When Patra came into the pens, Cleo growled, not letting her near until she had finished the vole. I fed them both. Freddy turned up in the near darkness just as they finished. I put in some more meat and shut down the pen door behind him as he chewed hungrily. His voluntary return to the pens while I was still there in the open was exceptional. Had he been scared away from the wood by Sylvesturr? I went down quickly and put some meat at the usual spot.

Not only had the meat gone next morning but the fresh remains of a woodpigeon had been moved eight yards from where strewn feathers showed it had been killed to a spot below a tangle of bracken and honeysuckle. A few yards further away was one of Sylvesturr's huge, tapered, twisted scats, bigger than anything Freddy ever released in the pens. I looked at my diaries: it was eight days since he had taken the last meat. I supposed a day or two either way was not important, for his visits would depend on the success of his hunting.

Through much of February Cleo and Freddy shared both pens at will, yet Patra stayed mostly in the small pen. At feeding time all three cats milled around together, with only Patra intelligent enough to reach into the meat bowl as I was washing out their dishes, hook out a handful and transfer her full bent claws to her mouth. On two occasions I saw Patra bang her paw down against Cleo over food, only to be promptly clouted with hard clawless swats from Freddy. Once, when she started into the den box while he was having a quiet siesta, he spat at her in a way his courteous old father would never have done.

February 16 was dull and windless, so again I let the wildcats out for a day off. The west wood meat was still there at the usual seven-day interval. I thought Sylvesturr might have graduated to eating fresh wild deer carrion, of which there was plenty. This would mean not only that he was almost completely weaned naturally to the wild in winter, the hardest time, but that the chances of a confrontation with Freddy were now far less. On each of the next three nights both Cleo and Patra returned to the pens at dusk to my feed calls and ate and drank their fill, but not Freddy. Worried by this new absence, I set the trap for him on the second night and also put a dish full of food on top of the pens. Next morning the trap meat was untouched but the food in the dish had all gone. Only a cat could have taken it, and I felt certain it was neither Sylvesturr nor Mia, who I was sure had long since left the area.

Moobli cornered Freddy in the rocky cairn below the escarpment next day. As his growls and spits came from between the rocks, Freddy sounded almost as fierce as his father. One hour after feed time, when only Patra had turned up to the pens, I went out with more food. Up came Cleo, and some way behind her Freddy! I kept very still. In went Cleo and Freddy, who seemed in fine condition, and I shut down the swing door.

On February 26 I noticed the cats had begun to behave oddly. Patra and Freddy had a brief fight, making loud '*rowwl*' noises at each other, before Patra flew into the small den box. Later Cleo also attacked Patra; now the claws were out and some fur flew. I felt sure the wildcat oestrus period was due and the sisterly bond was drawing to a close. It appeared rather inappropriate that they should start fighting on the day the first daffodils came out, heralding the approach of spring. Then at the dusk feed they all seemed amicable again.

It did not last. On the next two mornings I came out to find Freddy had kicked the heavy den door outwards, just as Sylvesturr had done before. On March 2 I saw Cleo launch a fierce attack on Patra, driving her into the den box where she crouched, growling. After Cleo had returned to the main pen, Patra poked her head out of the box and Freddy went in to attack her. Patra fought back, grabbed his head with both sets of claws and tried to bite, but he was too strong and drove her back into the box.

A few hours later I saw both Cleo and Patra sitting amicably a yard apart in the small pen, where Patra was now piling her droppings, not burying them like Cleo and Freddy. Suddenly Cleo glared at Patra, set her ears down, crouched and then pounced. Patra fled into the box again. In late afternoon, when I went out for another look, all three came milling to the front fencing and I thought all was well, but as soon as Freddy realized I was carrying no food, he looked at Patra's expectant face and again assaulted her, driving her once more into the den box. Were they attacking her because she was dirty with her droppings? Or because Cleo was in oestrus? Apart from the two attacks on Patra, she was certainly very playful all day, attacking emerging daffodils. She seemed skittish with her son, who was looking more and more like Sylvesturr with every passing day.

Clearly amicable sisterhood was now at an end. It had lasted twenty-one months. Patra again assumed the pinched spinsterish look she had worn after the birth of Cleo's kits, as if she knew she no longer fitted in. It seemed likely that we had found her two and a half miles down the loch five weeks earlier because the other two had driven her away.

As the days were lengthening, and small animals were emerging more and more as the occasional sunny spells stirred plants into new life, it would soon be time to release all the cats. I felt Patra should go first.

I carried her den box from the pens and took her in the boat to some thick woodland three miles away where there were many mice and voles. On the way we picked up a fresh deer calf carcass, and before releasing her, I axed it open on the haunches so that she could get at the meat easily. I felt sad as she went up the beach in short trotting bursts from bush to bush, '*mau*'ing loudly, but she had long since proved herself able to earn her own living.

She was back in thirty hours on the sacking bed in the woodshed. I softened when I saw her crouching there and fed her. Wondering if the earlier attacks had perhaps been a temporary aberration, I put her back in the pens. Within an hour Cleo had attacked her. She fought back, but only halfheartedly, as if she knew Cleo was right. A few minutes later Freddy chased her into the den box. It was no good; they would probably kill her between them, so out she came.

Patra now began behaving atrociously, like a spirited child that feels itself unwanted. She leaped on to the bird table every afternoon, intent upon avian annihilation despite eating and drinking as much as the other cats put together. She had become a compulsive eater, her stomach constantly distended, as if psychologically she was trying to make up for being the odd cat out. She raided the kitchen at every opportunity, once knocking over some bottles and smashing one on the concrete floor. She even left her scats on Moobli's bed.

Finally, after hearing from a local gamekeeper that a female wildcat had been caught accidentally in a fox snare in a riverside wood nine miles away, I took her there by boat and Land Rover. Foolish though it may sound, I found myself talking to her before the moment of final release, trying to explain that the time had come to let her go, that she would fill the niche left by another wildcat, that a young tom was known to be in the area!

She ran a few steps, looked back, gave a last '*mau*' and disappeared into the green curtain of foliage. There were many rabbits in the riverside fields and I felt sure she would make out all right. As we drove away, Moobli whined and stood looking sadly out of the rear window. I knew how he was feeling, for I felt the same, but it was in her best interests. She would not meet a mate in my area, for Sylvesturr would not breed with her. To have five wildcats running loose in my territory would certainly have meant a major upset to the overall balance of nature that I was trying to enhance.

Cleo and Freddy seemed more relaxed and happy in the pens after Patra had gone. On March 13 I noticed Cleo had undergone a spectacular colour change. The inside rear parts of her thighs had taken on a new brighter orangey hue, and the thicker hair made the back of her legs seem smoothly rounded. The underside of her tail, which she now held upwards more often, was also much ruddier. I was sure it was a seasonal phenomenon, to make her more attractive to the male. She was extremely active, rubbing herself over the daffodils, rocks and undergrowth. I checked the diaries − it was exactly one year ago that Cleo had taken refuge in his den with Sylvesturr, when I had been trying to put all the wildcats into the woodshed.

It seemed certain she was now in or rapidly approaching oestrus. If the 63 days' gestation (the most quoted figure) for wildcats was correct, Cleo would have mated with Sylvesturr on March 23. If the 63 to 69' days gestation theory (confirmed by Berne Zoo in Switzerland, where copulation had been observed) was correct, Cleo could have mated with Sylvesturr as early as March 17. All these dates fell into the week when all the wildcats were housed in the woodshed, with the females having access to Syl during the days when Moobli and I were safely away on the trip to London. If there was any chance of Cleo mating with Sylvesturr again I had to free her right now. I let her and Freddy out of the pens. After a gap of three weeks, the meat had begun to disappear from the west wood again. I hoped she and Syl would have a romantic rendezvous there.

My only real guide to managing the wildcats had been my experience in Canada with cougars − apart from the conflicting references to the animals in nature books. I knew that mountain lions often run with their cubs until the following year, but when the mother comes into oestrus in the spring, the incoming male often drives the cubs away. They are then totally on their own for the first time. I thought this would not be a bad thing to happen to

124

Freddy. And Cleo, feeling the urge to mate, would then feel it was right to let Freddy go.

The two cats ran free for several days. While Cleo came back at dusk for food in the pens, Freddy returned only well after dark. To make sure he got his rations, and that Cleo did not eat the lot, I left them in a dish on top of the pens and shut Cleo inside. But I soon realized it was not a good idea to incarcerate Cleo, even for a few hours, if Sylvesturr were to come looking for her.

In the early hours of March 17 I was woken by an awful yowling noise, a sound that gave a real meaning to the word 'caterwaul'. Then I heard Moobli scratching at the kitchen door. I shot out of bed but could see nothing in the darkness. I had read that male wildcats will call noisily during the breeding season; also that females will screech when wanting to mate. This was certainly no fox bark. Thrilled by the thought that Sylvesturr might have come back, or that Cleo was looking for him, I refrained from investigating the noise. Half an hour later, as I was dropping off to sleep, I heard the thin metallic '*awroori*' sounds wildcats make to contact each other yet not give away their positions. I wondered which of them it was.

For two more days there was still no evidence that Sylvesturr had actually returned, so I decided to take Cleo to him. It was a calm and sunny day, the first of real spring. Primroses had started to appear in sheltered places. Soon there would be plenty of natural prey about, and with Cleo in oestrus − I was sure she had made that awful screech, and probably from a desire to mate − she would be needing Sylvesturr. She deserved a real chance of freedom too, while she was still young.

I put her into the large den box in which she had given birth to her kits and released her from the boat on the edge of the woods at what I judged to be the far end of Sylvesturr's territory. She immediately ran up the shore into the trees, not pausing or walking about as had Patra, and did not wait to see where I was putting down a meat supply. I had a slight lump in my throat as she trotted away through the pines and firs without once looking back.

Cleo was back at 11 a.m. the following day! She had covered a good three miles of extremely rough country in less than 24 hours − a faster traveller than Patra had been. She went straight into the open pens and fell asleep in the main den. Later we found Freddy had taken a fish head from the previous night's food on the pen roof to right inside the trap, which I had left propped open in the west wood. Had he felt safer inside the box-cage, because Sylvesturr was about? Had Syl in fact followed Cleo home? I threw more sausage meat in the trap but did not set it.

For two days Force 10 gales came hurtling over from the south, blasting heavy rain across the loch. Freddy's nightly food remained untouched on the pen roof, as was the meat in the trap. Had Freddy left the area, or even been chased away?

I was rowing home in calm moonlight after meeting some friends on March 22 when I noticed what looked like a new rock on a high knoll below the west wood. It was rounded and lighter colour than the surrounding heather. Suddenly it changed shape and the top part of it moved. I saw two distinct ears, then it became smaller and melted away into the landscape. I was sure it was Sylvesturr, for it was too large to be either Cleo or Freddy. He had disappeared at a spot just above the den we had once found below the stout dwarf birch, which I had thought might be one of Syl's temporary hunting refuges. If Sylvesturr had indeed followed Cleo, and she was now out in the woods with Freddy, it seemed certain the kit would be in the way. If Sylvesturr caught him in the open, he might just kill him. If I set the trap, however, I might catch either Cleo or Sylvesturr instead, and the resulting psychological upset would ruin any mating attempt. It was a problem.

That night I opened an unexpected letter from Nobby Clarke, who had been head keeper of small mammals at London Zoo when I had first taken Sylvesturr away. He was now Head of the Animal Department at Edinburgh Zoo Park. He referred to Sylvesturr, the 'marvellous specimen of wildcat', and asked if I could help to provide a male wildcat, or female pine marten or otters, as it seemed a shame that a national zoo should be short of these particular animals. Coming when it did, the letter seemed a curious coincidence. I replied that I might let them have Freddy, provided I felt he was not likely to make it out here in the wilds on his own. Before I came to a final decision, I would telephone them first, I said, and discuss everything fully.

South-west gales blew all next day, but in the early hours of March 24 I was woken by loud '*mau*'s and '*awroori*'ings around the cottage, and in the morning all the new pen roof meat had gone. It seemed as if Freddy had been driven to return by sheer hunger, but hating the gales, he had waited for the first lull before making his move. Cleo chose to spend the day in the open pens.

Three days later, really worried about Freddy, I locked Cleo in the pens to make sure it really was him taking the roof-top meat. The food disappeared within an hour of darkness. Next morning I could see something had been in the open trap eating the remains of meat and the old fish that must have been nearly rotten. I hoped it was Freddy because I had to take the risk now. Surely, if he was in the area, Sylvesturr would be far too wild to go into the trap. I hauled it over to the pens, where Freddy was coming some nights, and set it carefully.

I went out early next morning and there he was, nicely caught. He had lost some weight after his 15 days of freedom. He yowled with anger when he saw me approach, flared but did not spit until I picked up the trap. Then he did so, loudly, and right in my ear. He landed in the pens and headed straight into the den, his head snaking up and down with each stride, like a small lion. Despite the slight loss of weight, his body was broad, his legs and paws more powerful than his mother's, and his head was big and square. His eyes were huge and golden, with great black centres, just like Sylvesturr's.

It was wonderful to see Cleo, who had watched the entire operation from the small pen, hurry into the main area to seek Freddy. As she passed by the den door, he saw her from inside and immediately came out (although I was still standing there) and began to follow Cleo among the grass and new primroses.

The change in Freddy's personality was astonishing. Throughout his 15 days of liberty he would not let us even see, never mind get near him. Within an hour or two of being back in the pens with Cleo, where he knew the wire fencing between us meant total security, he walked about a mere two yards away, glancing up at me occasionally with casual unconcern. He plodded doggedly after her, twisted his head against her body, lifted his tail, lowered it again, arched his back, flicked his tail again. My fears that they might fight after the long separation were not founded. That night I put meat down in the wood in case Sylvesturr was around.

One afternoon Freddy again followed Cleo about, crashing his head against her and raising his tail, but I noticed that after that first initial greeting Cleo never did this back to him. Several times he sniffed her rear parts. Cleo accepted this at first, but on the third occasion, when both were standing on the den box, she uttered a brief yowl and swatted him. He just lowered his head, took it without any reaction, then followed her again, his head going up and down. It was an oddly ponderous walk for a wildcat. If he was trying to mate with his mother, he was not having much luck.

When Cleo and Patra had been with Sylvesturr during his convalescence, and later when Cleo had taken refuge in his den, I had noticed that there had seemed to be a definite overlord and underling relationship between the old tom and the young females. I felt that female wildcats would not mate with any but a dominant mature male. I thought of Syl again, and went to check the new meat I had put out in the west wood.

It had all gone. In the mud near by was one of his unmistakable large prints, far too big to be Mia's. That convinced me. At dusk I herded Cleo into the den box, carried her to the wood, fed her near the unset trap, left more meat near by, and returned to feed Freddy.

When Cleo came back to the pens later, as I had thought she would, I chased her back to the wood, hard though it was to do. I blocked off the woodshed. If she was still in oestrus, I wanted her to have every chance with Sylvesturr. I felt sure he was not now in the area for nothing.

At the end of March I woke to see three whooper swans cruising down the loch and a pair of buzzards circling over the cottage. Chaffinches were chipping away in the bushes and, on the bird table, which was right on the edge of their territories, two male robins constantly fought and chased into the woods. A greater spotted woodpecker began a loud rat-tat-tat-tat to its mate on a dry snag tree. Bluebells were now sending up their first rich leaves, like green starfish upon the earth.

Cleo stayed away for four days, not even showing herself at dusk. I began to fear we had driven her away for good, but I refrained from letting Moobli try to track her.

In the early hours of April 3 I heard loud '*mau*'s near the house, and found Cleo walking round and round the pens seeking a way in, while the '*mau*'ing Freddy was trying to poke his head through the fencing. I hoped she had been running with and had mated with Sylvesturr. I let her in again.

Next morning I saw a large dying slow-worm in the open grass with a deep bite across its back to under its jaws. I wondered if Sylvesturr had attacked it and decided it was not edible. When it was dead I gave it to Cleo who, to my surprise, ate all but the last four

128

opposite: After putting Cleo up a tree, Moobli leaped up playfully.

above: Cleo growling at Moobli. Although used to him in the cottage or near the pens, the wildcats were afraid of the dog in the open.

below: Moobli located a wildcat skeleton in the woods to the west.

above: Cleo gave birth to four more kittens after mating with Sylvesturr in the wild. Here she picks up the runt, Liane.

below: Liane bowled over by the young tom, Miny, in a mock fight.

above: I tamed Liane by constantly bringing her into the cottage before letting her return to Cleo for milk and hunting training.

below: Liane on the desk in my study.

inches. Slow-worms, which are harmless legless lizards, could well be a wildcat food item in the wild.

As the days passed Cleo and Freddy spent hours gazing at the distant woods, at the trees along the loch shore and at the new hunting grounds among the emerald forests of bracken. I noticed they were now often sitting separately. The time had come for decision – to keep or free them, or let Freddy go to the Zoo.

On my next two supply trips I had telephone talks with Nobby Clarke and Roger Wheater, the Zoo's enthusiastic, modern-thinking director. They both wanted Freddy very much indeed, not only as an exhibit but because they had a lonely young female wildcat there, and wanted to try to breed from her. This put a whole new aspect to things. Cleo and Sylvesturr had produced two superb youngsters. Now Sylvesturr, Mia and Patra were free, and before long Cleo would also be at liberty. Freddy had constantly shown he was partially dependent on man by coming to the pens for food during his 15 days at large, which Sylvesturr had never done. He was also too large and fierce when in the open to have prowling around the house. Four free wildcats in the immediate area, among the nesting birds, was too many for a natural balance, and one day Freddy would undoubtedly come up against Sylvesturr. Win or lose, I wanted neither to perish nor to be injured. In the Edinburgh Zoo Park, which I knew to be one of the finest in Europe, he would have a far better chance of mating than in the wild.

I had often looked at Freddy and thought what a fine specimen he was. Unlike Sylvesturr, he was not wary and shy of man when he knew there was fencing between. Many thousands of youngsters went to that Zoo every year, some of whom might become tomorrow's active conservationists. If Freddy did sire kittens, they too would be a source of inspiration to young folk. I told Nobby Clarke I would bring Freddy on one condition: if he did not settle down happily in three weeks, or if the two cats did not like each other and fought, I would be free to take him back and, with care, release him to the wild in a good prey area.

So it was arranged. I had reared and rehabilitated four more of these rare creatures to live in the wild and put one into a Zoo where, if happy, he would also be useful. It was not, I felt, too bad a thing to have done.

I freed Cleo from the pens, left a food supply in the woodshed, then drove to Edinburgh.

10 · New Generation

Nobby Clarke met me on the high back path to the Zoo. He explained that Freddy would have to go into quarantine for a few days, while blood and urine tests were made, before joining the young female. We turned Freddy into a large cage, between a young leopard and a cougar cub, which seemed an oddly fitting coincidence. He immediately climbed up the bars, his eyes huge and black, his big horn-coloured claws thrusting him upwards.

'He's a really magnificent specimen, a junior edition of his old dad,' Clarke said with admiration. As we stared at his tawny underside, we both had the same thought: 'There's nothing wrong with his mating equipment either!'

Clarke showed me the enclosure where Freddy would live. It was three times the size of my own pens, with grass, hollow logs, bushes, flowers, and a long rocky den at the back, upon which a fine female wildcat, a trifle larger than Cleo or Patra, was chewing a piece of meat. It was situated in a quiet terrace kept for solely British mammals. As I had felt before, Nobby Clarke had a wonderful way with and understanding of animals. When I asked if he could actually touch the young leopard, he immediately opened its cage and cuddled it. The big half-grown cub sank its large claws into his jacket and nibbled his arm, but only in play. The animal allowed me to stroke it too. If Freddy settled down well, he clearly could not have been in finer hands.

I took no money for Freddy. I did not want to feel I was turning wildlife into a business. A small plaque with his new name − Sylvesturr 2 − and mine was put on the run. This somehow gave a touch of reality to all the isolated work with the wildcats which already seemed to be assuming a dream-like quality. As I drove on down towards London, I felt an overwhelming sadness that life with the wildcats was virtually over.

As if to show me that our wildcat days were anything but ended, Sylvesturr left one of his huge tapering scats for us to find in the middle of the path from the loch shore up to the cottage when I returned with Moobli early in May. I had telephoned Nobby Clarke from London before starting the journey home in the laden Land Rover. 'The cats have settled down perfectly together,' he told me. 'Young Sylvesturr 2 is still growing, eating like a horse, and when he thinks there's no one about is often quite playful.' I was greatly relieved.

The nesting birds were all settling down well in the woods, although the spring foliage was not yet fully grown. The front pasture was lushly verdant with new grasses, soft rush and the bottle green leaves of thousands of bluebells, some of which were hanging out their first flowers, as if heralding the colour of the summer skies to come.

Early next morning I saw Cleo stalking along just above the loch, her long striped tail hung in a low curve. She was perfectly silhouetted against the bright water as she hunted through the grass below the budding crimson rhododendron flowers.

I went out quietly and '*mau*'d to her. She stopped, looked up as if she could not believe her eyes, then '*mau*'d back in return. I kept very still and she walked a few steps up the pasture towards me, but then turned and walked to the west wood again. It was good to know she was all right. I decided to try and trap her overnight, to check her condition, but it was not necessary, for later we found her in the woodshed. Two weeks' absence had not made her heart grow fonder. She hissed and flared and dived into one of the den boxes as I went in. Covering its entrance, I carried her into the pens to let her stay there for a few days of really good feeding. Within a few hours she was her old semi-tame self again. As she fed I noticed she was plump and heavy round the gut.

I was doubly delighted − for not only was she almost certainly pregnant again by her ferocious and cussedly independent old lover, but with 60 square miles of forested, roadless wilderness behind the cottage, she had chosen to stay with us. As Cleo ate at my feet, I looked out over the murmuring woods to which Sylvesturr had returned to mate with his true but late-found love. Maybe even now he was not too far away, and I felt a great happiness.

My wildcat days began by chance, but I had at least done a little to help stem the tide of destruction that by the early part of the century had brought these rare and beautiful creatures to the brink of extinction.

I spent the next five weeks keeping a close watch on Cleo, who had begun to eat and drink almost twice as much as usual and was lying up in her den most of the time. I was sure that the early March oestrus and late May or early June birth was the normal wildcat reproductive pattern, for in middle or late May, when a female would be slowed down by pregnancy, there would be far more easy-to-catch surplus young birds, mice, voles and rabbits than at other times of the year.

On June 5 I heard that an eagle pair had been seen several times on the far slopes of a mountain to the west of my loch and decided to go and check the whole of its western face, despite having to wear brand new boots. Cleo had evidently spent some of the night in the west wood, for I found the remains of a young missel thrush in a clearing there. Its feathers had not been clipped, as though by a fox, but raked out in the wildcat manner. For an awful moment I wondered if Cleo had given birth to kittens somewhere in the wood and was just coming back to the pens for food. She certainly looked slightly thinner. Perhaps she had been suffering a false pregnancy and the swelling was now going down. Before I left on my trek I made sure the pen gate was tied open so that she could go in and out at will.

It proved an exceptionally hard day on the hill. I had to search between the 800 and 2000 ft levels and after covering 11 miles, scrambling up and down the sides of a steep gorge, all I found was an old ledge site where the nest had been blown out by the wind. Even the discovery of a patch of rare yellow globe flowers failed to alleviate my depression as I boated home again with blistered feet.

Before going indoors I peered into Cleo's den, where she had been resting up when I left.

An extraordinary sight met my eyes. What on earth was happening? It looked as if an albino mole had burrowed its way up into the den and was now resting on the surface hay, a grey-white rounded object tinged with pink. Cleo was licking it frantically while still lying on her side, as if the rest of her (which I could not see because of the door and its shadow) was somehow pinned down.

I raced indoors for my short-focus field glass and trained it through the den door. She had given birth — to three fine kits, which were suckling into the long buff fur of her belly, lined up like little furry piglets. The object I had seen was the foetal sac of a fourth kit, which Cleo was now vigorously licking and pulling away from the feebly struggling form.

As I continued to watch silently, anxious not to frighten her, she swallowed the remains of the sac (her natural and instinctive response, to keep the den clean and stop the scent reaching any possible predator) and kept licking the tiny kitten. It twittered like a little bird, waving its small limbs and struggling unsuccessfully to reach its mother's teats.

I prepared Cleo's evening meal and put it into the wire enclosure. I had no intention of disturbing the family that night, but I said to myself: 'That poor little mite will never survive.'

Cleo was loth to leave her kits. She came out, ate half the meat very quickly, drank a little milk, then hurried back to the kits who during her short absence had been groping around blindly to suckle each other's warm bodies.

Back in the cottage I poured myself a good stiff dram. The first words I recorded in my diary that day were: 'Here we go again. Cleo has stepped up her production 100 per cent!'

Next day I crawled through the gate, trying to avoid the new growing hogweeds, as their broad leaves would shelter the kits from the summer sun, and knelt in front of the wooden den door. Cleo, usually shy and fierce, had been astonishingly tame when she had given birth to Freddy and Mia, and I expected her to be the same now. To my surprise I was greeted by a low growling from inside the den. Perhaps she thought something other than myself was invading her den. I showed my face outside the entrance hole, but she continued growling, and even raised her lips in a flare.

Though similar, the kits were smaller than the year before's. They had big feet, broad heads with low-set ears and were marked with chestnut and browny-grey stripes and elongated spots on a buff background. Two were suckling, the others lay on their backs in the crook of Cleo's rear legs, little shiny pink pads sticking upwards. The kit furthest from the teats was the smallest. Its sides looked pinched and I wondered if it had had a suck yet. I would have to help this one somehow, but Cleo was in no mood for interference.

I crept out again, cut some small titbits of fresh meat and took them back. With these, the usual soothing talk and half an hour of patience, Cleo finally became docile again. After stroking her gently she actually let me touch the kits. I knew now that if they were picked up they would emit loud piercing 'meeoo's, and Cleo would instantly revert to anger. Instead, I gently but quickly hoicked one of the bigger kits off a teat when it had stopped sucking and put the smallest kit's mouth near the swollen pink nipple. Immediately it kicked like a TT rider trying to start his bike, and got its hard gums on the nipple. It then began to suck with such appetite that its whole body heaved like a suction pump. Cleo seemed to feel little of this, as if her teats were not ultra-sensitive.

With Cleo more trusting again, I managed to measure and sex the kits one by one. If I was quick I could examine them before they woke up and started squeaking for help. Sexing two-day-old kits is not easy for the amateur and mistakes can be made, but it turned out later I was right. The largest kit with the thickest stripe was a 7½in. female. The next two, both toms, were 7¼ins each, while the small runty female was a mere 6¾ins long. It was she who let the side down and whistled out a 'meeoo'. I hurriedly put her back near the teats as Cleo growled. She was the most perfectly marked kitten of them all, with a prettier, more cherubic face than the others and the promise of at least five good dark rings on her tail.

What should I call them? All kinds of ludicrous names ran through my mind. As I saw them all lined up again, with Cleo on her back, legs splayed out, abandoning her entire belly and its swollen milk glands to the kits, I settled for the most mundane names of all – Eeny, Meeny, Miny and Mo. Eeny was the big soft female, Meeny and Miny the two middle toms which looked alike, and Mo the weak little runt.

It seemed natural for the kits to be smaller than last year's as there were four instead of two. Cats carry their babies in a uterus that is divided into two horns and sometimes a mother may have three kits up one horn with only one kit in the other. This could

134

have happened in Cleo's case, with little Mo furthest up the horn as she was the last to be born.

Tiny Mo was very frail. During her first days I spent hours gaining Cleo's confidence, making sure Mo had a full chance to drink her fill, even if it meant slipping one of the other kits off a teat.

Once I went out to check the kits and received a nasty shock. The other three kits were lying asleep by their mother, only one with its mouth on a teat, but of little Mo there was no sign. Cleo growled when I reached over to feel the hay behind her recumbent form. Again I had to go to the cottage for meat. This time I dropped it more than a foot in front of her, so that Cleo had to stand to get it. As she moved and stepped forward, the suckling kit dropped off the teat and rolled on its back. Then I saw Mo lying still at the back of the den. I reached in and brought her forward. She struggled weakly and felt cold, but was still alive. I warmed her in my hands. When Cleo settled down again I put Mo on a teat, pulling two other kits away about a foot so that they would spend a minute or two groping their way back.

Wildcats are excellent mothers and will fight fearlessly against known foes or any threat to their young, but they follow the natural law of most predatory animals and will not make any special effort to help preserve a sick or weakling youngster. As I went back into the cottage, I had little doubt that in the wild poor runty Mo would by now have been dead.

The kits were only three days old when there occurred one of the most extraordinary of all the wildcat incidents. I was driving back to the boat with Moobli at the end of a supply trip, and was well past the riverside wood where I had released Patra early in March, when a golden eagle passed overhead, leisurely beating towards some rock faces above the wood. I had always thought there might be an eyrie up there somewhere but I could not follow the eagle's flight because of the trees. I stopped the Land Rover, intending to walk through the woods and scan the faces with my field glasses. We never got that far.

Suddenly Moobli put his nose down, zig-zagged about among the bushes and scrub cover of the wood, yawned noisily as he often did when starting out on a fresh wildcat scent and was waiting for the order to go ahead. I gave the order and off he went. As I hurried after him I knew that whatever he had scented could not be very far away, for he was moving urgently and tracking nose-high. I had just hissed at him, the quietest signal I had devised for making him go slower, when I heard him making the little anguished sounds in his throat that meant he had something at bay. I burst through the trees to find he had put a wildcat up a large birch tree, and there, lengthways on a branch some 15 feet above the ground, her striped tail switching from side to side, was Patra!

She was not spitting but her ears were laid down flat and she was making a low curdling growling sound of protest deep in her throat. I was sure it was Patra; it not only looked like her but Moobli had never yet put a totally wild wildcat up a tree. As she straddled the branch, I made the usual soothing sounds I had always made to her and Cleo. I noticed she was extremely fat, her stomach bulging out over both sides of the branch. Surely she was pregnant too!

Knowing she would stay up the tree for a while to make sure we had gone, I hurried Moobli back to the Land Rover, shut him in with one of his sterilized sausages, and went back to the birch tree. As I talked soothingly to her I wondered if it was possible that she could have mated with the young tom wildcat believed to be in her area. Well, there was one way to find out, and that was to try and catch her and bring her home.

I scattered a few pieces of meat ostentatiously below her tree, then boated home with Moobli for the box-cage trap I had used before for live-trapping the wildcats.

It was nearing dusk and some of the meat had gone when we returned. I laid a small trail of tiny scraps, then set the trap delicately with a juicy piece of red steak. We retired to a clearing over half a mile away, cooked something to eat on the vehicle's little bottle gas cooker, and retired for the night. Next day the trap was empty. We busied ourselves checking eagle eyries in another area before returning in the afternoon to reset the trap with fresh meat.

When we came back just after dawn the next morning, the door at the back of the trap was down and there, not spitting or dashing about, was Patra, safely caught. She crouched in the wooden box portion, fat as a furry rugby ball, with a look more of reproach than anger in her black-pupilled eyes. Wildcats have excellent memories and I was sure she recognized us. I covered the open cage part of the trap with a dark beach towel, so that she would not rush at the netting, and carried her in the trap back to the Land Rover, and then took her home in the boat.

I could not put Patra back with Cleo now she had kits. Luckily I still had half the fencing up in the woodshed, where I had once partitioned off Sylvesturr, and in less than an hour Patra was safely installed there with a large hay-filled den box. I did not think she would mind a temporary loss of freedom for it was proving to be a cold wet summer, and she would now be relieved of having to hunt before and after giving birth.

When I went to feed Cleo each evening, I spent some time in the pens with the family, sitting on the grass, bitten to the point of torture by midges, to see if I could win the confidence of the kits before their eyes opened. I noticed Cleo sometimes stood up to stretch and stayed high, as if consciously trying to make the kits stronger by forcing them to reach upwards for her teats. While she was eating, I removed one of the kits to just outside the den. Naturally it squealed. Cleo stopped eating, showing no belligerence and walked to the kit. After several delicate adjusting bites, she picked it up, not by the scruff of the neck but by placing her bottom jaw right under its neck, and very carefully carried it back into the den.

On June 10 south-westerly gales filled with rain began to rage around the cottage. They were so strong and cold that I became worried about draughts in the south-facing den. I decided to pursue my 'friendship with the kits' policy by bringing them all into the cottage. Wearing gloves in case Cleo turned nasty, I put the kits into deep hay in Cleo's old den box. She growled a little but immediately entered the box to carry them out again. Quickly I shut her in and brought them into my study-bedroom. Now they were away from the noisy wind, Cleo soon settled down, and I had a fine session tape-recording her '*brrrooo*' trills to them and their squeaks when seeking her teats.

Runt or not, little Mo was the first to try to flare if I suddenly scratched the box. I noticed that when Cleo had enough of them feeding she drew her upper rear leg right over her teats, thus closing the 'milk bar' to the kits. Eeny, the biggest, was now 8½ins long. Mo still seemed constantly to be forced to the outside, so I occasionally pulled one or other of the kits off Cleo's teats and put her on.

As Cleo seemed quite tame again, I decided to keep them all in overnight, maybe for several days if the gales kept up, and providing she used a litter box. Cleo ate her food normally but would not leave the den box for a drink until after dark.

It was hard to sleep that night. Cleo woke up just after 1 a.m. and started to wander about, shifting through my paper files. She used the litter box all right, as I could tell from the unsavoury noises after the initial scraping of the debris. About 10 minutes later she decided to drink the watered milk, lapping loudly, then to attack the dry biscuits, making such a racket as she crunched them up that sleep was impossible. Only the persisting gales and drenching rain prevented me from shoving them all back into the pens!

Next day, despite the weather, I had to battle up the loch for post and to keep an appointment with an excellent young keeper in a village to the south who had promised to show me an old eagle eyrie. Returning home soaked and tired, I opened the study door as Cleo shot from under my desk into the den box with a horrible growl. It took me a while to soothe her down again. The sudden opening of the door had scared her. Inside the den or pens she was reasonably tame, and inside the den box in the room she would also let me stroke her and the kits provided I moved slowly and gently, sooth-talking all the while. But outside the pens, or a few yards from the den box, she was as wild as ever, ears back, growling like a dynamo. One had always to be on guard and not go beyond certain well-defined limits.

When I went to feed Patra later in the woodshed, I was greeted by a fierce spit and a foot-stamp right from the mouth of her den box. She had seldom acted in this way towards me since she was a kitten. I wondered if it was because she was angry at being incarcerated. There was no way I could tell her I intended releasing both her and Cleo and the kits later in the summer, or that I was keeping and feeding them for their own good. Then I noticed that Patra looked a great deal thinner and my heart started beating a little faster. I shone my torch past her into the entrance of her box. She, just like Cleo, had given birth to kits in my absence. I could not see how many for they were deep in the box, and I was not going to step through the partition and take a close look with her in that mood. I would leave it till the morrow.

Back in the study, I opened my mail. There was a letter from Roger Wheater, Director of the Scottish National Zoo Park at Edinburgh, thanking me officially for presenting them with Freddy. 'You will be pleased to learn I am sure that the Wildcat has settled down well in its new surroundings and it is hoped that you will come to the Zoo at some future date in order to view your presentation . . . ' How wonderfully everything has worked out, I thought as I went to bed, happier to put up with Cleo's nocturnal noises and the occasional squeaks from the kits in my bedroom. With Cleo's two last year, and four this year, and now Patra's brood, we at Wildernesse seemed to be doing our share of putting a few more of these rare and beautiful creatures back into the wild. Freddy was the only one I would give to a zoo. How lucky we had been to catch Patra again only days before she had given birth.

When I went out to check Patra's kits next morning, the truth slowly dawned. I shone the torch past her grumbling form on to three kits, none as large as little Mo at birth. I could not believe it. No, it had to be a trick of the light coming through the window, or shadows of hazel sticks atop the log pile. But as I continued to train the beam I knew it was nothing to do with light or shadow. Patra's kits had *thick* black stripes, some nearly half an inch wide, the dark marks on their legs were blotches, their heads were smaller than Cleo's kits, with higher set ears, and their tails were also blotched and as thin as those of rats.

She had clearly not mated with any pure wildcat tom but with some plain old domestic feline!

Interesting though it was to have shed some light on an old controversy – for it is believed in some quarters that wildcats will never mate with domestics when free in the wild – I felt most disappointed. Perhaps her early life around Wildernesse with Moobli and myself had made her less discriminating. For a moment I toyed with the idea of drowning all but one of her kits, but I knew I had not the heart to do it. I felt sorry for Patra as I recalled her general air of irresponsibility, her comical but vain attempts to arouse Sylvesturr's interest once he had mated with Cleo. Poor old girl, she had never really got anything right! Never mind, although my meat bill was now around £7 a week, I would feed them all and release them when they were ready. (Months later, the farmer's wife on the land near where I had found Patra told me that a pure black feral domestic tom had adopted the area in the early spring. But this tom was found dead in April after a fight with another large feral ginger male.)

By their ninth day Cleo's kits were crawling well but could not yet lift their bodies enough to walk. Their eyes were still closed.

While little Mo was now 1½ins shorter than the toms Meeny and Miny, and 2ins shorter than the big female Eeny, I saw she was the first to use her little claws. Once I saw her rake some hay beneath herself. She was runty but not backward. The other three now lifted their heads and could spit audibly if they heard my approach. Although Mo had been the first to flare, she did not try to spit.

That night, because my room was now in need of the strongest fresh air spray on the market, I transferred Cleo, kits and den box to the small rear room. I did not want to put them back outside while the gales blew, and inside I could still make sure Mo got her share of milk.

At the age of ten days Eeny's eyes were two-thirds open, revealing the extraordinary bright china blue irises wildcat kittens have for about seven weeks before a greeny-grey tinge takes over. In wildcats this turns to the final yellow-gold at about five months.

The gales died down next day and a misty drizzle set in. I arrived home in the boat from a disappointing eagle trek, tired and soaked through. When I opened the rear room door to feed the wildcats I found some consolation. Although she was the runt of the litter, little Mo's eyes had started to open, a little Chinese slit showing bright blue in the gap nearest the nose. Eeeny's eyes were now fully open but not yet focusing. Before Cleo began her meal I saw her licking Mo's eyes to clear away the sticky secretions.

As I went nearer the other three kits lifted their heads, flaring and spitting, but the little runt just lifted her head, trembling weakly on its neck, trying to peer at me. She was not only prettier than the other kits, she was cuter and seemed to associate me with her mother and feeding. I wondered if perhaps she associated my soothing talk with the hand that had helped her so often to the teats. Certainly she seemed more even-tempered towards humans than her sister and brothers.

11 · *The Delectable Entertainer*

By the time the kits were two weeks old, and the family had been in the cottage for eight days, the powerful smell, and the fact that I would have to make a boat journey to a sandy beach to fetch more cat litter, made me feel we might all benefit by the cats returning to the pens. I did not want to protect them too much, for later in the summer they would have to start making their own way in the wild. They would need to learn that Highland rains were as much a part of summer as of the long grey winter. So when the drizzle ceased and the clouds cleared, giving way to blazing blue skies, I stuffed their den full of new hay, carried their box into the pens and opened it up.

Cleo immediately ran to the den, leaving all the kits where they were. I took them out one by one, set them on the grass and withdrew. All except little Mo began to 'maow' loudly. Cleo looked, her head going up and down, then came out and very gingerly carried each one into the den, taking Mo last.

By this time little differences in character and physique were beginning to show among the kits. Eeny, Meeny and Mo all had their eyes fully open, but the second tom Miny had only a slight gap in his right eye. Eeny, Meeny and Miny flared and spat loudly at any new approach of mine, and Miny's blindness did not prevent him from calling out the loudest when picked up, or from trying to scratch and bite. He was undoubtedly going to be the fiercest. Mo

141

was becoming the most active, and once even tried feebly to swat one of the other kits in play. All their foot pads were turning black.

That afternoon I went to check Patra's kits for she was now much tamer than on the day of their birth. To my surprise the eyes of all three kits were opening at eight days (a good two and a half days earlier than those of Cleo's pure brood) but the blue was much duller, the eyes smaller, with an opaque look about them. Their calls of protest at being handled were much weaker than those of Cleo's kits and their mouths were dull pink instead of bright red, but they were developing a good deal faster than the pure wildcat kittens.

Two days later I noticed that Miny's eyes were both open, and the other three kits were starting to focus and to look where they were going. None of them could walk properly but trundled along, bellies touching the hay, as they began to explore the den interior. When I called to them I was delighted to see that Mo recognized the imitation '*mau*'s and even took a few crawling steps in my direction.

By June 26 the kits' two lower canines were coming through and all but Mo tried to bite my fingers when I picked them up, hard nips which left the flesh white. Mo seemed by far the 'friendliest' and I spent more time stroking her than the others. When I went later with food, calling her as usual, Mo crawled to the curved hole in the den door and tried to climb over it towards me, thinking better of it when she saw the full four-inch drop on the other side! Two days later the kits' top canines were starting to break through and my enthusiasm for handling them waned considerably.

By the end of the month Eeny weighed 1¼ pounds, the middle two kits just over 1 lb, and little Mo no more than 14ozs. She was nicely built, as well as marked, despite her size, and her head was even larger in proportion than tom Miny's. She was also the first I saw to swat at the black tip of Cleo's tail. Mo also cuffed her sister's and brothers' tails as well.

During the first days of July I realized that Mo was no tamer towards me than the others. She was now showing a strong attachment to tough, thin-faced Miny. One afternoon I watched them playing. They bit each other, rolling over and over, then sat up swatting each other's faces with paws like little ping-pong bats sprouting claws. When I went closer to try and touch Mo, she reacted like a firecracker, spat and shot away a few inches, flaring as furiously as did Miny, the wildest one. I withdrew my hand, talked soothingly and tried again. The result was the same. Now all the kits were flaring, and even Cleo, as if affected by her kits' behaviour, had her ears back and was looking mean, though she was not growling. I left the pens.

Later I found Mo at the very back of the den, standing on her hind feet and trying to push her way into a small crevice in its larch slab roof. When she realized from the reactions of the other kits that there was something in front of the den, she pulled back, saw me and again spat. I thought I knew why: until then she had not been able to see me clearly, her eyes unable to focus on anything more than a foot or two away. Now she could see perfectly for several yards. While she had associated the sounds I made and the feel of my hands with being helped to the teats in her early days, the sudden looming sight of me scared her as much as it did the others.

Nevertheless I still had my own special feelings towards her. When, over the next two days, I found her behaving like Mia, Cleo's female kit of last year, and trying to escape through to the rear rocks to be on her own between feeds, I became worried. This early manifestation of the independence instinct, which can lead to a marauding fox or even an eagle snatching an unprotected wildcat kitten, occurs with some kittens more than others. That it should be developing first in the last born, the runt of the litter, seemed extraordinary. I spent the rest of the day blocking in the rear of the pens with small-mesh wire netting.

One day I tried an experiment. I wanted to see if a wildcat mother would accept or reject the kitten of another. Although individuals might vary, if one wildcat mother would foster another's kitten it could be a useful factor in any long-term breeding project. I moved Cleo and the kits into the cottage, and Patra with her hybrid kits into the pens.

Patra was now as tame as she had been at the time of her release. I determined to test the idea with her while keeping a close watch. Mo was much the same size as Patra's kits, and Cleo was after all Patra's sister, so I caught Mo. At first she tried to bite, then went submissive once she was picked up. I carried her into the pens. She immediately started to totter-walk into the den among her cousins, thick-striped and blotched, barging between them to seek a teat. I watched nervously, ready for quick action, but Patra showed no reaction whatsoever. It was as if she could not count or had known Mo all her young life. She did not even sniff at the strange kitten, and Mo was soon guzzling away with two of the hybrids. It was an interesting result, but I did not consider this brief introduction to be absolute proof of any theory about wildcat behaviour, and did not leave Mo in too long.

By July 11, at five weeks old, none of the kits was yet weaned but they all played and lay in the sun outside the den door with Cleo. The 'tail twitch' training had started in earnest now. Eeny still seemed the most advanced but was so good natured that she often let the other kits bowl her over without protest. Miny was definitely the ugliest, with his thin face and hard wiry body; he could now see the farthest. Whenever I approached, it was he who flared first and darted to the back of the den with whirring growls, closely followed by Mo, who still did not like my looming form, though she was the most submissive when picked up.

The year before, Freddy had been weaned at seven weeks old. If these kits followed the same pattern I would be able to release them in early August. Then my ideas on releasing all the wildcats changed.

One morning I watched the kits play, delighted to see little Mo was the fastest on her feet. She darted at the other kits, bowling them over backwards after playfully seizing them by the throat. In comparison, they still seemed rather tottery, making sudden dashes then falling over when they tried to stop, or looking about wildly after attacking heads of grass stems, as if to make sure no enemy was witnessing their real weakness.

After transplanting fifty cabbages, I caught Mo and brought her into the house for a photo session, picturing her on the bed, the desk, scratching her ear with a hind paw while lying down, trying to capture the greeny-grey tinge that was now creeping outwards in her eyes, banishing the bright blue. She showed little fear of being away from the family for the first time. Then, with Moobli in the house, I set her down on the grass in the front pasture and retreated a few steps. She looked about nervously, then started to run towards me with little '*mau*'s, afraid to be out on her own in a huge strange world.

Delighted at such progress, I put her back with the others. Then I picked up Eeny, but when I set her down on the grass she spat loudly and seemed most upset. I put her back. She instantly ran to her mother for reassurance, and Cleo licked her all over vigor-ously. Mo watched all this, then went forward and started licking

Eeny's tail! Then she licked her own paw and wiped her own face, twice.

At about 8.15 p.m. I fed Cleo as usual and then took the empty receptacles back into the cottage. When I returned Mo was watching her mother chewing the meat. Suddenly she advanced to the bowl, thrust her head in beside her mother's (Cleo allowed this without the slightest growl), picked up a piece of meat, chewed it, dropped it, then picked it up again and ate as if she had been eating all her life.

So Mo was now weaned. Little Mo, the sickly last-born of the litter, who had to be helped to the teats so that she would not die, was eating meat before her bigger brothers and sister. What an eventful day.

After a supply trip next afternoon, I hauled the boat on to its wooden runners and found all the kits lying in line sucking Cleo in the grass outside the den. When they had had enough, the three bigger kits went to sleep, but Mo started to walk about below the big shady hogweeds. I caught her, brought her into the cottage and tried to feed her cat meat from a spoon. To my delight, she sniffed it, then ate it all as I held the spoon in my hand.

I wanted to know if she would actually play with me, and stood up to fetch a two-foot-long eagle primary wing feather with a broken tip that I kept in the camera shelves. As soon as I moved off the bed, Mo flared in fear and ran to hide behind some sweaters lying near the wall, where she growled like a tiny electric dynamo. I brought the feather back, talked soothingly to her with the usual calming words, making sure she could see my hand coming towards her slowly, and managed to tickle her on the side of the head and under the chin gently with a finger. She looked nervous at first but, liking the caress, she calmed down again. I then showed her the tip of the feather with the other hand, making it dart gently about the bed just in front of her nose. Instantly she looked alert, ears pricked forward again. Then she started swiping out at it, making great round-arm cuffs with her claws out, much faster than a domestic kitten.

It was at that moment, when I knew I was becoming really fond of little Mo, that I decided I would try to tame her completely.

Next morning, when she was exactly six weeks old, Mo's training began in earnest. After the usual making-friends session in the pens,

I brought her indoors, set her on the bed and fed her a tiny piece of meat. I wanted to see if she would lap milk. As she watched the honey jar lid filled with a strange white liquid come to rest on the yellow bedspread a few inches away, she backed up, flaring slightly, before she caught the smell. Her head moving up and down as she sniffed, she edged furtively forward and licked the outer edge of the lid. This produced nothing of the taste which the smell had promised, so she bit the lid. Immediately it tipped up and her nose went straight into the milk. At that precise moment she must have been breathing in for twice she sneezed, so violently that she tottered sideways. Somehow a drop must have reached her mouth for she came forward again and was soon lapping rapidly with the loud ticking sound Cleo and Patra had made when they were lapping milk as kits. *Eureka*!

When she had drunk enough, she started to explore the bed and the sweaters I leave on it as extra 'blankets' on cold nights. As I slid my hand near, fingers twitching provocatively, she did an odd little dance − ears back, eyes large, making a half-circle backwards, and giving an occasional swift but feather-soft whack on to a finger with a clawless paw.

I knew that if I was to try and tame her to the house she would have to accept Moobli, who was now waiting anxiously but quietly outside the door, wondering what on earth was going on. Warning him to be quiet and a 'good boy', I let him in. Mo immediately flared, then reared as high as she could on her front legs, gave a loud spit and glared. Moobli just kept still a few yards from her, and she seemed to realize that this huge animal she had often seen had never done her any harm before, and slowly subsided. After half an hour I put Mo back into the pens.

My plan was to spend more and more time alone with her each day, yet always return her to Cleo and her family afterwards. I also wanted to keep Moobli in the act. Despite his gentle quiet nature, he was an exceptionally powerful Alsatian, measuring 6ft 4½ins nose to tail-tip. His inch-long canines were set in a massive bear-like head, and he could crack a red deer's thigh bone with one bite. I did not want to risk any feelings of jealousy on his part.

In the evening I brought Mo in again. She seemed slightly more amenable than before, playing with my moving hand, clawing and nibbling at my fingers. As I stroked her constantly and gently, she actually started to purr. I let Moobli in again, but it was hardly necessary to tell him to stay still for he seemed as interested in her as I was. His expression was one of total fascination and kindness. With ears cocked, he watched her from the foot of the bed, not attempting to touch or lick her. Although Mo often struggled, bit and scratched when in the hand, I did not resist or treat her roughly but persisted with loving caresses and soothing words. The only way such an animal could be tamed was by constant love, irrespective of what one received in return. The wildcat has bred right into its instincts over hundreds of years an innate distrust and hatred of its main persecutor, man. The slightest attempt at defensive retaliation on my part would have aroused and heightened those instincts in Mo. Here the love had to be expressed in action, not just attitude, as I had practised with ferocious old Sylvesturr. Both Cleo and Patra had been fierce and mistrusting through kittenhood, only becoming semi-tame after months of patience. The fact that Cleo accepted my close presence more often than not had clearly rubbed off on little Mo, giving me a slight advantage in the process of taming her.

I was now letting Cleo run free on some afternoons, as she made it clear she wanted to leave the kits and go off to hunt. While she was away the kits bunched up together in the far corner of the den and never set foot outside until she returned.

Next day I brought Mo in early. I thought she would have learned after the last mishap with the milk lid, but again she bit it first, put her nose into it, then spilled some on her left foot. She sneezed, withdrew a few inches, then shook her foot violently to get rid of the cold liquid. She then went forward and lapped most of it up quite naturally. The odd sequel to this was that almost every time Mo approached milk to drink she shook her foot hard first, a strange habit that lasted over the years. That morning, after eating and drinking her fill, she nestled close to me as I was lying quietly on the bed. I took her outside later so I could sunbathe on a camp bed. With Moobli sitting quietly several yards away, I set Mo on the grass, where she showed the same reaction, walking about, searching for cover, and every so often looking at me and '*mau*'ing for me to do something about it. Finally she settled for the shadow under the camp bed. Moobli dearly wanted to pick her up or lick her and his tongue came out instinctively, but when he made a slight move towards her, she flared and he stayed where he was.

After half an hour I put her back, wriggling through the mesh, into the pens. Mo looked at her sister and brothers (Cleo was away hunting) then back at me. She '*mau*'d and came struggling through the fencing again to reach me! I felt it was another little victory.

Two hours later I brought Mo indoors again. She could now climb up the tumbled blankets of the unmade bed and get on top under her own power, using claws for body hauling for the first time. But when she wanted to come down again she was not strong enough to jump. She '*mau*'d loudly. As I did nothing to help, she half climbed, half slid down the blankets backwards. She searched under the bed, ranged the floor, then settled for a brief sleep in a fold in the hanging blankets.

When she had slept enough and started walking about again, I took her on the bed for a caressing session. She purred loudly like a tiny motor, rolled, kicked out at my hands with her feet, clutched them with her claws, bit my finger playfully and squirmed against the combined inertia of my body, arm and hand while upside-down, her determined little jaw making her resemble a miniature lion. When I put her back in the pens and fed Cleo, I noticed big soft female Eeny was now also eating meat. It seemed odd that fire-cracker Miny, the fiercest, thinnest but strongest kit, should be the last to be weaned.

Over the next three days little Mo became more familiar with the study-bedroom as her second home. She recognized the meat and milk dishes and ate and drank readily. Sometimes she went into playful little dances on the blue carpet. These dances were crazy and delightfully entertaining to watch. She walked about the floor, then suddenly splayed her front feet outwards, arched her back as high as she could, separated her toes as wide as possible with claws sheathed, sleeked her ears right back, and with a big-eyed surprised look went into a fantastically fast dance in which she shot forwards and sideways before making her rear feet execute a hilarious circular waltz of their own. All the while her tail was upraised for some two inches above its base, then dangled down in a lovely curve, with all the guard hairs fluffed up like a flue brush.

Occasionally she would caper towards a thrown matchbox or rolled acorn, pounce on it with high '*Eeya!*' shrieks, bite it, then bat it about the floor at a dizzying speed. Suddenly she would break off and with a surprising leap land on top of the bed, hurtle round it, then leap off again to stalk towards me very slowly with an 'evil' look, before capering lightly away and taking refuge under the bed or behind the den box.

So amusing were these antics to me as I sat at my desk that at times I found myself trying hard to stifle a loud laugh, for one sound from me would have cut them dead. Yet I looked forward to them more and more. When a man lives alone in the wilds, as I had done for many years, genuinely light-hearted moments are few and far between. I was grateful to my little waif for bringing back the gift of laughter, and as my affection grew, I knew I could no longer go on calling her plain old Mo.

I suppose many single men have an image in their minds of their 'ideal' girl, an image seldom realized. I had met, won and lost mine, yet the mental picture, based partly upon memory, persisted. She was a tall shapely athlete, with great green-blue eyes and long thick tawny hair, redolent of health and sun and sand and sea and jungle. The name I had given this fading-dream woman was Liane. When I now saw my little tawny kitten, eyes flashing green-blue in the lamplight, performing her superb little dances so effortlessly, and heard her shrieking '*Eeya!*' as she pounced with mock ferocity on her playthings, the two sounds and images came together in my mind. The very word 'Liane' could sound very much like '*mau*', the wildcat summons call, when spoken in a high feline tone. Thus little Mo became Liane from that day forth.

12 · *Parting of the Ways*

On the morning of July 19 Cleo returned from hunting with a dead vole. She showed it to the kits and then started batting it about with her paws, as if encouraging them to be fierce and chase it. When Meeny picked it up with one clawed paw and looked at it, Cleo hooked it away and made the tom chase it properly. Cleo then ate the head, as if showing them it was food, and allowed Eeny to drive her off it with high whirring growls.

This inducement to ferocity on Cleo's part was the prelude to the kits accompanying her while hunting, so that she could teach them to recognize rightful prey and to pounce correctly. Hunting training was essential to all the kits. Even if Liane did become tame, I wanted her to hunt naturally too. I could not separate her completely from the family just yet. Oddly enough the tom Miny, who was the most ferocious towards Moobli or myself, stayed out of all this.

I left Liane with the others all next day, noting that she was the first to eat and drink from Cleo's stainless steel bowl. She had to crane her head over its four-inch-high edge and try to swallow with her throat pressed against it. None of the other kits were lapping milk yet. Later I was amused to see Liane sucking at Cleo's teats as she lay on her side in the grass, but unlike the others she kept her eyes open, cutely peeping through her mother's fur at my or Moobli's movements.

After a week of southerly gales and drizzle, I put Liane into the

150

hay of the sunny front pasture for some photos of her alone. At first she crept through the herbage away from me, but when I had taken a few shots and called 'Liane' in an abrupt squeaky voice, she came bounding back – perhaps because I was the only thing she knew in the whole new terrifying horizon.

When I put her back in the pens, the other kits gave her a boisterous welcome. With fat-faced stoical Eeny looking on, the two toms Meeny and Miny capered up to her and bowled her over with mock growls, and for a minute or two I could not see which kit was which. As I tried to take pictures, Liane broke away, and started to climb up the fencing. She peered out at me, then forced her way through the mesh and ran to where I stood, leaving Cleo and the two brawling kits behind, watching. What an astonishing breakthrough that seemed. Maybe the two toms were behaving a little too roughly towards her and she realized that she could find peace and gentleness with me.

Next morning I had her indoors again. After putting her on the bed, I ignored her and did some writing. She dozed for half an hour before, suddenly, I heard loud '*mau*'s and saw her standing on the edge of the bed as if she had never climbed off it in her life. She glared at me, wondering how to bridge the gap, then leaped to the floor, capered across, and with a little jump on to the arm of my chair, hauled herself on to my lap, where she went to sleep. It seemed I had finally won her trust, but the physical act of typing became impossible, for the jerky movements scared her. I had to resort to drafting my work with a pen.

Later, however, she blotted her copybook, or rather my bed, for the first time. Squatting with great delicacy, and with blissfully half-closed eyes, she spread a large puddle over the bedspread. For some reason she refused to go to the litter box of sawdust which Cleo had used when I first had the family in the house. Perhaps she had been with me too much and so missed the training wildcat kits usually gain by watching the mother perform her ablutions. That afternoon, Liane used the toilet area in the pens, and there she did scrape grass and leaves over it. So again I felt I should not separate her from Cleo just yet.

By now Patra's hybrid kits were more advanced than Cleo's, although they were only two-thirds of their size. I could not keep them cooped up in the partitioned shed, so I opened up the whole shed for them. I tried putting them in a separate pen that ran cross-

151

ways to Cleo's main enclosure; while I had proved Patra would accept one of Cleo's kits, Cleo simply would not accept the close proximity of her sister. Every time she saw Patra near the double mesh she launched an attack, trying to claw her way through.

This action upset all the kittens and made them bolt for their respective dens. The kits could have crawled through the mesh, and might thus get hurt, so the experiment lasted less than a day. Back went Patra and her brood to the woodshed, and down the loch I had to go for more sand and gravel for their litter areas, for they were now using half a sack of it a week between them. My meat bill was soaring too, and I was beginning to look forward to the time when I could release all the wildcats.

With Cleo spending most of her days out alone in the woods and returning regularly around 6 p.m. to feed the kits, I brought Liane into the study again on July 22. She showed me a new variation of what I had come to call her 'Zorba' dance. She still darted and shot about the floor with her paws twisted outwards, but she also had a slower version in which she swung her front legs out sideways like a fat girl running, and advanced and retreated in an odd minuet.

Around 9 p.m. Liane began '*mau*'ing loudly as I worked at my desk and for the first time made a strange chirring noice in her throat, like a juvenile imitation of her mother's greeting '*brrrooo*' trill. I thought she was missing the family. When I lay on the bed, she jumped up and cuddled close, purring. She twisted on her back and pushed at my beard with her front paws. It seemed she had just felt neglected. As I lay still, she looked intently at my eyes blinking, then shot out both paws, her claws protruding slightly, as if trying to stop the movements of my eyelids. If this became a habit it could be dangerous when she grew bigger, but a quick 'Na!' and a human hiss after the third time stopped her.

After her meal, I removed the shavings on top of the sawdust in her little box and replaced them with an inch of short hay clippings. To my relief, she now used the box − fully. Later, with Moobli stretched out on the floor after his gargantuan meal, his huge paws sticking out straight like the cabriole legs of a piano, I noticed the room had become strangely quiet. Liane had found the warm living comfort of Moobli's great bushy tail, had put both paws over it with her head between them, and had gone to sleep! He was well aware of this, of course, and was looking at me sideways, the whites of his eyes showing with the strain of peering at me in that fashion without moving his head and disturbing his little friend! His tail was to become a regular dozing place for the little kitten over the next few evenings. Moobli never once showed any jealousy and behaved like an angel.

With a low mist hanging over the hills and loch, I boated out for supplies next day, then went to explore the rocky cairns and woods that ran for almost a mile along the single track road near the sea, where Cleo and Patra had been found as kittens two years earlier. I was looking for the den of a huge old tom wildcat I had seen two years before that, and which had eluded me on two previous searches. That afternoon I found it, between huge boulders below a cliff. To the right of the entrance a dry mossy rock held the greening bones and skulls of rabbits and small birds. It did not appear to have been used recently. It occurred to me, as I watched some rabbits hopping in the fields towards the sea, that this area would be a good place in which to release Cleo and her brood.

When I returned home at dusk, Cleo and her kits, including Liane, had all gone! Had she taken them off into the wild already? In panic, I raced round her hunting area in the west wood with a torch, ordering Moobli to 'Track the pussy coots!' He did his best, but the frequent leg cocking on tufts, and the scent he picked up from mossy rocks, told me that all he was finding were recent fox trails. Only later, when I went to fetch his biscuit meal and nightly meat sausage from the rear workshop, did I discover what had happened.

Cleo had carried each one of the kits into the workshop, the door of which I had foolishly left open, and had installed them on the piles of sacks (which I used for bird hides) near the free food supply! She reacted to me as usual when not in the pens, flared and hissed, backed into a corner with ears flat, then shot past me and vanished into the night. I had a hard task rounding up the kits into a den box, but finally I got all four back into the pens and left the gate open. Cleo was back in half an hour and I closed the gate in case she tried to spirit them off somewhere else during the night.

On my way back to the house with the paraffin lamp, I remembered that I had not yet fed Patra and her three kits in the woodshed. There was a sudden flurry in the grass by the shed wall. As Moobli went forward instinctively, a small striped shape shot across the path, its little claws scrabbling on the earth as it forced its way through a tiny hole at ground level and back inside. It was one of

Patra's kits. They too had the wanderlust upon them, and while Patra could not get out, it seemed her kits were now investigating the world outside on their own. I blocked up the hole.

I now had to think carefully about all their futures.

In the early morning three days later, an extraordinary event happened which made me hasten my plans. I had just dressed when I caught a glimpse of a large bird floating silently past the window, barely thirty yards above the front pasture. Hoping it might be an eagle, and not just a buzzard, I screwed the big telephoto lens on to my camera and, closing the door on Moobli who was whining oddly, stole outside for a shot. I was just in time to see the bird (a large female buzzard) sailing serenely over the west wood. But when I looked over to the wildcat pens an astounding sight met my eyes.

There in the smaller pen, partially obscured by the brambles, stood Cleo, her tail as thick as a bottle and her ears back, growling in a way I had never heard before. She was standing high, ready to attack. Facing her just outside the pens, and glaring with its big orange eyes as if trying to mesmerize her, was the red-brown form of a large fox. It was visibly wilting before the ferocious wildcat stare and very slowly was starting to back up. I was far too close with the big lens to try for a photo.

Although the kits were clearly safe in the den, my main thought was to get that fox out of there and teach it a lesson it would not forget. I drew back slowly, then tiptoed swiftly to the door. As Moobli shot past me I hissed, 'Go on, boy. See him off!'

By the time I reached the corner again both fox and Moobli had gone, racing eastwards to the main burn and its waterfalls. Moobli had an astonishing turn of speed when he needed it. I ran as hard as I could, stumbling through the long bracken on the north hill, hampered by the camera and long lens. Then I heard Moobli's deep baying bark in the east wood. Cursing my mere human speed, I reached the burn in time to see Moobli floundering out of the far side of a pool, the fox just a foot in front of him, and Moobli's jaws clamped on to the very tip of the fox's tail. As Moobli struggled to get his footing out of the pool, the fox tore itself free, bounded forward and made a tremendous leap of at least 10 feet on to an almost sheer slab of rock, hooked its forepaws over the top and vanished into the herbage on the far side of the burn. With the fox's tail hairs still sticking to his mouth, Moobli whined and danced about. He knew he could not make such a leap from the standing position and was about to rush downstream to cross the water flow when I called him off. He had no chance, for the long-legged fox can run as fast as a hare. Knowing the ground and its trails intimately, it would in that quarter-minute have been several hundred yards away through the thick bracken and summer growth.

The fox had obviously come sneaking around in the hope of picking off one of the kits, possibly Patra's, which had been straying through that little hole for several nights. I did not think it would return during the daytime again after such an experience, yet it was probably cunning enough to know Moobli was normally kept in the cottage at night. It just might return in the dark a few days later for another attempt.

Cleo had proved herself fearless when confronting the fox, and could probably protect her kits from it, but what if it returned with a mate? I could no longer leave the pen gate open for her to hunt alone in case the fox, or foxes, got to the kits while she was absent, or she herself took the kits away. She and her kits, and Patra's, would have to be kept penned in for a few days longer.

I now made my final decision about their release. I would keep little Liane but set free Cleo and the other three kits amid the rocky cairns and woods near the rabbit-filled fields by the sea. Patra and her kits would be set at liberty in a large conifer wood on the far side of the loch where there were many voles, mice and other prey. I would leave a food supply for both families each week until it ceased to be taken.

The immediate problem was Liane. Being the smallest kit, she could still wriggle through the mesh of the enclosure. She was in more danger from the fox than the others. The answer was both simple and expedient. She was now well used to the study-bedroom after her daytime visits, so from now on it would be her permanent home. I would have to live with the young wildcat for many weeks until she was large enough to look after herself, but if all went well the process of taming her would be enhanced. I would now have to trap voles or mice for her hunting training, but until Cleo was finally released, Liane could spend daytime periods in the pens. Every time I went on a trek or supply trip she would stay in the room.

155

Having worked this out, I caught Liane and brought her indoors. She was very playful for about an hour, then chirred loudly and leaped on to my lap and went to sleep. Carefully I transferred her to the hay box and did not hear a sound from her all night.

I was woken by a sudden thump on the bed and strange pokes all over my body. Liane had leaped up and was investigating the strange humps and bumps now below her on the formally flat bed. Heart beating fast, I did not want to scare her off, yet my face was exposed. I kept still. She crept right up to my face, watched my eyes blinking and once again shot out a paw to stop the movement. 'Na!' I hissed, and she leaped two feet backwards, then started one of her Zorba dances over the bedspread, advancing and retreating, ears back, looking ferocious. I swizzled my hands about under the bed-clothes and she watched every movement, leaping and chasing after them with swift jerky movements, like a big squirrel. She 'caught' my fingers with both sets of claws and bit down into the clothes. I was thankful for their covering.

Presently she tired of this and began to nuzzle round my face and beard, smacking her lips. It was the noise wildcat kittens make when they want some food. Then she forced herself down past my chin into the bed itself, as if looking for a dark place she could explore. I wiggled my toes, she felt where the movement was coming from and like a mole burrowed down to them. The next thing I knew she was biting my toes! I soon stopped moving them and started twiddling my fingers instead. I felt her forcing her way up towards the movement. Suddenly I felt a sharp, excruciating pain as, en route to my fingers, she encountered something else of interest, a naked hairless mouse no doubt, and bit me in a most tender spot. For years I had slept naked, summer and winter, but if this bed burrowing was to become a regular early morning occurrence, and if I did not wish to surrender my masculine equipment to a wildcat, it would be necessary to change the habit. From then on I slept in my underpants. On this first occasion, however, I managed to grit my teeth and stay still, finally enticing her back up to my neck area with frantic finger twiddling of my left hand.

Before long she emerged by my face, looked over at the window, and leaped down with a fast sideways tail-dangling caper. She shot across the carpet, up on to the chair, and found a new resting place on my work files on the window shelf. Here she dozed for about half an hour, allowing me to get up and dress, then started grooming herself with long licks up and down her shoulders and forelegs.

When she started playing about on the floor, I put down my large shaving mirror, magnifying side outwards, to see what would happen. At my movement she shot with a hiss to the top of my clothes case under the bed, and from this perch sniffed with bobbing head the strange new shiny object on the carpet. Overcome by curiosity, she jumped down, walked round to the side of it, as if not wanting to stalk it directly, then came in front of the mirror. The sudden appearance of a huge wildcat's face, twice the size of her own, made her flare and leap about two feet backwards. When nothing happened, once more she crept forward, saw the face begin to appear again and ducked back. Each time she grew bolder until she was staring at the strange cat full in the face, and sniffing it. Most peculiar – no scent! Within four minutes she was reaching behind the mirror with her claws for the other big kitten and was clearly mystified. Within ten more minutes she had somehow worked out that the other kitten's movements corresponded exactly with her own, that it was therefore something only to do with *herself*, and she never played with the mirror image again.

After she had eaten and drunk, she scratched at the floor, looked round, spotted the sawdust and hay-filled litter box and went to perform, her tail jerking up and down like a pump handle. That completed, she delicately raked debris over her leavings with her left foot. She used the box and covered her wastes in this way for the next two days. I was delighted – prematurely, as it turned out.

By now the early blue of her eyes had been banished to the outer edges and the replacement greeny-grey was gaining a lighter gold tinge. The few spots mingling with the stripes down her sides were elongating into the final shorter stripes of her adult coat. The tramlines of dashes that swelled out and receded again to the dark brown line down her back were also starting to merge together. While still a runt compared with the others, she was fast, well built for her size and seemed to be thriving on the fare I gave her.

One fine but sunless day I carried her up to the pens and dropped her through the camera hole after removing one of the wire strands. She ran straight into the den where Cleo greeted her with a murmured '*brrrooo*', not even getting up, as if the kit had never left her side. Liane then barged in among the other kits, who also showed

157

no surprise. Although one kit was suckling, Liane made no attempt to get milk. I was sure now that I could separate Liane totally without problems, and at night I brought her back into the cottage again.

Shortly after that, Moobli and I returned from an unsuccessful search for a new badgers' sett to find chaos. The far corner of my study was a mass of white where all my files had been ripped open and tossed about, as if by a whirlwind. Sheets of paper were lying everywhere, with very few left on the shelves. The mischievous cause of all this rumpus, who had clearly had a fine old time on her own, was lying neatly curled up on what was now her favourite bed – my desk chair.

'You can't discipline a wildcat,' I repeated to myself as the lovely little brute greeted me with a '*chirr*' and stretched herself lazily. Well, I would feed the other cats before I tried to restore order.

When I went to the woodshed, I found that the bottom half of the double door had somehow come open and Patra and her entire brood had vanished. Moobli found them in seconds, ensconced in the workshop, the kits dashing everywhere. Patra snarled, spat and dashed through the door into the north hill bracken. I forbade Moobli to go after her. She had broken into the carton of sterilized meat, and between them they had devoured two whole sausages. They had used one of the sacks as a communal loo. As I rounded up the swollen kits and put them back into the woodshed, leaving the top door open for Patra to join them later in the dark, I knew the time for her final release was nigh.

It took me a full three hours to sort the papers into the correct files. Meanwhile the wanton little miss, full of beans after her meal that evening, discovered that a sheet of paper lying on the carpet made a jolly good toboggan if leaped on at speed with all four feet braced. When finally I sat down to type out my diary, I found she was not prepared to give up her new bed to her huge foster parent, at least not without a struggle. She leaped on to the arm and forced her way down beside me, making me shift up into a cramped position to make room for her! There she stayed stubbornly and went to sleep, only the hot lump by my backside reminding me now and again that she was still there.

Around dawn next morning, after playing moles under the bedclothes again, I heard Liane land with a little thud on the floor and gratefully turned over for another fifty winks. Suddenly there was a great deal of swishing. She was at the files again. As I looked up, I saw that she had worked a thin hardcover file so it rested halfway over a small divider on the shelves and had become a see-saw! She walked up to one end and down it went, then to the other and down went that end. She did this several times, enjoying herself thoroughly, until the papers suddenly slithered out on to the floor. The great crash sent her scurrying for shelter on the suitcase under the bed.

I soon learned that her peaks of greatest activity, when she indulged herself in file-shuffling, Zorba dancing, sledging along on paper sheets, swiping out and biting the tassels on the dangling bedspread, were at 10 p.m., 1 a.m. and 7 a.m. Unfortunately, they did not coincide with mine, but when one lives by choice with a young lady of independent mind, one has to make a few adjustments.

Patra did not return until the evening after we had found her in the workshop. She had left the kits alone for nearly twenty-four hours. They were certainly ready to go free, and I felt sure Patra would turn vicious towards them if closed up again in the woodshed.

On the last day of July I enticed them with meat into a den box, and in blazing sunshine took them by boat over the long conifer wood on the far side of the loch. Patra growled for most of the way, pushing her claws through the ventilation holes of the box.

With a parcel of sterilized meat sausages in my pack, I carried the box of cats up a steep bank and over half a mile of difficult terrain between the small spruces and tussocks until we reached the first green open patch. Setting the box in a thicket, and spreading the meat around so that Patra could see it, I opened the door and said, 'Goodbye, old girl.' Then I took off quickly back to the boat. If I had stayed looking at them I might have changed my mind.

I felt little emotion as we boated home. I intended to renew their meat supply on fishing trips, and would probably see them again. Moobli lay in the well of the boat looking miserable.

I cleaned out the entire woodshed and the litter area – good fertilizer for the fruit trees – and then went to see what new havoc little bossy boots had created in my study. As I peeped through the window, the place seemed quiet and in perfect order. There she was, lying all alone on the green cushion of my chair, her big ears twitching slightly, pink nose between her big paws, little sides heaving as she breathed. It was almost as if she was keeping my chair warm.

From her warm cramped perch beside me, she now launched into new kinds of mischief. She took to leaping on the desk and chasing the moving typewriter carriage, flicking at the ends of the paper, swatting my typing fingers. Once she seemed to leap from nowhere and land with her front quarters right inside the well of the machine as I was in full spate, so that two of the hefty sharp keys hit her. She squawked, leaped out, shook her paw in pain, and never tried that particular stunt again. Instead she took to Zorba dancing on the desk itself. After one intricate dervish-like double pirouette, she swiped my tin of Biros and pencils into the fireplace. She also started burrowing through the loose files, like a huge shrew going berserk and hurling up debris from a woodland floor. She used her claws more often too, usually to hook off paper clips. Once she hooked the photograph of a woman friend out, flung it up into the air, batted at it with her claws, her paws as broad and spiky as huge black sundew leaves, and waltzing about on her rear feet only, whapping down upon it time and again with her front feet, before chewing it to shreds.

Yet she was a fastidious eater, like her mother, not greedy like her Auntie Patra had been. She ate only what she needed. At night she still spent time sleeping draped over Moobli's bushy tail, so that he dared not move for fear of upsetting her. Then she would wake, look at me, haul herself up the old coat on the back of my chair and force her way down beside me.

I still took her into the front meadow for walks. If it was drizzling, or Moobli went too near, she hared straight back into the house. This was a useful reaction for it meant she now regarded the study as home, and I hoped she would continue to do so in mature life.

Before I finally released Cleo and the other three kits, I wanted to make absolutely sure Liane no longer needed her mother and I resorted to a cunning trick. I put her into the pens with the others for a short period each afternoon, with only the roughest of food: stodgy meat sausage, with plain water in the bowls. The other cats would eat and drink but Liane, used to the best, sniffed and turned up her nose at the rough fare. I then removed her again and fed her the choicest meats and milk in the study. Afterwards I returned to the pens to feed the other cats good food and milk too. Liane did not

above: If I moved suddenly, Liane would flare on her bed of my sweaters.

below: Back in the pen, Liane clutched bramble leaves with her forepaws while forestalling an attack from Miny with a karate-style kick.

above: Liane snoozing on Moobli's warm furry body, which he bore with great patience.

below: Liane with her favourite toy, a hunk of tightly rolled cardboard suspended from a cord.

know this, of course. I think she came to realize that only in the study would she receive the fare she liked most, not with her real family. It was sneaky but effective.

One night I returned from a fishing trip with Moobli to find Cleo and the kits had disappeared. Moobli soon traced them. Cleo had forced her way through a loose wire in the camera hole and had carried each of the kits into the newly vacated woodshed, her home when she herself had been a kit. Eventually I got them all back into the pens. It was time for them to go free too, for it was now essential the kits learn to hunt in the wilds with their mother.

Next day I went out to the pens wearing leather gauntlets (now necessary with Cleo's kits) and got Eeny and Meeny into the big den box easily enough. Cleo followed them in to eat the bait meat, but Miny hid in a rock cleft at the back of the den. I managed to haul him out by the root of the tail and seized his neck scruff as he bawled and tried to bite. I thrust him into the box with the others. We boated and drove to the site I had selected, the rocky cairns in the woodlands by the rabbit fields, where I staggered with the box up to the disused wildcat den. Cleo could use it if she wished or find another.

I set out the meat sausage supply where she could see it, opened the front door flap of the box and retired some twenty-five yards away to watch. At first Cleo stayed crouched, her kits all behind her with saucer eyes, looking fearfully around. Slowly she eased herself out. She put her feet on top of the box and with eyes huge and black-pupilled looked cautiously at the strange new area. She knew it was goodbye this time; she knew by the distance the boat and Land Rover had travelled that I meant it now; there was no going back.

She went back into the box among her wide-eyed kits, as if she did not want to leave. I walked forward again, picked her up with soothing words and gently set her on a rock below the den after kissing her neck. Then she went, sneaking low, and was out of sight in seconds. Twenty yards away she started calling her kits, '*maoo, maoo.*' They answered with little '*mau*'s and, one by one, filed over the rocks and through the thick grasses. My last sight of them was of Miny's backside before they disappeared for ever.

'Goodbye Cleo,' I said, feeling a terrible lump in my throat. 'God bless and look after you, dear old lady.'

And that was that.

As I closed the box and carried it back, Moobli looked as if he could not believe what I was doing. He made a move forward with his head low, as if he wanted to track them as of old, but I called him back. If I felt sad as we drove away and boated home, Moobli seemed even more downcast. He lay in the boat, forcing himself to sleep as he always did when unhappy. His eyes were red and blood-shot when I woke him. 'It's for their own good, old son,' I tried to explain. How he loved running out ahead of me each morning to check that his charges were still there.

Although I set fresh sterilized meats for Patra and Cleo and their kits on my next few fishing and supply trips, Cleo's remained untouched after two weeks and Patra's after three, and I brought the den box home again. We never saw either wildcat again.

For more than two years the lives of Cleo and Patra had been intertwined with ours. Now all we had left was little Liane.

13 · A Chapter of Accidents

For the whole of August Liane lived in the room with me, except when accompanied on outdoor excursions. As she grew stronger (weighing over three pounds by the middle of the month) there were times when 'little Liane' was as much as I could cope with.

On the very night I returned from releasing her mother, she semed to know that her family was no longer outside as usual and that she was now on her own with us. She was more wary and kept her distance. I had to learn that a deep underlying love was not in itself sufficient when dealing with an animal that is wild and independent by nature. That love had to be constantly communicated in every movement and action. I am convinced that wildcats somehow know when the status quo they have been used to is about to change, even if there is no outward sign.

I knew she knew her mother had gone, and this knowledge made me nervous. When I picked her up and stroked her, she suddenly and for no apparent reason yowled noisily, scratched, and sank her teeth hard into my right forefinger. I reacted instinctively, protectively, without thought, and threw her away. She hit the floor and rolled over, spitting and growling with a high whirring sound, and dashed for refuge to the suitcase under the bed. There she crouched hidden by the 'curtain' of the tasselled bedspread. When I lifted it up, trying to make friends, again she spat and slammed down her foot against me, just as her father Sylvesturr had done throughout his life at the approach of a human.

I thought I had undone all the work of taming her and cursed my stupid reaction. I sucked and washed my gashed finger, then put some meat and milk by the side of the case. For two hours she just stayed there, refusing to touch it. I knew better than to make any more approaches, left Moobli in the kitchen (where he normally slept) and just stayed working at my desk, not daring to go to bed in case the noise above frightened her even more.

At about 2 a.m. I heard a movement. She had sneaked out and was lapping her milk. I watched from the corner of my eye as she ate some of the meat too. Then she took a few steps towards me, seemed to think better of it, and leaped on to her second best bed, a pile of sweaters on an old sea chest. When she was asleep I tiptoed quietly over and slid between my own blankets.

Next morning I awoke to find her still there. Pretending not to look at her, and doing without breakfast so as to avoid opening and closing the door, I moved quietly to my desk for some typing, a sound she was well used to. Suddenly there was a little '*mau*', a thump on the back of the swivel chair, and she was beside me, trying to force her way down between me and the arm. Apart from shifting up to make room, I made no move to touch her. The next thing I knew she was clawing at my right arm as I typed. I kept typing with that arm while I sneaked a finger of my left hand over and darted it about on my sleeve. She immediately started to claw at it, but in play now. By just ignoring her it seemed I had won her back.

During the next few days her play became even more intricate. She knocked my plastic slide-viewing lens off the desk and began batting it about the floor. It was the first time she had chased a large hard object in this way. She seemed far faster than a domestic kitten, her movements delicate but deadly accurate.

To replace Cleo's black tail tip, I made another plaything for her, a bright green and red stiff magazine cover rolled into a hard ball and suspended on nylon fishing line from a string near her litter box. She played with this for hours, dancing, swatting, flirting, waiting for it to swing overhead as she ducked low, then whacking out at it after a swift turn, her eyes huge, intent and black. Sometimes she dived on it with both sets of claws, pinning it down to the floor, then doing a forward roll with both feet, her teeth fixed into it.

At night, with the paraffin lamp hissing away, I noticed her looking at moving shadows on the white walls. I made strange animal objects – pecking birds, fluttering butterflies – with finger shadows and she leaped on to the bed and began to chase them. On the second night she deduced that they were not 'real', far sooner than it had taken Moobli to work this out when he was a pup, and began to look from them to my hands.

Of course, the dozing, sometimes snoring form of Moobli proved too much of a temptation for her. He was becoming slightly jealous of her, and did not like being ordered to 'sit' every time he nosed towards her out of interest. When I saw her dancing deliberately near him, and he was lying watching her in the lion couchant position with his head up, I became worried: one chop from those mighty jaws and inch-long canines would have ended her nine lives in a trice. She sleeked her ears back, did a backwards waltz, then danced in and delivered a quick left and right with clawless paws to his huge muzzle. He merely blinked and drew his head back half an inch. Again she went in, right, left, right, and away, and he actually seemed to enjoy it. His mouth dropped open in a huge grin, his long pink tongue lolled out and he started panting as he often did in a warm room. When Liane saw the great mouth and teeth she did a reflex leap right over his head and landed on the bed. Moobli saw me looking at him approvingly and started wagging his great tail. This sight proved too much for Liane and down she jumped, dived straight on to it, clutched, bit, rolled over, then started kicking at it with her hind feet. The dog did not think much of this treatment and whined *sotto voce*, but he let her get away with it. For two weeks it became a regular feature of Liane's nightly play – if Cleo's tail represented a vole then Moobli's was a big hare – but never once did the long-suffering dog snap at her.

Another game she invented was to throw herself on her back right under his nose, lie with her legs splayed out and whack out with each paw at his chin. If his nose went too close, she flared while still lying on her back on the floor! One night, however, Moobli decided to cut out this latest caper and whoofed right in her ear. At that close range it must have sounded worse than a thunderclap! She was on the suitcase under the bed so fast he never saw her go. I felt it essential to stay out of these dog and wildcat play sessions, for it was important they worked out their own adjustment and came to trust each other.

Every time the urge came upon her now (seldom more than

once a day) Liane used the sawdust hay box, never performing her ablutions anywhere else in the room. It seemed she was perfectly trained, for which I was grateful. She not only scraped hay over her wastes but also tried to rake debris over her left-over food too, a real wildcat trait.

She stared at the flickering flames of the wood fire nervously, showing no signs of wanting to sit near on the mat, like a domestic cat. I noticed other differences: she did not erect her tail hard when stroked, and never 'kneaded dough' with her front paws on my lap.

Thinking it would do her good to have a long spell in the fresh air, I put her into the pens alone for three hours while I wrote indoors. When I went out again she set up a great racket, '*mau*'ing loudly and trying to claw her way out through the mesh. I went round to the back, opened the gate, and she shot into my arms, '*mau*'ing, purring, sniffing at my nose and eyes and gazing into my face as if to be sure it was really me after such an age! When I brought her indoors again, the fuss continued, though she never rubbed herself against me like a domestic cat.

Although by mid-August she was still rather small for a wildcat (only 1ft 8ins long at 13 weeks of age) she was strong enough to inflict considerable damage if she really wanted to. Her Zorba dances now had an air of ferocity about them. The initial ears-back coy look, as she drifted and waltzed about with turned-out toes, was supplanted by a really nasty black-eyed look as she dived on to my hand, clawed hard with both sets and pulled her head down for a bite, which was sometimes quite hard. Then she would dance away again, sideways, looking back archly as if to say, 'Now, now. How DARE you!' − as if I had attacked her! In she would come again, pounce with a loud '*Eeya*', clutch, bite and kick, and be away again in a trice. It was lovely to watch, painful to experience (though she seldom drew blood), and I fervently hoped she would not do it when mature. I found at this time that she would accept a light tap on her backside, providing it was in play and no harder than she would have received from her mother. This usually stopped her biting too hard. She was full of confidence in her own den. In fact she was just about taking over the joint!

Although she could climb quite well the logs that were propped up against the outer wall, it was not until August 9, when I refused to lift her down again, that she learned how to descend under her own power. Her instinct was to go down forwards, but not being a squirrel with reversible rear feet, she could not. So she tried going half sideways, slipped a bit, clung on without moving, slipped sideways again, and finally completed the manoeuvre backwards, having difficulty prising each set of claws clear as she went down. She learned quickly, for next day she did it correctly without a second's thought.

Some days, when everything had gone well and it was fine and dry, I could call her out to me from the cottage and across eighty yards of the front meadow. She hated wind but did not mind light rain. If the vegetation was really soaked, she would walk along reluctantly, shaking her feet free of moisture every few steps.

One night, when chasing her hefty cardboard ball, she must have tripped for she fell right over into her food, getting cat meat and meal into her fur. She had to be cleaned up like a naughty child. To be accurate, much of the time it was like having a recalcitrant teenager on my hands. As her litter box was now too small for her, I changed it for a large plastic baby bath I had found on a dump, half filling it with sawdust and the hay covering she preferred. She took to it like a charm, but to my chagrin not as a litter bin. Instead she cuffed clouds of hay and sawdust everywhere and used it to lie in, elbows hooked over the sides as she swatted out at her swinging ball. I noticed that her tapetum (the screens at the back of an animal's eye which in darkness reflect helpful light back on to what it is looking at) were now flashing in the lamp beams with a bright blue-green light.

Once when she was playing in this way, she started to make terrible yowling screeches, not kitten noises at all, but more like a full grown cat being strangled. At first I thought it was a new 'play' cry of ferocity, but she was rolling about on the floor, apparently in pain. She had swatted the nylon line above the ball too hard and it had swung round twice, wrapping itself tightly round her foot. The harder she pulled to get away the more it hurt. When I tried to help she yowled louder, spat and tried to bite me, but I managed to cut the line and free her.

Although she seemed to recover quickly, jumping on to her chair bed beside me, she slept far longer than usual that night and ate like a canary next day; she even looked thinner. She sneezed twice too, which was worrying. For all her boisterous play, I had to remember she was still a runt and delicate for a wildcat. In the wild she would never have reached the weaning stage.

167

The incident taught me never to leave her alone in the room too long, and when I went out on treks or supply trips, I made sure the line was well out of reach. It would be awful if it ever caught round her neck.

Trouble seldom comes in a single package. A few evenings later, I felt she was not having enough hard exercise in the room, and wanted to make sure her claws and leg muscles were developing the sort of strength they would need in the wild. So at dusk, when her eyes were at their best, I put her on the trunk of a long, slim ash tree south-east of the cottage and clapped my hands lightly, hoping she would climb up a little way. Moobli heard the clap, thought it was a signal to him, and came dashing up. The sight of the fast-moving Alsatian apparently coming for her galvanized Liane into action and she shot up the trunk like a squirrel. I called to her, but she kept climbing higher. Then she looked down, frightened by the height. She spotted a small branch at about thirty feet, and with slipping claws, obviously tired, gained its safety. She looked down at us, a lost, tiny little figure, terrified at the unaccustomed height, and began to 'mau' plaintively.

At first I thought I could call her back, for she had managed to climb down the seven-foot larch logs upended in the porch. Those, however, had been at a slant; the perpendicular smooth trunk of the ash tree was a different proposition. I called and called, and she walked back and forth a few paces on the branch, still crying out. She looked as if she would try to back down, then funked it. I had no ladder at that time, just a triangular heavy scaffold device I had made for painting my roof; there was no way I could prop that up against a vertical tree trunk. After several minutes, she looked as if she might just try to jump down. I went to fetch a blanket in the hope that I could drape it over my outstretched arms and so catch her if she did.

I had gone only two steps when I heard a rush of air and a horrible thwacking sound. She had jumped, apparently making for me, but, because I was moving, had missed. Instead of landing on the soft earth, the front part of her body struck a big rock which was only thinly covered with moss. She yowled, kicked, fell over while instinctively trying to get on to her feet, then lay on her side. As I stared in disbelief, her guts seemed to be swelling up. In awful remorse, I picked her up, stroking, kissing, talking to her, and carried her back into the room.

She was not breathing and I thought she was dead. Suddenly her sides began to heave fast as breath began to be sucked into her winded lungs. She was stunned, out cold, one eye totally shut, her mouth open. I felt she must have a fractured skull, and would still die. I laid her on some soft sweaters and nursed her for an hour. I felt her little body gently all over but could find no obviously broken bones. The swollen stomach made me fear that she had suffered internal damage, though I could see no blood in her mouth or anus.

In the morning I woke early to find she was still alive and could just about walk, though she was weak, tottery, and her left eye was swollen shut. She was very subdued all day and could not eat until nightfall. She was wary of me, as if it had been all my fault – as to a large extent it was. The following dawn I woke feeling stifled; she was draped across my neck. She began to purr again and sniffed my nose and eyes, smacking her lips and looking for milk. I quickly fetched her some. In three days her eye was back to normal, and she resumed usual play and her Zorba dances, but the ferocious and shrieking attacks on my hands ceased. As far as taming her was concerned, the fall seemed to have helped.

By the third week in August she was putting on weight again, becoming quite hefty and looking more like a wildcat. I let her have free run of the whole area, and she soon leaped through the window and discovered the woodshed for the first time. Sometimes I fed her in the pens so that she would remain used to being in them, especially if later she became fierce. Occasionally she would flare or spit at my sudden approach if she had not seen me for a few hours. I could never forget that underneath the apparently successful taming she was still a wildcat.

Every night Liane slept in my room, usually leaping on to my sweatered back from the floor and making the chirring note of greeting, demanding to be petted. Often she licked my fingers or face frantically with her eyes closed. She was now more affectionate than any domestic cat I had known and displayed more variation in her play: she was far more demanding. Outside in the sun she often panted like a dog, her flanks heaving, mouth open showing her bright red tongue and throat. The interim greeny-grey of her eyes was now almost entirely replaced by the final gold that would grow paler with age.

Towards the end of the month Liane developed digestive trouble. Her droppings were very loose, and she refused to eat or drink. She began to lose weight rapidly. She sometimes slept 13 hours at a stretch, ate almost nothing, and began to urinate on the carpet and to look even thinner. Using a vet's hypodermic syringe without the needle, I forced some milk with a pinch of aureomycin and half a powdered cat condition tablet down her throat twice a day. When she remained loose, I added a little kaolin and chlorodyne – the great foreign travel antidote to runny human stomachs – into the syringe mixture as well. She was bad-tempered and bit my hands several times.

Luckily, the new 'medicine' seemed to do the trick. Obviously feeling more sprightly, on the third day, she chose to go into the pens of her own accord for a few hours. That night I set a piece of half-cooked steak on my desk chair as a little treat, but she only ate half of it. As Moobli was staring at her eating, drooling slightly at the smell of the steak, I said, 'Go on, boy. Eat your food.' He sneaked up to the chair and very delicately with the tips of his front teeth slid the steak away. Liane's expression should have been photographed. He had never taken her food before. She leaped up, flared and went to clout his muzzle, but he was away on to his bed in the kitchen with the meat. The next piece I gave her she ate very quickly with little growls as she chewed away with her side carnassials.

Later, she leaped on me, purring loudly, and I caressed and stroked her. She seemed fatter already. (Her morphological balance was most delicate and she could lose or gain weight in a matter of hours.) She jumped on to the bed, watched the battery record player's turntable going round – with Giuseppe di Stefano's magnificent tenor filling the room with '*Che Gelida Manina*' – then leaped right on top of it. The tenor voice dropped to a deep growling bass. She went round once, leaped off and capered round the bed. Oh, this was a great new trick! She had just jumped on to it again when I reached her and lifted her on to the floor. She was now in the mood for games; she boxed a few rounds with Moobli's tail, and for the first time even chased a buzzing fly across the bed.

I was delighted to see her spirits restored, but was worried about the need to make a trip down to London. There seemed no alternative to taking her with us. Her sleeping den box would have to go too, so would a new litter bowl filled with sawdust and hay (the baby bath was too big for the crowded Land Rover). When we boated down the loch, into the first rain in nearly two months,

Liane '*mau*'d and pushed her big claws through the ventilation holes in her box, just as Patra used to do.

I did not want to leave Liane in the Land Rover amid the noisy fuming traffic of London for the few days of our stay, so I telephoned the owner of the Hampstead hotel where I had stayed in the past and where Moobli had been accepted. He was an understanding man and liked animals.

'Of course we'd *love* to have a young wildcat here,' he said. 'We have two rather "wild" cats of our own. Just so long as it doesn't bite the maids – we have a hard time finding good ones!'

But how would Liane take to the long jolting drive, the racket of trucks whizzing past on the motorways? As we set off I watched her carefully. She put her paws up on the windscreen to peer out at the passing trees and roadside. She capered about inside the vehicle, throwing herself in front of Moobli's dignified head as he lay on the bed at the back, and clouting his chin or clipping his ear as she passed. When she wanted to relieve herself, she hopped over the seats to the right bowl and squatted elegantly, tail upraised, and even covered it up again. A swift brief uplift of the front hot weather panels cleared the air. Far from being ill or frightened, she was no problem at all. Once she even jumped on to my lap and put her paws on the wheel to peer ahead, as if she were driving.

We had set off in the afternoon and reached one of my 'gipsy dormitories' by late evening – a gravel pit outside Dent in Yorkshire. I cooked supper on the camp stove, fed the animals and banished Moobli to the three front seats for the night, while Liane slept (as she often did) on the bed beside me, outside the covers. As we completed the drive next morning it was entertaining to see the different expressions of car drivers when they saw a wildcat staring at them out of the window.

Liane took happily to the thick carpeted luxury of the hotel room, just as Moobli had assumed it to be part of his aristocratic heritage on his first visit. She ate and drank all I gave her and made no mess except in the litter box.

I awoke at six next morning to find the sun streaming in the window and Liane lying on her back by my side, her paws bent on her chest and her head resting on the pillow. I had known a few odd girl friends in my time but this was ridiculous. A foot in my eye, a claw in my mouth to wake me up. How charming!

For the next nine days, while I dashed about my appointments,

Liane and Moobli entertained each other in the Land Rover. As soon as folk heard I had a young wildcat outside, out she had to come, and I would lug her box from the parking meters down long streets and into different buildings to show them. She rose to each occasion, putting on hilarious performances, growling, purring, chasing paper over desk tops, delighting the various office staffs. She really seemed to appreciate performing for an audience rather than just plain old me.

One late afternoon, however, we came close to losing Liane for good. I stopped as usual to throw sticks for Moobli in the area of Hyde Park by the Serpentine bridge, a green grassy place he liked. As he chased and brought back the small branches, something made me look across the road to the Land Rover. To my horror I saw Liane stand on the driver's seat, peer at us, and then squeeze through the slightly open window, pushing it back with a strength I did not think she possessed. The next moment she was down and running through the fast-moving traffic towards us. A taxi clapped on its brakes, tyres screeching, and she made a huge leap 15 feet into the air and landed on the grass. Terrified by the screeching noise and the great black object that had borne down upon her, Liane scooted straight up a sycamore tree to its first fork, and there she stayed.

Moobli saw her too and reared up the tree, whining. Seeing us staring upwards, passers-by gathered and before long we were at the centre of a small crowd.

'What an odd-looking cat,' someone said.

'I've never seen a fawn striped cat like that before,' said another.

I played it all down. 'Oh, she's just an ordinary kitten,' I said. 'She'll come down if we move away.'

Eventually the gathering dispersed, but it was dusk before Liane finally came down, finding backward footholds on the pieces of rough scaly bark. Then she ran to us with her squirmy '*chirr*' note. It had been a close shave for her with that taxi.

On the way home we visited Edinburgh Zoo Park. I wanted to see Freddy, the tom kit I had let the Zoo have to be a companion for their female in the spring. Unfortunately he had not yet mated with her, probably because he needed some months to settle down. Nor did I see him.

'He comes out at night more, spends most of the day in the den at the back. But he's in fine shape,' I was assured by Nobby Clarke, head of the animal department.

When we reached my home loch next morning, strong north-east gales were blowing noisily over the hills. All I wanted to do now was get home to Wildernesse, for Moobli and Liane had endured more than enough of living in the Land Rover. I hauled the small boat down over branches, screwed on the 4 h.p. outboard, carried eight loads of materials and gear down to the shore and put everything in the boat. Then I set Liane in her box on the centre seat in front of me and, with Moobli in the bow, set off.

At first, the oncoming waves were not too bad, but as we turned the bend leading into the wider middle mile and a half of the loch, the waves grew deeper, white-crested, and ran heavily against us. I realized I could not fight the waves directly with a laden boat and the low-powered engine, so I slid with them to the north, then cut east again where the curve of the land point ahead reduced the power of the waves. Even so, with the engine flat out, we only banged along at half walking pace.

Near the steeper rock bluffs on the shore, the waves piled up into deeper troughs and the bow nearly went under each time it slid down one and hit into the next. We made it to the lee of an island, where I refilled the tank with petrol. We had just headed past the long gravel spit and turned north-east for the last three-mile run to Wildernesse, with the gales now dead against us, when the engine suddenly cut out. Frantically I got it going again by using the choke, cursing the fact that I had left my valuable long oars in the cottage, and off we banged again. We had just passed the second curving land spit, about two miles from home, when the engine faltered and cut out again. This time nothing would make it restart.

I grabbed a frying pan from one of the bags and paddled desperately to keep the bow to the waves, but the boat swerved slowly broadside. We were totally swamped by the crashing water, and down we went. I clutched Liane's box by its carrying handle and one of the briefcases (containing my most valuable possessions – my wildlife notes, diaries, and costly photos) and leaped as far as I could from the sinking boat towards the shore. I was then 25 yards from the beach and struggling in about 14 feet of water. For a few moments I thought I would not make it. Then I remembered that for years, whenever Moobli and I had been swimming together, I had trained him to swim near me. I would grab his tail and make him tow me towards the shore, his natural reaction anyway when his tail was seized.

'Come here, Moobli. Come here!' I gasped as he paddled around with his powerful web-footed trudgeon stroke.

He came, eyes white and snorting like a bear, and swerved off again. I grabbed the end of his tail with the hand that held the briefcase. In this fashion, trying to hold Liane's box high with the other hand, kicking madly the hardest breaststroke kicks I had ever made, we reached the gravelly beach.

Gasping and spitting out water, heart pounding as if it would burst out of my chest, I just lay there for a few minutes regaining my breath. Poor little Liane was crouched in her box, soaked to the skin and terrified. Luckily only a few inches of water had gone through the upper ventilation holes, and I tipped her box up to let it all drain out.

Miraculously the boat had done a nose dive, keening in sideways, bow towards the shore, its rope lying snaked in only six feet of water. I could not get wetter than I already was, so I peeled off my soaked jacket, dived for the rope then heaved the boat slowly towards the beach. Luckily the heavy items were all still in it and my pack and lighter objects had floated on to the land spit. I unloaded everything from the boat, stacking it all high on the beach, and let the water out of the briefcases. The boat, filled with water, was too heavy to haul out, or even tip up, so I would have to come back with the baler.

We had now to walk the rough route to Wildernesse with Liane and my essential belongings. I would then have to return with some oil, for I felt sure the engine had broken down because I had failed to put enough oil into its fuel mix. I could not carry Liane in her big square awkward box for two miles, so I took the top items out of my pack, put her bedraggled and oddly quiescent form into it with some dry clothes and strapped down the top. Then with pack on and both hands filled with heavy briefcases, we set off to walk through the lochside alders and over the treacherous tussocks and rocks.

Halfway home I set the loads down for a rest and to give Liane some air. She had gone.

'Didn't you see her?' I yelled furiously at Moobli, who had been walking behind me. 'You damn fool!'

She must have jumped straight out into a tree for him neither to have seen nor scented her. I looked back the way we had come and '*mau*'d loudly, but there was no answer.

174

'Track her, Moobli,' I shouted to the shivering dog. 'Track the pussy coots!'

He tried, but picked up no scent at all. He looked miserable, all in, and I realized I should not have shouted at him.

Angry at myself, and shivering in the cold winds, as if an electric charge was running through me, I knew there was nothing for it but to get my valuable notes home fast and spread out to dry, before changing into dry clothes and returning with oil for the engine and a baling tin.

After all the long drives and hectic times in London, with Liane flourishing when I had least expected it, now, at the very last moment, she had escaped into the wild just two miles from home. What a damn sad and silly day!

14 · Liane, a Cat from the Wild

On returning to the land spit with oil, baler and a broken oar for a paddle, I almost gave up hope of finding Liane because Moobli seemed totally unable to track her. I searched high and low over the steep wooded sides of the lochside hills, 'mau'ing like a mother wildcat gone crazy. Then, to my surprise, I heard little answering 'mau's.

Liane was up a thick dying alder tree 40 yards from the shore. Keeping Moobli back, I called softly to her. When I went close she scuffled down to me, clinging hard to the lichen-covered trunk as I lifted her off. It seemed a chance in a million that we had her back, for she was not yet old enough to have found her way home to Wildernesse alone. I put her back in her box, baled out the boat, and put oil into the engine fuel. As I was loading up again another mishap occurred. My third briefcase, a moth-eaten relic, slipped from my over-full grasp and burst open on a rock, and the gales blew away several sheets of photos. I chased over the beach and hoped I had rounded up every one of them. Then I kicked the boat off as hard as I could, leaving Moobli to run along the shore.

After 200 yards the engine cut out again. Drifting in the tossing waves, with the boat now light enough to avoid being swamped, I removed, blew out and refitted the petrol pipe. Still no good. The gales blew me back another quarter mile, but I managed to paddle

176

above: Liane panting like a dog in the warm sunshine.

below: Exhibiting a dancing and mock-hunting display, fluffing out her tail in the weak watery sunshine.

left: By late September Liane was hunting the woods at night but often came through the window for a reassuring cuddle.

below: Once, when I dropped a pan, she flared. I always had to remember that she was a wildcat.

above right: She loved to scuff and gallop about in the snow.

below right: Performing a graceful ballerina-like stretch on the gravel-filled punchbag.

above: By the end of May she had become an expert hunter of mice and voles.

below: Even at one year old, she did not really like being held up.

half-sideways into the slight lee of a small bay, where I unloaded everything again and stacked it all below the shelter of some trees.

Now I had to walk back again with another heavy load. This time I did not put Liane into the pack but in a pillow case tied round my neck. She must have been as tired as I was for she relaxed and even went to sleep cradled in one arm, waking only when I had to use that hand for hauling myself up the steeper slopes.

It took the rest of the day to dry everything out – my notes, diaries, camera, lenses and sheets of photos. Each of the glass slides had to be opened individually and dried. The final disaster was the discovery that two sheets of photos, one containing rare pictures of wild otters swimming, the other of Cleo and her young kits together, were still missing. I never saw them again.

By nightfall Liane was in fine spirits again, eating and drinking heartily, playing in the study with all her old toys and the letter files, and scuffing out the hay from her plastic baby bath.

Next day I carried the heavy 20 h.p. outboard down to the shore, hauled the big boat down to the water and went back to retrieve everything and the small boat. It was a sunny morning and I draped my soaked clothes and laundry over the bramble bushes that were now filled with blackberries. Even my breakfast cereals had to be dried out in the sun.

On September 16 Liane caught her first shrew in the bracken jungles fringing the east wood. She did not play with it half-alive, as a domestic cat will do, but brought it into the study dead. Then she did play with it, throwing it high into the air with both paws and batting out as it fell again. To my surprise (for few animals will actually eat the musky scented shrew) she eventually ate most of it on the carpet.

She was now three months and ten days old. Due to the artificial environment in which I had kept her through kittenhood, she was slightly more backward at hunting than she would have been in the wild.

My plan was to allow her full run of the house and outside too; she could choose to come in when she wished yet also develop her hunting skills naturally. It was clear that her system needed live prey. While she still used her litter box in the study-bedroom, her increasing size and weight ($4\frac{1}{2}$lbs), together with her high protein meat diet, produced defecating performances of such magnitude and pungent odour that a heavy strain was being placed on our close indoor friendship! This is as much a problem with animals as it is with young children. During the next five weeks my efforts to 'house train' Liane ranged from temporary success to hilarious incident and total frustration. She regarded the study-bedroom as her true home: the great outdoors was only for hunting, her loo was indoors! I now had to try to reverse the habit.

At first I put her litter box in the kitchen, and while she was shut in there with Moobli she used it. But when she was outside during the day, she would suddenly hare into the study and, finding her litter box gone, jump into the cold ashes of the fire!

For a few days I shut her in the kitchen with Moobli at night and left the back door open so that both could go outside when they wished. She now performed in the shavings on the workshop floor, so I swept them all up. Then she used Moobli's bed, obviously with no protest from him. I decided to try more forceful means. I let her sleep again in my room, but when she went to perform in the fireplace, I tapped her behind lightly, as I would in play when she became too boisterous, and put her outside. This treatment failed utterly, for it was not play and it just made her wilder. So then, as soon as she showed any signs, I hurried her into the pens and shut the gate. She would have to go outside, and maybe would learn that outdoors was better for such purposes; indoors was just for sleeping, playing and where she could expect some affection from her foster parent.

She still leaped on me for caresses every evening. One of her favourite games was to lie in the valley between my knees, completely upside down, her head hanging over the edge, belly exposed, legs in the air and staying totally still as if she were dead, while I tickled and poked her gently. She was not in the least ticklish.

On September 18 I watched from the windows as she stalked a short-tailed vole at the rear of the cottage. She stayed still while it came out of its hole and wobble-tottered along as if on tiptoe. Then she tensed her muscles, sprang with both clawed paws stretched out, trapped it down, pulled it back for the death bite on the skull and dropped it. All the while her pupils were wide and as black as jet, despite the daylight. I wanted to see if she would let me have the vole, but she flared, growled, picked it up in her mouth and ran into the woodshed where she ate all but the tail and part of the little rear haunches. I did not mind, for it was good to see her skills and new independence increasing.

She was now catching large insects such as bluebottle flies, which she chased with lightning dashes, her claws slashing out until she struck them down. Then she ate them. Insects appear to make up a fair part of the diet of young wildcats, and the speed and reflexes needed for a successful catch stand them in good stead for serious hunting.

One afternoon, when I was sunbathing by some logs I had cut and left to mature, I suddenly felt sharp pains in my left hand. Liane was under the logs and making mock attacks on my fingers. She was unusually playful, throwing herself on her back and swiping out with paws at full stretch, rolling over and over as she bit a finger lightly. None of this really hurt, and she was now such a lovely animal I could forgive her almost anything. When she had finished playing she climbed right on to me, her foot pads cold on my skin, and lay with her warm furry head against my neck. Such blissful and trusting moments were more than reward enough for the problems and long hours of patience.

After I had seen her catch two more voles on September 26, Liane went voluntarily into the pens. Again I shut her in, this time for the night, hoping now that she had chosen to enter she might regard it as a good litter area. It did not work. Although she '*mau*'d raucously and leaped into my arms next morning, when I went to cook lunch I found she had used her hall litter box for the main deposit but had made a large puddle on the fire-lighting papers. She spent the afternoon climbing among the east wood hazel bushes, working up a huge appetite. After eating, she finished the usual hand caressing session in the study by furiously licking her forelegs and shoulders before trying to soak my letter files. She squawked indignantly when I picked her up and put her outside none too gently.

A few days later we invented a new game. I picked her up and threw her towards the thick larch pole of my wind generator: she sailed through the air, landed and clung on as if it was a magnet. Then she climbed down and ran back for me to throw her again. A few more tricks like that and she would be a music hall turn! She also developed a propensity for giving me sudden surprises as I was not looking — such as leaping on to me out of nowhere I leaned against the porch logs for a little sun after hours of typing.

I now tried new training ploys. I fed her every meal in the pens, so she began to go there when hungry; if she sneaked back into the house to 'perform', I held her close to the mess, said 'Bad girl!' and clapped my hands, sending her high-tailing outside again. This worked for about two days. Then I found her making a large pool on Moobli's towel. Performing on clothes and towels was really too much. In the hope of discouraging her at least from doing that, I pulled the towel from beneath her. She squawked and shot outside.

That night she was not in the pens or the woodshed and did not return for food. During the day a huge golden eagle had flown low from east to west behind the cottage, pursued by two ravens. Scared that the eagle might come back and spot Liane, or that a big fox would get her, I set Moobli to track her. We eventually found her by torchlight in total darkness a good 40 feet up in a thick oak tree on the north hill. She refused to come down.

In the morning I woke to hear loud '*mau*'s and got up to let her into the house. She ignored me and her litter box in the open hall and promptly ran to squat in the letter files. I pulled her out by the base of the tail and was bitten on the hand. Judging by the size of the pool she made outside she must have been saving it up all night. Moobli, too, was feeling the way I did about all this. That afternoon he came whining into the study and I went out with him to find Liane at it again on his bed. She fled outside at my entrance. I was glad that Moobli had not got angry with her. I was beginning to learn that she just would not seek out a litter box unless she and the box were kept in the same room all the time, but I decided to persist a few weeks longer. That night I set litter boxes in the hall and in every room.

It was now early October and the red deer stags were roaring on the mountain slopes as they trotted round the perimeters of their harems of hinds. On a trek, Moobli and I paused behind a rock to watch a nine-pointer chase one hind in a half-circle, calling short barking '*but but but*'s, as if spitting at her. Then he turned off to one side, stretched his head and neck out straight and roared his challenge across the glens. The alder leaves had been falling from the trees along the shore for three days now, and the first beech and ash leaves began to drift down too. The next strong winds would start the spectacular falls of autumn.

When we returned, Liane came into the house briefly, as if just saying hello, then went straight out again. With delight, I saw her at her toilet in the pens. When I approached with food, she dashed to the front fencing with a loud '*brrrooo*' chirr and clawed playfully at my hands. She looked healthier after her long spells outside, her fur had grown thicker and her eyes were almost as large and black as old Sylvesturr's.

On October 9, in the light of a weak and watery sun, Liane showed me a new dance routine in the open area between the cottage and the pens. It was the first time she had danced out of doors. With ears back, toes pointed outwards like a ballerina, she hopped, ran and drifted about, pouncing on leaves and tufts of grass, her tail high but curved and fluffed out to almost three inches thick. At times she looked like a mad earless hare. I shot off a whole roll of film, standing well back so that she felt quite free. I had to use a 300 mm. lens and it was hard to focus on her flying form. When I bowled a small apple towards her she chased it like a dog, cupped it in her paws, bit into it, then leaped away and stalked it again, stiff-legged. She pounced once more but did not bite again. She ignored it thereafter. The tart acid taste of the fruit obviously did not suit her palate.

All next day Moobli and I were away on a stag trek. When we returned, Liane's evening play session in the study had an element of real ferocity about it. She glared at my hand, then growled as she charged it, a real karate attack. She clutched, bit and kicked with her rear feet, rolled on her back and flared, certainly not trying to hurt but looking terribly fierce all the time. Then suddenly she lay on her side, both forelegs stuck out stiffly, and let me stroke her chin.

Her bad habits began again two days later. She ate her evening meal, climbed into some new blankets in her bed box, raised her tail and let go. After that I found Liane had done it again. This time on my bed. She had ignored all the litter boxes. I could not sit back and let her get away with it. Even if it meant her becoming wilder and more alienated, she would have to learn. So I pushed her nose in it, and was rewarded with a loud spit and claws in my arm. With gauntlets on, I shoved her outside again.

She kept it up during the next few days, and so did I. It seemed then as if she was starting to accept her nose being pushed into it, as a sort of ritual, the price she had to pay for the pleasure of peeing and shitting anywhere indoors. It had no deterrent effect whatever. On stormy nights she ate in the kitchen, looked fierce and wild when nature's urge overtook her, looked for somewhere out of sight to go, went, and only then ran out of the house.

For the next three nights Liane ranged along the area of the shore. The water and waves no longer scared her. She was evidently catching plenty of food, for she ate barely half the meals I gave her. She slept by day, usually in the den of the open pens where she had been born, and hunted most of the night, only coming back for a meal if she had been unsuccessful.

One morning she came in as I was preparing her food, ignored her boxes and used my best clean beach towel for her major business. I controlled myself, washed the towel with silent curses as she dashed outside again, then fed her in the pens. I went into the kitchen after lunch and, like the proverbial fat man who doesn't see the banana skin, put my foot into one of Liane's brand new giant offerings and nearly brained myself on the concrete. As it was, I merely pulled a thigh tendon. She was still in the room and my fall scared her, so that she leaped to the window seat spitting and flaring.

Two days later I made the final attempt. Perhaps she would not use the hay of her litter boxes now as it was the material of her bedding in the pens. I put down one box with sawdust in it, one with bare earth, and another with grassy turf. Then I brought her into the study to see if we could recapture the careless joy of days we had shared in the room when she was a small kitten. I fed her, but within two minutes she was on the bed, ignoring all boxes and squatting. To me it seemed as if she was keeping her bed clean while prepared, almost deliberately, to make a mess on what she knew to be mine. Somehow I kept to my new resolution never to try to discipline her again.

Liane knew she had done wrong. She looked at me with glowering eyes, hissed as I got up from my chair, then confused between me as foster parent and me as threat, ran about trying to hide. She looked just like old Sylvesturr, the same ferocious gloomy expression on her face, the jutting lower jaw so characteristic of the wildcat. I kept talking to her soothingly, wheedling my way back into her confidence, and after a quarter-hour of stroking and fussing, she was finally purring again. I then quietly let her out of the door and cleaned up the mess.

I accepted then that the bedroom days were too imprinted, the earlier training to the house too successful. It was impossible to reverse it all now so that she performed only outside and never in the house. As a kitten she had used her litter box regularly when it and she had been at all times in the one room. Once she started to range outside alone, the choice of rooms, inviting surfaces and boxes when she returned indoors was just too much for her.

My fondly nurtured image of her returning from hunts for only caresses, play sessions and a snooze on my lap went up in smoke. I had to admit defeat at the last hurdle: although I had hand-tamed her, I totally failed to house-train a wildcat.

From now on Liane's visits indoors would need to be supervised and her main headquarters would have to be outside in the pens. She seemed to prefer them to the woodshed. With winter only weeks away, I decided to improve the rocky den for her. I drove a square post into the ground and nailed a new aluminium roofing sheet lengthways over the top of the den so it projected three feet at the front as a protection from the rain. Then I built a second door about a foot inside the den, with its hole set on the opposite side to the entrance on the main door: whichever way the wind blew, there could now be no draughts. Loads of bracken were laid two feet thick over the roofing sheet and I filled the den with new dry hay, stuffing it into every tiny crevice so it was really warm and cosy. Liane took to it immediately.

Late at night, however, as rain began to fall, she came '*mau*'ing loudly round the porch to come and sleep indoors, as she usually did on wet and windy nights. This presented problems. I did not want to banish her from the cottage and our company when she sought them. Nor did I want to shut her in the pens in case she became bitter, morose and fierce, like old Sylvesturr. So I compromised. For the first few nights I put Moobli's bedblankets in the hall, shut the kitchen, rear room and study doors and left the front door open.

When I went out early on the next two mornings Moobli was sprawled out asleep, and there, lying right across him, was little pussy poos herself! Now she was denied my proximity as a sleeping partner, she had decided to adopt Moobli as a replacement. Far from minding, he seemed inordinately proud of her choice. I fed her in the pens, this would be the normal pattern from then on. She still liked the pens as a daytime refuge, and made a nest in the bracken on top of the aluminium sheet where, on sunny days, she would doze for hours, basking in the warmth, safe from any sudden disturbance from Moobli.

It was odd that she had chosen to sleep across him in the hall, for when they were outside her attitude towards him was much the same as Cleo's and Patra's had been when he suddenly loomed near by – she was scared. Once, when I had not seen her all day, I set Moobli to track her. He found her in the large rhododendron bush by the path, and when she ran to some old ruined walls near the west wood, he naturally followed. She was bigger and heavier now and, it seemed, could keep him at bay, for when I caught up I saw his tongue was bleeding. As usual, he was showing no belligerence; he just wanted to get close and sniff her. She was letting him know that while friendship between a huge male Alsatian and a young female wildcat was possible, it had to be when *she* chose and on *her* terms.

I gave her the fresh carcass of an ageing red squirrel which, sadly, had died in the woods, to see if she would regard it as food. She sniffed it all over, then carried it up to the den roof bracken, pulled it under her rear end and went to sleep. Later, I saw that she had taken it to the ground and buried it under dead bracken. She left it alone all next day. When I went out with her food around 7 p.m., I found she had disappeared. Tracking her with Moobli revealed that she was hunting in the west wood for the first time.

Evidently she caught nothing, for next morning she ate part of the gut of the squirrel. By 3 p.m. she had eaten all the gut, the lungs and much of the back meat. As I watched, she crunched through the spine and ate most of it, leaving just the head, forelegs, rear legs and tail. Her preferences seemed quite different from those of humans, who tend to eat the leg meat of an animal first. She ate the heart last, then covered up the remains, as wildcats do for protection from crows, ravens and insect and slug scavengers.

The first winter snows fell upon the high tops of the mountains on November 2. Liane made a voluntary change in her sleeping quarters, using the old hay box in the woodshed for the first time. She came indoors occasionally at dusk, after '*mau*'ing at the study window, for brief stroking and purring sessions, but as soon as she was set down on the floor again, she showed no desire to sleep on the bed or the sea chest sweaters and leaped on to the window shelf to be allowed out. I left her alone for long periods now, as she seemed to be adjusting well to her new life outside. If I bothered her too much in her new-found independence I might just lose her.

By November 15 the nights were drawing in, so that I had to

light the paraffin lamp by 4 p.m. With south-westerly gales blowing driving rain into the pens, Liane transferred her main head-quarters to the woodshed. Despite her problems in the cottage, she kept the shed floor clean. I was delighted by this. Now, when I went away on a brief research trip, I could lock her in the shed with a food and drink supply, leaving special exit holes for her to go in and out at will. This meant she would always have a safe refuge, which she would not have with the gate tied open in the pens. From then on I fed her just one meal in the evenings in the woodshed. For the rest of that winter, Liane ran totally free, though I still had many chances to watch her interesting behaviour.

She took to leaping on the window sill at night to catch the sturdy brown December moths, which were common in my woods and were attracted to my light. She knocked them down with her paws, then chomped them up like breakfast cereal.

During the first days of December winter laid its bitter chill upon the land. Sleety snow fell heavily, straight down, dark and grey like flakes of zinc. The clouds, blue-dark over the iceberg mountains, allowed little light on to the snow that now covered everything down to the 700ft level and lay in patches over the ground outside Wildernesse. Webs of white mist hung wraith-like over the glens and my water system froze up, forcing me down to the loch for buckets of water.

The cold made Liane hungrier. She was gaining weight too – just over five pounds now – with hefty shoulders and forelegs. One day she did something she had never done before. She sprang on to the bird table after a great tit, which escaped easily and denounced her with scolding, scissoring notes from the safety of a little willow bush. I snapped a towel at her and she snarled and dashed into the pens. I shut her in all day in the hope she would get the idea that the bird table was out of bounds. Possibly she did for she did not leap on it again for well over a year.

In the early hours of December 10, after heavy snow had fallen all night, I was woken by a loud penetrating scream, '*Kaah Kahhf*', halway between a bark and a cat being strangled. Despite the bitter cold I dashed to the window but could see nothing in the near-dark. Next morning Moobli and I tracked all over the front pasture and the two woods. We found big padded five-toe badger tracks leading from the west wood to the east, where we lost them because there was little snow under the trees. Then we made a more surprising

185

discovery – large wildcat tracks in the snow, measuring just under 1½ins across and in places nearly 4ins deep.

They could only be Sylvesturr's! The tracks started from the east wood and went to the rhododendron bush south-east of the cottage, where they vanished into the snowless areas below the thick broad leaves. Moobli scented around, stopping when I told him to as I did not want him stepping into the tracks, and we picked them up again on the edge of the glade below the huge Norway spruce that dominated the east wood. From there they headed over the pasture, crossed the badger tracks below my vegetable garden, and disappeared among thick swathes of brown bracken. Most astonishing of all was that halfway across the pasture, Liane's smaller tracks, often barely breaking the snow surface, appeared from the east edge of the cottage, joined his and went side by side with them to the vegetable patch. Here she separated and headed north again, back past the cottage to the woodshed, where we found her asleep. Had she actually met Sylvesturr or just gone the same way at a different time? Could the old tom have come back looking for Cleo, or was he now interested in Liane? Whatever was happening, I was delighted by this evidence that the old curmudgeon was still alive.

That evening I broke my resolution never to try and catch him again and set the box-cage trap. I could check his condition and maybe feed him in the pens before releasing him again. I doubted the chances of success, for he knew the trap well and had a memory like a computer.

Liane was now extremely active, darting about and playing in the snow while I tried to take pictures. I was surprised to see her carefully cover up her droppings, raking a mound of snow over them with both front feet.

Next morning tracks showed that Liane had been in the trap, which had not worked, and all the meat had gone. She had clearly scented it from over 100 yards away because for four snowy days she had certainly not been in that area. After my experiments with the other wildcats, it now seemed conclusive that these animals do use scent for finding carrion in winter.

There were no further tracks of Sylvesturr's in the snow patches that were left after several hours of fine, sleety drizzle.

I could not find Liane in any of her usual haunts on December 18. I hurried round the woods, searching for her without success. On returning, I found she had gone into the cottage of her own accord and was sleeping on my bed. Suspiciously, I sniffed the air – nothing. She lay looking up at me with half-closed eyes, as if saying, 'I can come in and behave you know!'

On Christmas Day I took Moobli on a short hard trek up the steep ridges and rock faces to the west in bright sunshine. We checked a rocky den at 400 feet, which Mia had used shortly after she had left, but there was no sign of recent activity. We did, however, find the new sett of the badger that foraged the woods at night.

That night I brought Liane into the study and the three of us had a fine little party, Liane stuffing herself on turkey giblets, then capering about the floor, more ponderously than she had as a kitten, and clouting Moobli's muzzle with her paws. She was much bigger now, and hit harder; I could hear the blows land as he flicked his huge head this way and that.

He took it well for a while before finally deciding to enter the festive mood himself and respond in kind. Instead of trying to bite, he sat back on his haunches and swiped out with one of his own vast paws, downwards, so that one of her mock attacks ended with her spinning – and flaring – across the room. That was enough, for she leaped on to my lap as I typed my daily diary and after a few minutes '*mau*'d to go out. I opened the window. She stood for a few moments on the sill, her eyes penetrating the darkness as mine could not, then dropped down into the more real and exciting world of the night, to prowl the silent woods alone.

15 · She Knew I Loved Her

Moobli and I saw the New Year in by camping out in the woods —
my yearly ritual of renewing close contact with nature, which
seemed more appropriate to my wilderness life than drinking
heavily and singing 'Auld Lang Syne' to myself. It was a bitterly
cold night. Even the condensation inside the tent froze into icicles.
On our return Liane behaved as if we had been away a month.

She reared up at the window, '*mau*'ing and stretching her white
jaw upwards until I let her in. As I read a book at my desk, she lay
in my arms reaching out jerkily to touch Moobli's box-like
muzzle with her paws, as if to reassure herself that he was back
too. She was extremely affectionate that evening. When I held her
up in front of me, she placed both paws on each of my closed
eyes. She did not like being held up like that and could have taken
both eyes out with just one clutch, but she just held them there.
She knew I loved her. Then she stayed totally still, her big golden
eyes gazing into mine only inches away. It is an extraordinary experience, looking closely into the eyes of a ferocious and reputedly
untamable animal like a wildcat.

I found, too, that she liked to have the nape of her neck and the
short hairs of her head given quick hard little pinches. She squirmed
with pleasure, giving faint little '*mau*'s, but I stopped when I suddenly realized why she liked this — it gave her the kind of feeling she
would get from the love bites of a tom during mating!

On January 14 I knew the biting cold fine spell, which had resulted in my water system being frozen for several weeks, was coming to an end. Deer using the west wood for shelter from the freezing north-east winds moved up the slopes and disappeared over the ridges to the north-east. They know better than any man when the weather is going to change and, sure enough, the wind switched to the south and the water started running freely in the pipe from the burn.

Three nights later snow began to fall again, and we used it to track Liane's nightly ranging. She was now prowling along the loch shore before dawn and had established a litter area just above the waves as if to mark one edge of her territory.

One night, as I returned home with Moobli from a shopping trip by the light of a half moon, Liane danced right down the path to greet us. The moment the boat touched the grassy bank, she hared back to the woodshed. Starting off six yards behind her, Moobli lost a further four by the time Liane reached the top of the path. Far from being scared of the great 'wolf' behind her, she capered out from the gap between the shed and the cottage wall and gave him a couple of light cuffs round the muzzle, as if saying, 'You're just not fast enough, old man!'

It surprised me that she could outsprint Moobli over a short run. In later months we turned this into a game: I would carry Liane down to the shore, tell Moobli to sit while she scooted as fast as a hare, and then off would go Moobli after her. He never caught up with her. Like most felines (except possibly the lion), wildcats have small lungs, and on a long run out in the open he would have worn her down within 200 yards.

In mid-February, with gales and incessant rain blasting from the east, Liane seemed to have evacuated the woodshed. She ignored the den in the pens and hollowed out a new home for herself in the thick bracken below the aluminium sheet at the back of the pens. She also made a hole in its north side so she could see out. Perhaps she had hoped this would be her 'secret' den, for when I peered into this hole her large golden eyes glowered at me with a most unfriend-ly look.

I wondered if her move could have something to do with the normal wildcat mating season, and Liane just wanted to be more alone. The trouble was she occasionally stayed in it, or hunted from it, leaving her nightly food untouched in the woodshed.

It was vital for Liane to keep using the woodshed as her main headquarters for I would shortly have to leave her for a few days to deliver my photos and book to my publisher, and to complete some biological research at the British Museum. Liane was now too large and unpredictable to inflict on any London hotel. Besides, she would probably be happier with a proper food supply on the territory she had come to know well than in the traffic-filled city.

The new hole I made in the woodshed wall enabled her to sneak in along the foot-wide gap between woodshed and house rather than expose herself in the open as she squeezed through holes in the outer walls. I also hid her haybox between the stacked firewood logs. It took her two days to find the new hole, but then she began to use it regularly: she also liked the new position of the hay box. From then on she only used her bracken den for an occasional daytime snooze.

When Moobli and I left for London in late February Liane had enough food for a month. I said a fond *au revoir*, locked the doors and set off up the loch.

When we returned ten days later Liane was fine, though a little thinner. She had eaten all the meat and fish but plenty of biscuits and three sausages were left. That night she behaved like a lost child recovering its parents. She came through the study window, clawed up my sweater, '*chirr*'ing and '*mau*'ing and looking up into my face as if to assure herself it was really me after her longest time alone. I tried to put her on to the sea chest sweaters while I typed my diaries but she insisted on staying in my lap even as my fingers flailed at the keys.

I was perplexed to find next day that Liane had torn open a large sack of sheep nuts which I kept in the woodshed to feed to sickly sheep or deer we found. It looked as if she had deliberately scraped the nuts right across the floor. Certainly she had not done it to make a litter area for there were no droppings in the shed. What on earth made her do it? Was she eating them! A day or two later I had my answer. I peeped over the lower door to find her sitting hunched between two logs, her eyes black and staring, her whole attitude one of keyed-up expectancy, clearly waiting for mice or voles to come and feed on the sheep nuts. There could be no other reason for ripping open and burrowing into the treble-thick paper sack except to attract her prey. While I could have attributed such foresight to a fox, it seemed extraordinary that such qualities were also possessed by a wildcat. Indeed, by dusk she had two large woodmice lying beside the nuts.

Spring came late that year after the long hard winter. The first daffodils appeared on March 17, when I saw the large female buzzard soaring over the cottage and south-westwards across the loch. Presently I heard the short high piercing '*keeyoo*' of the smaller male as it hastened along in her wake, calling loudly as they disappeared from sight.

Despite her enthusiastic welcome on her return, Liane became more wary after a few days and far more active than usual, often returning to the woodshed to eat before immediately taking off again into the woods. Her window visits at night were fewer and instead of coming in, she just 'fought' my hand through the gap, gave my fingers a few playful bites, and then dived away into the dark. Several times at dusk I saw her in the open areas making odd brief squats on the ground. When on March 26 she came through the window for a brief cuddling at the desk, I thought I had found the solution to this behaviour. As I stroked her tail area, she exuded a strongly scented sticky liquid that was certainly not urine. She also kicked her rear legs backwards, each one separately, which she had never done before. A quick pinching movement on the nape or to short hairs on her head, which she had always liked, now produced a tail-raising squirmy movement of her rear, as if she was ready for mating.

Male wildcats have special scent glands from which they produce a secretion which, when mixed with the urine, they spray on to trees, bushes or grass tufts, either to warn other males to stay away or else to inform females of their presence. It now seemed highly likely that females have a similar ability, hence Liane's short squattings. Clearly she was in oestrus and was leaving her scent around to attract a male, or to let one know she was there. Later that night I went out to find her perched in the willow bush near the cottage, as if waiting for a certain little fellow to pass by! There was no evidence of Sylvesturr in the area. In any case, wildcat males are monogamous and he would be looking for Cleo.

By early April Liane had lost her appetite, as is usual with wildcats in the mating season. Her fast lasted just under three weeks, then she appeared again on the window sill at nights, '*mau*'ing to

191

come in and '*chirr*'ing noisily at every touch of my hands as she slept on my lap at the desk.

One day in early May, as Moobli and I were travelling up the loch to look for eagle eyries, we found a lamb that had been attacked by a fox. We even saw the fox leap up the bank of the burn bordering the long wood and disappear between the trees. I had to restrain Moobli from chasing after it, for I knew he had no chance of catching a fox with a 200yd start in woodland, and I did not want him lost for hours.

The lamb had been attacked in the throat. The wound was not bleeding badly, yet the fox's teeth had torn a deep hole just above the front left shoulder, so that its trachea was exposed. It would not recover without medical treatment. I took the lamb home and named her Clarrie. She put up a stout fight for life, responding quickly to bottles of warm milk and water, and feeds of grass or my garden vegetable leaves.

Three days later I decided to let her graze outside in the sunny and warm fresh air. I did not want her to totter off and die, or to be attacked by the fox again, so I put her in the wildcat pens. Her wound was still weeping, but she was soon moving about, clipping off the herbage with both upward and downward jerks of her head.

My slight worry now was how Liane would react to the presence of a lamb around the cottage. While it is often said that wildcats will take small lambs, I had never heard of it happening in my area. In any case, Liane was still runty for a wildcat, and Clarrie was a hefty little animal of about seven weeks old. There seemed little danger – apart, perhaps, from the blood scent of her wounds.

To my surprise I did not see Liane for two days. Her food in the woodshed disappeared but all the milk was left.

I went round the woods with Moobli but did not find her. She would not have left the area without good reason. Perhaps she had seen the strange big white animal in her pens and this had triggered the wild streak in her to assert itself at last. The rear haunch of a newly dead calf had been stripped of hair for a few inches, far more neatly than by any fox, and some meat eaten.

After being away for three days, Liane returned to the woodshed on the night of May 13, hungry and so thirsty that, despite the burns and lochside, she drank nearly half a pint of milk. I wondered if she had found Sylvesturr in the long wood and, with Cleo gone, had perhaps made him an offer he could not refuse.

192

above: After Moobli had saved the lamb from an attacking fox, it would plump down on the cool floor of the hall in the hot days of July.

below: Liane clawed and chewed at the haunch of a red deer hind.

above: Yawning in the pens just before she came into oestrus, Liane then tried to 'stand' for Moobli.

below left: She sometimes had a distant look after roaming away for a few days.

below right: White fur in a pelage indicating interbreeding with domestic cats gone wild.

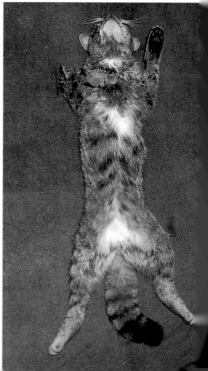

By now Clarrie was quite tame. She had eaten all the suitable vegetation in the pens, so I let her graze round the cottage.

I soon found my fears that Liane might attack her to be unfounded. Twice, when the front door was closed, I found Clarrie escaping the midday heat of the sun by wedging herself into the shady gap between the woodshed and the cottage wall. Liane was so scared of her that she walked up and down '*mau*'ing and would not go into the woodshed while the lamb was so near her entrance hole.

Occasionally, when Clarrie was grazing near the cottage, Liane would stalk carefully towards her through the masses of blooming bluebells, making sure she went no nearer than four yards. With her head going up and down like a badger scenting the air when first emerging from its sett, she would peer at the odd, white, but apparently amiable creature that had suddenly invaded her life and spent most nights in *her* pens.

Not until May 22 did it appear that Liane had finally accepted the stoical lamb. While typing at my desk, I noticed that Moobli, who was lying outside, had his ears pricked forward as he watched something by the cottage wall. I crept out in time to see Clarrie standing by the pens and Liane walk slowly from the woodshed and very gingerly, most tenderly, sniff Clarrie's nose. Then, as if overcome by her own daring, she suddenly danced away with dangling tail back into the shed. Clarrie seemed not one whit alarmed by the wildcat's nearness and calmly toddled off up the north hill, grazing as she went.

When wild life expert Geoffrey Kinns came to stay with me for a few days on his way to photograph eagles on the island of Skye, he told me I was crazy to regard Liane as a runt.

'Wildcats vary greatly in size, as you found when you examined the pelts at the Museum,' he reminded me. 'She's a superb specimen.'

Geoffrey worked as an artist at the Natural History Museum in London and was one of the finest wildlife photographers in the country. Despite losing a leg in the Rhine crossing of 1945, he was still carrying a 45 lb pack at the age of 55 in pursuit of his remarkable pictures (often published anonymously) of almost every species of mammal, amphibian and reptile, as well as the rare birds, to be found in Britain. He asked if he could take some 16 mm. movies of Liane, and we spent some time filming her behaving as if she were trying for an Oscar. She danced about, played with Moobli, sniffed

Clarrie's nose again and began catching young slow-worms from a family born beneath my timber pile. She went for a common gull which landed on the bird table after a crust, missing its tail by an inch. The gull uttered a loud screech, knowing it had suffered a close shave with death, but the incident happened too fast for us to film it.

We drove to the Highland Wildlife Park at Kingussie, where some eight wildcats were kept in a large enclosure. While I felt they would not breed in such a situation, it was fascinating to see so many versions of Liane living amicably together. When the time came, I would certainly find a mate here for Liane, I thought.

After Geoffrey had left for Skye, I dug the composted garden over ready for planting and with the help of the two fine young keepers, began the rounds of the seventeen golden eagle eyries I had located in my area, in which a total of four eaglets were being reared. We erected a hide of natural materials some 45 feet away from one eyrie, on a cliff ledge which had small dwarf trees growing from it. I had to go 13 miles by boat, drive 12 and walk 6 miles on each return visit. There was little time for anything else during those weeks, but I obtained the best pictures and observations so far of these astonishing birds. Because I wanted to observe eagles at dusk and dawn, I spent five nights in the hide on the ledge while poor old Moobli waited in the Land Rover where the road ended. (These and many other more spectacular eagle adventures are described in my books *Golden Eagle Years* and *On Wing and Wild Water*.)

Returning from the eyrie one evening, I went to the spot where I had released Cleo and her other three kits but did not see any of them. The keeper of the land told me that the rabbit population in the fields seemed to have diminished, and one night a wildcat had been seen on top of a fence post near the road. From his description, and knowing Cleo sometimes liked to climb on to a pole or stump to have a good look round, I deduced she was surviving well.

Encouraged by this, I went back a few days later to keep a lookout some 50 yards from the disused wildcat den, spending the night in the Land Rover. I was watching the rocky cairn by the roadside at dawn, tired from the hard nights out on the cliff ledge, when suddenly I saw a plump young wildcat emerge from the herbage, look nervously about, creep along a few yards, then vanish back into the undergrowth. To my astonishment, another young wildcat with a thinner face came out, followed almost exactly in the tracks of the first, and also vanished. I felt sure the first was Eeny and the second the slim and wiry Miny. Would Cleo or Meeny also show themselves? I waited another half hour but saw no more of them.

I could, I suppose, have set the box-cage live trap for them, but if at least three of them were surviving, we had done well enough. Besides, I had plenty on my hands then with the eagle work and Clarrie and Liane at home.

16 · The End of the Affair

Liane was now well into her second year and had become extremely active. Sometimes I saw her at dusk chasing insects and large moths across the ground, leaping up into the air after them, as if warming up her skills before going off on a proper hunt. She was firmer, plumper, yet not as large as Cleo. She was obviously hunting well for she occasionally left my meat in the woodshed, staying away two days at a time.

Wildcats are not fully mature until two years old, and it seemed she was into a new growth phase. She now weighed over six pounds. None of this weight increase, I was glad to note, was due to enlarged milk glands. If Sylvesturr had come back to the area, or she had met him in his own wood in early May, he had certainly not made her pregnant. My arrangements for a rather odd trip would have had to be cancelled if Liane had been expecting kittens.

Since a book about my years in the Canadian wilderness had been published in North America, I had received many letters, including invitations from two distinguished ecologists to visit them in the eastern United States. I also wanted to see again the log cabin I had built on the Canadian Pacific coast and some old friends there. So as to travel freely across the vast continent without the worry or cost of hotels, I bought an old milk truck, installed a couple of shelves, a gas cooker, water supply, and a piece of plastic foam for a bed, and it was ready to drive away from the Golden Guernsey Dairy in Milwaukee.

I arranged for a neighbouring farmworker to boat down to Wildernesse once a week to feed Liane while I was away. He took Clarrie to join five other orphan lambs on the farm. Moobli was to stay with friends he knew and liked in Sussex. I left Liane when hunting was at its easiest, and I knew my friend would not let me down. Even so, my thoughts often returned to her as I clocked up the 4,500 miles over the Rockies to Vancouver and back.

I returned to the loch, with Moobli in the Land Rover, exhausted and looking forward to some quiet days at home. My friend told me that during the third week Liane had stopped eating the food he set out for her, in fact he had never once seen her. The laden boat biffed up the loch against the waves produced by a strong easterly breeze. All was peace at Wildernesse. A family of woodcocks shot up from a clearing in the bracken and winged their way into the west wood. The bramble bushes were loaded down with blackberries. I hastened to the woodshed and looked into the den in the pens.

There was no sign of Liane.

Next day we searched both the woods. Apart from fox droppings (full of blackberries) near an old deer carcass below the west wood, Moobli could find no scents at all.

Three days later we boated down the loch again to fetch the rest of my gear from the Land Rover. We were delayed by visiting my friend again and had to come home in the moonlight. As I would be indoors catching up with my writing for the next few days, I let Moobli off for a hard run of the last two miles home. I watched him loping along like a great wolf in the silver light over the boggy, rocky and tussock-filled ground where a man could hardly walk. A dull-coloured animal, like a large hare, seemed suddenly to dash down the hill and chase him for a few steps before darting back up into the bracken again. How odd, I thought. It was probably just a trick of the light.

I wandered drowsily round to the woodshed next morning feeling sure that Liane, who had been staying away a day or two at a time before we had left, was now gone for good.

Suddenly I heard a loud '*mau*'ing, and there she was, back in her hay-box bed. She leaped out with a loud '*brrrooo*' chirr, sharpening her claws briefly on a slanting log, and started walking about me with loud caterwauling cries. She was thinner than before. She reached up and buried her claws painfully in my thigh, then leaped into my arms.

197

I fed her all the raw and tinned meats and milk she would eat, after which she fell into a deep sleep in the hay-box. It was then I noticed some small dog footprints in muddy open spots a few yards from the shed. Perhaps someone with dogs had visited the area and that had driven her away. It seemed strange she should leave the area in which she had been born, for it was clearly Liane I had seen one and a half miles up the loch the previous evening. Perhaps she had gone to look for us? It was odd, too, that she had stopped eating the good food my friend had left out, which was now teeming with sexton beetles.

For the next six weeks Liane seemed permanently hungry, 'mau'ing loudly for food and eating half as much as Moobli. She quickly replaced her lost weight and more. By late November she tipped the scales at 7¼lbs.

Despite her raucous welcome, she seemed far more wary and wild now when caught in the open. One evening she came to the window sill at dusk just as I was pouring some milk into a mug of tea, and I let her in. She turned and knocked the mug of tea flying. As the hot liquid touched her feet, I picked her up to get her out of the mess and – as I had often done when she was a kitten – threw her across on to the bed. This time she spat loudly in mid-air, then crouched angrily, her ears back, eyes narrowed, and continued to growl. I knew better than to react with resentment, or even to try to mollify her. I told Moobli to stay where he was and I ignored her. A few seconds later she jumped on to the window sill and I quietly let her out.

I just hoped this setback would not last.

It was now the rutting season, when the big master stags come down from the high hills where they have spent the summer together and seek their harems of hinds. It had been a long fine summer and the stags seemed to be late this year, for we had heard the usual rutting roars only twice. One sunny day Moobli and I set out into the hills to see if the main numbers had come down yet from the high tops. When we returned with what I felt sure would be particularly good deer photos, I had a flannel bath in the kitchen and cut my hair with the aid of two mirrors while lying on a camp bed outside, before settling down to sunbathe. A few minutes later I felt a tickling sensation. Liane had padded round from the woodshed and installed herself in the warm space between my thighs. She squirmed and rolled, and twisted her head upside-down. Her movements tickled so much I could hardly bear it. But feeling this should make up for her reversion in the study a few evenings earlier, I let her please herself, bit my lip and stuck it. I tried to pick her up, to bring her on to my chest, and she '*mau*'d, as if annoyed that I had interrupted her idea of the way friendship could be expressed out in the open. When I let her go she ran back to the woodshed.

It was clear now that the separation during my longest-ever absence from the Highlands had induced the return of some of her wildcat instincts. Like a youth called up in wartime, she had realized it was a harsh and lonely world when one had to rely on one's own inner resources, and that independence made one strong. She had, in short, grown up. The period had done her good, but from now on our friendship would be on her terms as much as mine.

Liane still seemed to be eating so much food that I thought perhaps Sylvesturr was joining her at night to help clean up the bowls. I found fresh wildcat droppings in the east wood, far too large to be Liane's, and certainly not those of a fox. If Sylvesturr was around I did not want to scare him away again by setting the live trap, especially if he was also visiting Liane to take some of her food. On the second night I noticed Liane's bowl was only half empty yet her stomach was distended. Something had to be taking what she left behind.

There was one safe way to find out: keep watch. I closed both doors of the woodshed and placed a hazel wand with a wooden square at one end as a 'gate' near her entrance hole. I retired to the dark of the workshop. If I saw the big tom go through the hole, my plan was to sneak out and block it up, thus trapping him in the shed. I could then check his condition and maybe photograph him. For three nights not a shadow of the old boy did I see. On two other nights I went out after midnight and closed the gap anyway, but all I saw was Liane gazing at me sleepily, wondering what on earth the sudden new visits in the middle of the night were for! Then there were no more big wildcat scats in the woods. It seemed Sylvesturr had eluded me yet again.

In early December Liane gave further proof that wildcats like fresh carrion. After a period of heavy south-westerly gales, hail and sleet, when the loch level rose five feet in two days, requiring both boats to be manhandled up the shore out of reach of the waves, I found a huge freshly dead hind in the long wood to the west. Her forequarters had been chewed by a fox and the stomach removed, but as the big rear haunches were fresh, I skinned them and took them home for the animals. I hung them from a rope across the roof beams in the woodshed. Later I found Liane standing with her rear feet on the hay box, her front claws embedded in one of the haunches, fiercely chewing the red meat.

The taste and smell of blood made her wilder, and she growled when I lifted the leg away. She kept clinging to it, her body taut, as if made of elastic. When I moved her hay box so she could no longer reach, she leaped on to the haunches and chewed large holes in them. She even used my shoulders as a high perch, snaffling a few more bites as I was holding her, and even growling slightly. I could feel the power of her jaws as they bit into the flesh, and was extremely glad she was friendly. She entered a new growth phase too, and by mid-January weighed just over eight pounds.

For the rest of the winter Liane ran totally free but remained partly dependent on us for food. Days went by and we barely saw her. Then, suddenly, she would appear on the window sill again, seeking reassuring contact and play, which was now conducted with gloved hands. Once assured that all was well with us and the status quo had not changed, out she went again to pursue her own life.

In early March Liane came into her second-year oestrus. She was clearly feeling the urge to mate far more strongly than in the previous spring, for she constantly rubbed herself over twigs and grass tufts, rolled on the ground with her head completely upside-down, oblivious of its wet surface, performed little somersaults, and made loud growls of frustration. She even walked about growling on half-bent legs, her tail high in the air, backside quivering side-ways, and tried to 'stand' for Moobli. The dopey old dog stood there with a big lop-sided affectionate grin, like a great horse over its foal, enjoying her sudden matiness without the slightest idea of what was causing it. She also went into the wildcat's usual springtime fast.

Though I anticipated this, I had expected it to occur a few days later; I knew just where I would borrow a mate for her. Were not the eight wildcats at the Kingussie Highland Wildlife Park somewhat overcrowded, and were they not well used to human beings? Surely the park would let me have a surplus male for a few weeks, or maybe sell me one for good, if he and Liane got along?

On my next supply trip I telephoned the director, Eddie Orbell. I received a nasty shock.

'We would have let you have one,' he told me, 'but the blizzards and heavy snowfalls this winter broke down the enclosure and all the wildcats escaped! We set traps of course, but were only able to get three back – two females and one tom. Obviously we can't let you have him!'

I returned home, chiding myself for not checking earlier. It was probably the end of any chance of a mate for Liane that spring season, unless old Sylvesturr would mate with her now that Cleo had gone. I felt this was unlikely, but I was not unduly worried. Liane was still a young wildcat and it would do her no harm to wait until she was more mature, in her third year.

By March 24, still fasting and eating only half her normal rations, it seemed Liane's oestrus period was over. She came in through the window for the first time in several days, but there were now no loud chirring 'brroo's when she was touched, and she behaved more placidly. Within a few days she was playing like a kitten again during sunny periods, often in the open pens. She darted to my hands through the mesh, clasped them gently between her paws, claws always sheathed now, gave a gentle love bite or two, then hared off again to stalk rustling grasses, crouching down so low that she looked like a thrown wet rag, so closely did her body fit into the contours of the ground.

Often, when I threw heavy sticks to give Moobli hard exercise, she would watch them flying through the air, moving fitfully, as if torn between the desire to see and the desire to flee. Occasionally she made token runs after Moobli as he pounded past and up the north hill, but as he thundered back with the stick, she scooted into the safety of the shed gap. She seemed even more interested when I threw a round rubber ball for Moobli. I rolled it towards her. To my surprise she darted over it, gave it a few round-arm cuffs and clutched and rolled over it, looking more like a large monkey than a cat. It was the first time she had played with a ball, and she soon lost interest in it.

By April 1 she looked slimmer and I found she had lost a pound of her winter weight since January. Two days later she began her spring moult, almost bare patches appearing under her limbs and front flanks. Her new growing coat was of much lighter colour, the guard hairs buff and yellow.

Although I thought her oestrus period was over, on April 5 I saw her again trying to 'stand' for Moobli as we were about to set out on a twenty-mile journey to see a keeper about eagles. I called Moobli down to the boat and we set off. It was late when we returned to the anchored boat in almost pitch darkness. With a heavy south wind blowing, I decided to sleep in the Land Rover until daylight.

When we returned to Wildernesse, Liane was nowhere to be found. Some daffodil blooms near the woodshed had been snapped off their stalks and her food and milk tins were still half full. Had someone come and taken her? I searched the area but found no footprints apart from my own. In a muddy patch near the west wood I saw a deep but obscured track, the mud so soft and fallen in that I could not tell whether it had been made by a large wildcat or a fox, or by a dog. Moobli picked up a scent but it petered out once we were on the dry needle-covered floor of the wood.

When she failed to appear on the second or the third day I became really worried. I hiked along the lochside and up along all the ridges and rockfaces beyond the west wood, continuously imitating the wildcat 'mau' calls. Suddenly I thought I heard a faint answering 'mau' coming against the wind from a cairn of large boulders to the north-west. I looked at Moobli. His ears were pricked forward and he was also looking in that direction.

We climbed up and Moobli found a scent; he zig-zagged between the great tangle of rocks, where again it appeared to peter out. When I continued the search, 'mau'ing loudly, there was no answer. If Liane was with Sylvesturr in one of the several possible dens in the large area of rockfall, perhaps he had a way of telling her to keep quiet. After another hour of searching without result, we returned home, and I put fresh meat and milk in her bowls.

Next morning, after hail had been hitting the tin roof for much of the night, I found a blanket of snow covering the ground. I felt sad that Liane had gone. If she stayed away in this weather without feeding, she would probably become too weak to return even if she wanted to. I walked round to the pens: there were no tracks in the snow and no signs of her in the den. The shed also looked empty, though some of the meat and all the milk had gone.

Then I heard a long drawn out 'mau'. I looked up. Liane was sitting like a silver ghost on the largest log of the woodpile in the dark at the back of the shed. It was like seeing an old friend come back from the dead. I 'mau'd in reply, but she looked scared, dropped to the floor and began to flee for the exit hole, as if I were a stranger. I stayed still, '*mau*'ing gently, and finally she came slowly towards me. She looked frightened, tired and was much thinner.

It took a full five minutes to warm up her wet body with my hands and get her purring again. I felt joy and relief, realizing just how fond I had become of her. It was wonderful to touch her long soft fur again and to feel her larynx vibrating against my own throat with her loud purrs.

If she had been with Sylvesturr, or maybe even another tom that had migrated to the area, he might come back again to visit her. If so, I wanted to catch him and establish the fact beyond doubt. I set the baited old box–cage and shut Liane in the pens.

Heavy snow fell overnight and I walked out into a white world on April 10. I was surprised to find clear wildcat tracks leading from the east wood almost up to Liane's pen. They were too small to have been made by Sylvesturr. They came to a stop about a yard from the pen then turned uphill where they were soon lost amid the tangles of old brown bracken. The animal had ignored the trap, which was all frozen up, so it would not have worked anyway. I recalled then that during the past four years I had found evidence of wildcats in the lochside woods two miles to the east of us.

I let Liane run free for a few hours each day and shut her in the pen at dusk. When the trap remained untouched, and no more tracks or droppings appeared during the next three nights, I let her out at night again.

I was sure her oestrus period was now completely over. I realized too that Liane could have just gone away to search for a mate. Perhaps she had not been with Sylvesturr at all, nor any other tom. She could have been acting on instinct.

These theories seemed to be correct, for during the next five weeks Liane showed no inclination to wander. But then, to my surprise, she came into oestrus again for a *third* time, on May 15. That morning she started growling and moving sensually over grass tufts with her tail high. Once more she tried to 'stand' for Moobli when he came near. Two days later she disappeared again. At first I was not too concerned, as the weather was now fine. On the fourth day I set out with Moobli early in the morning, when scent is strongest in the dew, and tried to track her through the woods, pastures and up the slopes and ridges above in a half-mile circle. He found no traces whatever, and looked uninterested, as if he knew she was miles away and had gone by choice. Nevertheless, I kept setting out her food each night in the woodshed.

Liane was nearly two years old, strong and healthy after a life of good feeding, and I was sure now that she had been desperate to mate and had gone deliberately to look for a tom. If true, it was most interesting that female wildcats would go in search of males in this way, as was the discovery that her oestrus period had erupted three times, the second after a gap of twelve days and the third after a lapse of some thirty-five days. If this happened with unmated females in the wild, and they mated during such a third oestrus, the average of 66 days' gestation for the wildcat would put birth at around July 21. It would not be ideal timing, but a good mother would still have time enough to rear her kits and teach them to hunt for themselves before the onset of harsh Highland winter in late November or December.

I was now not only busy with eagles but also studying some foxes, and spent the night of May 25 several miles away. When Moobli and I returned next day, in the first drizzle for ten days, I went to check the woodshed from old habit.

She was back again, this time in her haybox. She greeted me with a loud chirr of welcome. Having polished off all the food and milk I had left in her bowls, she leapt out and started calling raucously for more. Again she was thin and had sheep ticks on her brow and behind her left ear. Yet within ten days she was back to her old weight.

As the weeks passed there were no recurrences of her oestrus. Neither was she pregnant. It seemed clear she had not mated with Sylvesturr, if he was still alive, nor any other wild tom. I knew then it was probable that one day Liane would leave us, especially if she found a mate in the wilds. I gave this much thought and decided against trying to live-trap a wild male for her, not only because it would mean keeping it in miserable and unnatural imprisonment but also because there would be no guarantee that under such conditions the two would mate anyway. If Liane wanted to obey the call of the wild, then that was her right.

Despite these little dramas, our friendship with Liane continued to flourish through the summer. Moobli spent long periods lying down watching her, and she devised a hilarious new game for them to play. She walked towards him slowly until right below him, turned on her back and cuffed his indulgent face, turned on to her front again, stayed still for a few seconds, then shot off with a mighty scuffing of earth, so fast that he could never catch up with her. Then she would come capering around the other side of the cottage, her body high off the ground, tail dangling like a fat streamer, and dart into the gap by the woodshed to greet his tardy arrival with another playful cuff. If he became too boisterous, her claws came out and she stamped and spat. He soon backed off.

I now believed in her extra-sensory perception, for if ever I planned to go away for a few days or on overnight treks, she always came to the window sill the night before. Then she would insist on coming in to be stroked, looking up into my face and thrusting her chin into my beard with little lip-smacking noises, making her chirring notes of affection, just to establish we were still good friends.

Occasionally, after she had been hunting alone in the woods all day, she still came in and slept overnight on the bed covers beside me, curling up in the warm bend between my legs and body. She would wake me before dawn with loud '*mau*'s to be let out again.

Liane now adopted the woodshed as her main quarters, only going into the open pens on warm days to bask in the bracken of her sun bed on the den's roof. This was fortunate, for in late May there had been a slight disruption to her life. I had the first of four young vixens, all of which had been caught by a foot in gin traps, and which I intended to nurse back to health and release into the wild in forestry areas where there were no sheep. I told the full story in my book *Out of the Wild*, but part of it bears brief retelling here.

For three weeks I kept the young fox in the kitchen. During fine days I let it run on a collar at the end of a 15ft length of rope attached to the base of the bird table. At first I thought there would be no problems, but on June 10, as I was sitting at my desk, I heard a deep growling noise through the closed window. Liane had come round from the woodshed, her tail fluffed out, ears back and mouth open, showing her fangs. She stalked the vixen with a stiff-legged sideways gait, then launched a fast and furious attack. She bowled the fox right over, bit hard into the back of its neck and was away again in a flash. The fox, unhurt, actually went sniffing towards her, but as Liane was preparing for another assault, I opened the window fast and scared her away. Four days later the fox escaped, but it made a successful return to the wild, and even mated with the dominant fox of the region.

When I acquired three other young vixens, I could not have so many in the kitchen and decided to put them in the wildcat pens. One day I again heard growling noises from my desk. I rushed out to see Liane flat on top of the roof netting, growling with black-pupilled eyes, and even trying to reach down and slash at the foxes with the claws of her right front paw. The vixens showed no reaction, as if they knew they were safe behind the thick wire netting. Liane seemed ready to have a go at all three of them. It was clear that wildcats regard foxes as enemies, or perhaps Liane just did not like them being on her territory.

Eventually one vixen escaped and was fatally wounded by wild foxes up on the hill. The other two escaped in strange circumstances when I took them with me to London in August.

Before departing, I set out the usual food, milk and water in the woodshed. My friend at the neighbouring farm again undertook to make the boat journey to replenish Liane's supplies, and also to bring up the loch three Edinburgh acquaintances of mine who wanted to use Wildernesse for a weekend. I said a fond goodbye to Liane, sure she would be all right during these warm summer days. She was catching most of her own food now, for there was plenty of prey about.

Returning home on September 6, I hurried to the woodshed before unloading the boat. There was no sign of Liane. Later my friend told me he had not once seen her. He had stopped coming when he saw her food untouched, and then had fallen ill. He also told me that instead of three people staying at Wildernesse that weekend there had been a party of eleven in my home, which annoyed me. Maybe the disturbance of so many strangers had caused Liane to leave. When I telephoned one of these folk later, I was told they had not seen anything of her either.

Twice a week for a month Moobli and I searched the shoreline and trekked the hills and woods, but we could find no tracks, scats nor any other signs of her. These treks also revealed that the two dens of Sylvesturr's I knew in the long wood were now unoccupied and had not been used for some time. There had been no positive signs of him in our woods since the previous November. Our searches then had to be suspended for a while.

On October 4, as I was chasing after Moobli, who I thought might be on Liane's scent trail, my right foot hit a large tussock the wrong way and down I went. The ligaments were torn so badly that

I was unable to move the boat for nine days. Even after hospital treatment I had to hobble round with a stick for several weeks.

My one hope was that Liane would return when the really cold weather began to set in. This hope was never fulfilled. Later in the month I dashed to Spain where my father had fallen ill and had no one to look after him.

It was not until late February that I returned to Wildernesse, and still there were no signs that Liane had returned. A check on Sylvesturr's dens in the long wood showed they were still unoccupied. I had to admit that after three years of freedom in the wild the old curmudgeon himself was probably dead. We made a few more searches for Liane over the following weeks but they all proved futile.

We never saw her again.

My one consolation lay in the fact that she had come into oestrus three times in the previous spring, and on each occasion had stayed away for several days at a time. It was possible that she had finally left to seek a mate in the wild, or had even gone away with a wild tom which had sought her. I remembered then that during the past four years I had found considerable evidence of wildcats in the steep woodlands that stretched for two miles to the east of us. I made a systematic search through my diaries, and the results were most revealing.

In that time I had found wildcat prints in the mud round a deer carcass near the shore, the remains of a barn owl which because its feathers had been ripped out, not chewed, had certainly not been killed by a fox, and near by the unmistakable claw marks made by a stretching wildcat on the trunk of a small birch. The following winter I had found many close-together tracks of a wildcat in scuffed-up snow on rocky ledges right above the part of the woods where the owl had been slaughtered. These tracks indicated that the animal had been creeping along, belly low and with very short steps, while peering and scenting for roosting pipits or other birds in the clumps of thick heather. In May the year before, Moobli and I had found the tracks of an adult wildcat and a kitten in sandy mud on the bank of the river that lay beyond the woods. It was possible the male of this pair had now lost his partner and was ranging widely for a new mate. Nor could I forget the large wildcat tracks in the snow that had led to Liane's pen.

207

Even as I write this, seven years later, I still miss my little waif, as indeed I miss all my wildcats, but when I look at the surrounding woods and hills I like to think she is out there somewhere, living a wildcat's natural life. She probably is.

In five years I raised two kittens, gave magnificent old Sylvesturr a choice of two mates, by one of which he had six kittens, and his eventual freedom. I tamed one wildcat and released eight of these rare creatures back to the wild. It still seems a worthwhile thing to have done.

Postscript

Three years after Liane's disappearance perhaps I could have been
forgiven for believing that my life with wildcats was completely
over. I was mistaken, for both *Wildlife* magazine and *The Living
Countryside* magazine commissioned me to write full articles on the
species, based on my studies and experience. These attracted some
attention, and I received a note from BBC reporter Ted Harrison
who wanted to record a programme with me for the BBC Natural
History Unit's Radio 4 wildlife series *The Living World*. I replied
that he should drive up the forestry track on the far side of the loch
and keep hooting until he saw me launch my boat.

On October 22 I was walking through the east wood when I
found what looked like a typical four-toed wildcat track in a small
patch of mud. Had Liane finally returned? Next day I hauled the old
box-cage live trap from festooning undergrowth, repaired its
rotting sides with new wood, and set it. Three days later I heard
faint hooting opposite. Ted Harrison had arrived.

I boated him over and we recorded a programme about my
wildcat years, some of it standing by the track. I played him tapes of
the kittens squeaking, Liane giving her trilling '*brrrooo*' greeting call,
and even of old Sylvesturr growling, hissing and spitting in his
usual defiance. The programme went out, was repeated, and the
BBC even bought for their archives the rights to Sylvesturr's chill-
ing performance. I heard it played twice in later programmes, no

doubt frightening the daylights out of urban listeners as much as it had me on first hearing it.

On the last day of the month the trap caught not Liane, or any other wildcat, but a pine marten. I did not set it again. I realized then that the track could have been made by the marten, which has big feet for its size. Although martens have five toes, as any experienced animal tracker knows, it is quite possible for a five-toed animal to leave a four-toed track, depending on the way the animal is moving or on the type of terrain. The outside toe sometimes does not show.

More than a year later I received a letter from the Nature Conservancy Council's Scottish H.Q. in Edinburgh, signed by Nigel Easterbee, in which he said he was co-ordinating the Council's intended survey of the distribution of the wildcat in Britain. He wanted to meet people who had an interest in these animals, to gain information; could I spare time to see him if he came across to the west? I replied that I was always glad to help the N.C.C. (as I was then doing with a survey on golden eagles). I mentioned my two books on wildcats, how I had dealt with their distribution and other controversies, and had also campaigned for their protection in articles and radio talks. Because the unpredictable and ferocious winter gales meant that I could not guarantee to boat out and meet him on any particular day, we postponed our meeting until the spring.

On May 3, as I was setting off into the woods to cut firewood in a dry spell, I saw lights flashing opposite. Nigel Easterbee, who turned out to be a staff scientist with the N.C.C., had driven all the way from Edinburgh and had to be back the same night. He helped me get in some firewood and I gave him all the wildcat information I could. I pin-pointed on his map the ten sightings I had made of these animals in the wild. I also told him that, while the Institute of Terrestrial Ecology's distribution map of the mid-1970s showed no wildcats for the Ardnamurchan peninsula, there were probably as many as 50 pairs there.

When Nigel said he did not as yet know a great deal about wildcats, I explained that there were two main controversies. The prevailing scientific view at the time was that they did not interbreed with feral domestic cats in the wild, although they had been known to do so in zoos. It had never been proved that any resulting hybrids were fertile. The other was that wildcats have multiple broods, that is more than one litter a year. I said that I disagreed with both theories. My investigation into 99 wildcat pelts, showing more scrawny and fused tails in the modern animals, had indicated that interbreeding had been going on for many years. And my own breeding of wildcats had shown that they normally mate in March and give birth to kits in late May or June. The kits run with their mother for three months or more. (I had seen Freddy trying to get suck from his mother at the age of four months.) Therefore it would be almost impossible for a wildcat to have a second litter and rear the kits to be strong enough to cope with winter conditions in so short a time.

I explained that I had dealt fully with both these controversies, and others, in the 10,000 word Appendix to my book *My Wilderness Wildcats*, which had been published six years earlier, and had touched on them again in *Liane*, published two years after the first book. (See excerpts in the new Appendix to this book.) I was surprised when Nigel said he had not read the detailed Appendix or either book, although he had tried to get them, as I had donated the first book to the N.C.C. library in London the year after its publication. He said he would now like to have the books, so I sold him copies at one third the retail price. I said I hoped he would find them useful. We had lunch and before he left I took him down the loch to see Sylvesturr's den. It was still empty.

In June Nigel wrote to thank me for seeing him, then gave me some astonishing, and disturbing, news:

> I followed up the kitten that Freddy sired but it's a disappointing story. The Edinburgh Zoo mated Freddy with a female whose parentage could be traced back a couple of generations without any suspicion of domestic blood. Furthermore the original ancestors of the female I am told were genuine wildcats. Anyway the apparently suspicious kitten was produced and the Zoo gave it to a woman who lived on a farm near Annan in Dumfries-shire. I rang this woman to arrange a photographic session with her cat, only to find that she lost it within one week of its arrival! I could have screamed . . .

This was the first inkling I had that Freddy had sired any kittens at the Zoo. There might be a suggestion afoot now that I had bred hybrid wildcats. In a long letter I reminded Nigel of my Appendix in which, after a lot of work, I had concluded that wildcats had been interbreeding with feral domestics for a long time. I had also tried to scotch the theory of multiple broods, for although wildcats

211

were *capable* of multiple broods, they would be very rare in the wild, and *both* broods could not survive in any one year. I wrote:

> There is no more reason for supposing Freddy had domestic blood than for the female he mated with. He *might*, but not from the ancestors I know of, so might the female have had a gene or two. You must also bear in mind the great variation in pelage as revealed by the British Museum collection of wildcat skins. If you were anxious to photograph the grey kitten then it must also be of value to photograph the other two who were *not* grey!

I added that if the female's parents and grandparents were all well known, then surely that would indicate some proximity to man, and thus a possibility of a bit of domestic blood creeping in? 'My wildcats lived six miles from the nearest neighbour, who did not have a cat anyway. It is true, however, that Patra must have mated with a domestic tom because she did have a piebald litter. But she was free then, up the loch.' I said that I would very much like it if some method were evolved of giving Freddy, or any captive wildcat, some kind of chromosome test, so that we would be certain about pedigree:

> In any case, if it is *proved* that Freddy or the female, or else some cat in either of their pasts, *had* some domestic blood, then the belief that *hybrids* can't breed would be scotched on the head finally ... As I say, I feel Freddy is pure wildcat but I don't know what went on in his (or the female's) distant past. The odd genes can be thrown up at any time as I'm sure you will know by now. You say the other two kits looked pure wildcat? It would be fascinating, and important, to see if they can breed too. So I hope they are kept for that purpose anyway. It is also interesting that the woman who got the 'grey' kitten lost it in a week — not much domestic blood about a kitten that goes wild so fast and I wonder how old it was ...

After this I also wrote to Roger Wheater, director of Edinburgh Zoo Park, asking for details of the kits Freddy had sired. I said that if it was felt Freddy had domestic blood they could let me have him back.

Roger's reply was interesting and also surprising. He told me that Freddy had sired one litter by the adult female with which we had hoped he would mate, but it was from the second siring, father with daughter, that the grey kitten had appeared:

> I am sure you will understand that we could not keep this kitten in the group, although I think the reality is that many of our wild cats, especially those found near human habitation, are almost bound to have some domestic cat history. [The point I had made six years earlier in my Appendix.]
>
> Miranda [Miranda Stevenson, the Curator of Mammals] tells me that matings between father and daughter that produce as in this case evidence of a domestic strain will be the responsibility of the father as he will be passing on the domestic gene and if it is a recessive one it will manifest itself in the way it did. There is no question of any hybrid as the wildcat and domestic cat are relatively close and all they would produce is hybrid vigour rather than infertility . . .

He appended a list of the wildcat births. This surprised me even more. It revealed that Freddy had sired 7 litters between 1978 and 1982, totalling 17 kits. Of these, 6 litters were to Sugar, the female I had taken Freddy to mate with at the Zoo, and she had had 15 of these kits, of which 5 had died. It was when he mated with his 1978-born daughter Rebel in 1979 (it was interesting that a male wildcat would mate with his daughter and that she could bear a litter in her first year) that the grey kitten had been thrown off.

There was no response to my suggestion that they might let me have Freddy back! It seemed proof enough that he was regarded as a normal wildcat, from which it was worth breeding.

In any event, I was delighted that Freddy had now sired seven litters, and if among 17 kits he had thrown off only one grey, and that to his own one-year-old daughter, I felt that any domestic strain in him, or the daughter's mother, would be extremely slight.

In September I received another long and helpful letter from Nigel Easterbee. He said he had found my Appendix useful, and had examined the skins of two hybrid specimens in the Royal Scottish Museum, which originated from a captive breeding programme carried out at Edinburgh Zoo during the 1920s:

> One of these skins was from a wildcat x domestic cat and the other was the progeny of the hybrid (wild x domestic) x domestic. This shows that, in captivity at least, wild and domestic

cats can interbreed and also that the hybrids are fertile. The degree to which hybridisation has gone on in the wild is a subject of some debate, as I'm sure you can appreciate, and a major problem in any investigation of this phenomenon is the lack of material which can be assumed to be a good 'wild', since even the oldest specimens in the museums may have had some domestic blood in them. Perhaps this is a rather pessimistic view, but interactions with domestic cats have probably been going on for a long time . . .

I had made all these points in the Appendix to *My Wilderness Wildcats* six years earlier, and do so again at the end of this book. I had also covered them in articles, radio interviews and letters to enquirers during the past five years. Nigel's letter continued:

I will not be writing or uttering anything about the possibilities of you having bred hybrid wildcats. Regardless of whether Freddy or ultimately his father? had some domestic genes, in no way diminishes your achievements in breeding these animals. I have heard that Roger Wheater has written to you, and I hope he has explained the procedure for crossing animals carrying recessive genes which can point to the origins of such a trait.

He told me that if he had been able to photograph the grey kitten then he would certainly have wished to photograph the other two kittens. He went on to say:

A method for screening cats to determine their status would be very useful but nothing so far has been developed. Chromosome tests, as I understand it, would, in this context, necessitate killing the animal to obtain suitable material. An attempt to distinguish wild and domestic cats using immuno-electrophoresis on blood serum proteins that was carried out recently was not successful. Finally, the craniometric methods that I am looking into can distinguish wild and domestic but not, it appears hybrids; these methods are naturally destructive.

He ended by saying the main survey of distribution was proceeding well, and that my Appendix had been acknowledged in a 1979 thesis on wildcats which he had recently inspected.

I replied thanking him for his kind reassurances and said I was delighted that he seemed to be coming to the same conclusions about wildcats interbreeding with domestics that I had reached in my Appendix, and was taking the question of hybrids being fertile a lot further. I directed him towards my own evidence on the matter: 'I think if you examined all the pelts in the Natural History Museum, you would be able to spend more time than I could afford and might be able to shine a lot more light, using your more up to date scientific methods.'

Since both Roger Wheater and Miranda Stevenson had invited me to go to see Freddy and the other wildcats, I took time off to visit Edinburgh Zoo in November. Freddy watched me as I made all the old sounds he had known, pricking up his ears and even walking nearer. He probably did not 'recognize' me but certainly some memory cells were triggered. They all looked perfect specimens to me, big, in fine health, and with superb bushy blunt-tipped tails.

In late April, five and a half years after Liane's disappearance, a keeper friend and I were searching through a pinewood some miles west of the cottage when we found and positively identified a wildcat den. Some bones from a dead hind had been hauled into the holes below a jumbled cairn of rocks. Two yards away two piles of thick corded scats lay draped over each other. Often a wildcat will repeatedly deposit its droppings over those of its partner, the action seeming to have something to do with maintaining the pair bond. There were also fresh four-toed tracks on the sandy shore below the den.

I wondered if one of the cats might be Liane, who would be nearly eight years old now. I later baited the area with meat. Although I put in two daily watches (each of several hours) from a high bluff above the den, I did not see either of the wildcats. Being busy with eagles, I did not return to the area until May 13. I found that in the interim one of the wildcats had swum over to a near-by islet and had eaten the first egg of a pair of rare black-throated divers. The shell lay crunched into tiny fragments beside the nest, and there was a tell-tale wildcat footprint in the mud near by. The den was now empty. With the onset of fine warmer weather I felt sure the wildcats had moved higher into the hills.

While the chances are few, I still treasure the hope I may once more see my little waif, now restored to her natural state in the wild, if it is only a distant glimpse in the gloaming.

Appendix

In 1976 I wrote that in the Scottish wildcat, *Felis silvestris grampia*, Britain has an indigenous mammal as truly wild, independent and magnificent as any animal in the world. While lynxes, tigers, lions and leopards can become amenable to man's discipline in captivity, the wildcat does not. A sub-species of the European wildcat, *Felis silvestris silvestris*, it is usually larger and darker coloured than its European and Asian relatives.

Besides the Scottish Highlands, wildcats are found today in France, Spain, Germany, most of central and southern Europe, including Roumania, but not Scandinavia and south and west Russia into Asia.

Wildcats formerly lived all over England, Wales and Scotland, though they were never natives of Ireland, and they co-existed with the mammoth, cave lion and bear, the reindeer and wolf for thousands of years before the domestic cat was introduced to western Europe around 1200 B.C. Their fossil remains have been found in up to 2-million-year-old Pleistocene deposits at Gray's Thurrock, Essex, the Bleadon caves of the Mendips, Cresswell Crags in Derbyshire, Ravenscliff in Glamorgan and rocks of the Weald at Ightham in Kent.

Known variously as the Wood Cat, Cat of the Mountains, the British Tiger, or Bore Cat, wildcats were common in England and Wales up to the end of the fifteenth century. Records exist dating from 1127 of their skins being used for lining clothes. King John, Richard II and Edward II and III granted licences for hunting wolves, foxes, martens and wildcats in many English counties. Increasing human population and the thinning, felling and burning of forest cover from the Iron Age to the nineteenth century for timber and grazing land, drove the wildcat north to its final fastnesses in

Scotland — a migration that had first begun with the retreating glaciers of the Ice Age towards the end of the Pleistocene and start of the Holocene era over 10,000 years ago.

By the turn of the century naturalists were predicting its extinction in Britain. In England wildcats were extinct in Northampton by 1712, considerably diminished in Cumberland by 1790, the last one killed near Loweswater in the Lake District in 1843, and extinct in the Hambledon Hills, Yorkshire, by 1881. In Wales this species was almost extinct by 1826 though one was trapped in Montgomeryshire in 1864.

In 1881, Harvie Brown recorded the wildcat as extinct south-east of a rough line from Oban, up the Brander Pass to Dalmally, along the Perth border, including Rannoch Moor, to the junction of the counties of Perth, Forfar (Angus) and Aberdeen, then north-east to Tomintoul in Banff, then north-west again to Inverness.

Such was the situation through the early 1900s, with the cat clinging on in its last remote areas in north-west Argyll, Kintyre, Stirling, west Inverness-shire and western Ross. The more intelligent land owners, such as the Earls of Seafield, realized the preservation of a fascinating but dwindling native mammal was worth the loss of a few brace of sport grouse and afforded the wildcat some protection. The Great War was its main saviour, for many keepers were then away after a different target.

The plantings by the new Forestry Commission gave the endangered wildcat population a further boost for not only were they tolerated for their predation on rabbits, voles and ground birds which ate young seedlings, but the woods gave them new shelter and encouraged an increase in a large variety of prey. World War Two also provided some amnesty.

In his excellent 1961 survey, from Aberdeen University, Dr David Jenkins received 135 full replies to 248 questionnaires he sent to Highland estates. He reported the wildcat present in small numbers in Aberdeenshire, common locally in parts of Angus (particularly Glen Clova, and spreading to Glen Lethnot and Glen Esk), rare in Argyll but maybe on the increase in newly forested areas, six killed on one estate in Caithness in 1960, widely distributed in woods and on moors in Inverness-shire and maybe fairly widespread over high ground in Banff, a sudden increase on some moors and hills in Kinross and Kincardine in the late 1950s, widespread but in small numbers in Perthshire, uncommon in Ross and Cromarty and in Sutherland but some evidence of a spread southwards into Stirlingshire.

Since then the institute of Terrestrial Ecology in Huntingdon conducted a survey and produced a distribution as at spring 1977, indicating that the wildcat still had a long way to go before it reached its southern range prior to 1900 where it was known eastwards from the tip of Kintyre, Ayrshire, Renfrew, more rarely in Lanark, Dumfries and Berwick. None the less there were indications of a spread to areas where wildcats had been rare for well over a century. Then the strongholds were in central and north Argyll, north Stirling and south-west Perth, south Aberdeen, north Angus, south and north-east Inverness-shire, with a great increase in Moray and Banff. Ross and Cromarty have fair populations widely distributed, which spread into south and central Sutherland

The wildcat has few natural enemies to control the population numbers other than man. Dr Jenkins reported that one estate, Glenmazeran, killed 86 wildcats in the years 1950, 1953, 1958 and 1960 – 35 of them in 1958.

An occasional large fox may be cunning enough to take a kitten when they first begin to wander away from the mother on brief independent outings from the age of two months but such predation would be insignificant. (Foxes several times came near my wildcat litters when normally they never approached the cottage in summer.) Most adult wildcats could easily repel a fox, or escape, their reactions being much faster.

The golden eagle probably has a slight effect on populations. Wildcat kits have been recorded in eyries but it is extremely rare. MacNally described an encounter when an eagle was seen to swoop down on a wildcat in the open some half-dozen times but the cat retaliated, swiping out with its claws, until the eagle retired. Geoffrey Kinns was given an eye-witness account of a wildcat springing on to an eagle's back after it had snatched one of its kittens, both being shot in the air by a watching keeper. Pioneer naturalist Seton Gordon described a fight between the two in his book *The Golden Eagle*, when the cat was killed after its severe injuries caused it to run round in circles. The eagle was also later found dead.

A great controversy remains. To what significant extent, if any, has the Scottish wildcat interbred with feral domestic cats, of which there have long been a large number in the Highlands? And to what extent has such interbreeding affected total populations and, in particular, the purity of the original true wildcat race? How many of the modern sightings are of hybrids? There is a strong body of learned opinion, dating back to the late nineteenth century, that the wildcat population is heterogenous, not homogenous, the diverse elements being due to the admixture of domestic blood. Hence, for instance, the wildcat's proven ability to have more than one litter a year. There is an equally strong body of opinion that such interbreeding is extremely rare, that its effect would probably be infinitesimal as it has not yet been proved that the hybrids are fertile.

A new Nature Conservancy Council's survey of the wildcat, supervised by Dr Nigel Easterbee, was begun in 1982 and shows that in recent years the animal has spread even further to recolonize its former territories in areas north of Glasgow and Edinburgh, in south Perthshire, the Oban area, and right down to the Mull of Kintyre. Could an increase in hybrids account for this recolonisation nearer to cities and centres of human population? It seems to me that the views I expressed some ten years ago still apply, but before going further it would be as well to examine the central debate concerning the wildcat's breeding cycle.

Despite assertions by a few authorities that wildcats can have two or even three annual litters, my own observations lead me to side with Millais, Pitt, Morris and Cocks (see the Bibliography) that the true Scottish wildcat normally breeds only once a year, mating in late February or early March. In Millais's *The Mammals of Great Britain and Ireland* Alfred Heneage Cocks says that he first bred wildcats in Britain and raised them almost every year from 1875 to 1904. He was first to set the gestation period at 65 to 68 days (since confirmed at 63 to 69 days) as opposed to a usual 50 to 58 days for the domestic cat. Cocks never observed a female come into season during the summer: 'Many years when, owing to the death of the young or the fact that the pair have not bred together in the spring, I've kept a female and male together all summer, they have shown no inclination to breed.'

The zoologist L. Harrison Matthews examined several female wildcats and found two in an-oestrus for February 16 and 28, two in pro-oestrus for March 1 and 29, and five actually pregnant animals in March. He rightly concludes oestrus must normally occur during the first half of March. But there was one lactating animal for May 25 which was also in oestrus, and another in lactation an-oestrus for August 29. This valuable evidence shows it is biologically possible for wildcats to have more than one litter a year, though it does not prove that they do so.

Although Millais records perplexity at seeing young Scottish wildcats in October, which had clearly been born in late August or early September, the later scientific supposition that these kits 'must have been members of *second* litters born late in the summer', is perhaps not correct. They could just as easily, and far more likely in my opinion, have been *first* litter kits born late. For many reasons, the mother may not have mated at all in the spring. Patra showed great interest in Sylvesturr in May, perhaps coming into oestrus again because her early spring oestrus was not, as it were, consummated, though this is only surmise.

My own experience shows that wildcat kits may not be fully weaned until 2½ to 3½ months old, and certainly even the earliest leavers (like Mia) need to run and learn with their mother for at least 3½ months, but more usually 4 or even 5 months, before they are strong enough, their claws sufficiently hardened and developed, to hunt on their own and scoot up trees out of danger. I also believe efficient night hunting takes some time to learn. Zoo mothers have been known to drive their kits off at three months, but this could be partly due to the confined conditions. Toms appear to need their mothers more — my young Freddy stayed close to his mother through the winter and early spring too when, during periods of freedom, he could easily have left. Millais also felt kits run with their mother until September. So the assertion that Scottish wildcats bear kits in May and a second litter about August seems extraordinarily optimistic and is certainly not proven.

In an attempt to clarify this controversy, I examined two papers on the zoo breeding of wildcats – from Berne Zoo, Switzerland, between 1960 and 1967 and from Prague Zoo, Czechoslovakia, in 1963–7. It is fascinating to note that out of the thirty-two litters (16 at each zoo) there were only *three* cases of two litters a year. The one Berne female which had kits in April and also in August 1961 died at the age of four. The fecund female at Prague destroyed her first litter in the spring of 1963 but reared a second litter in August that year. In 1964 the same female cared for her spring litter until the kits were taken away from her in early June, then in August gave birth to a second litter of only one kit, which died the day after its birth. Prague's Curator of Mammals Jiri Volf comments: 'From this it can be deduced that, physiologically, she was unprepared to rear a second litter that year; but other factors may well have been involved.'

Monika Meyer-Holzapfel, Berne Zoo director, records that they did not separate males from females when they had young, 'for the female is sufficiently aggressive during this period to chase the male away from the nest box'. She also writes: 'The birth season lasts from March to August. This means if a birth occurs in August, it may not necessarily be the second litter of the year: it may equally be the first litter of the year.'

From breeding and releasing my own animals, it does not seem possible for a wildcat to rear a family successfully in some two months, then have another and rear that too. Having late summer or autumn kits cannot be the norm for they would hardly be developed enough in time to cope with winter conditions.

All this evidence leads me to conclude that in the harsh conditions of the wild, having a second litter in any one year, though possible, is most unlikely, but to rear both successfully is almost impossible. Could mating with domestic cats gone wild be confusing the statistics?

Wildcats *will* breed with domestics in captivity. Cocks bred some pretty hybrids from a male wildcat and a female domestic Persian cat in 1903, and a year later with a female Abyssinian cat. Frances Pitt records she mated her wildcat male Satan to a domestic cat. She bred a number of hybrids which were not as fierce as their sire but 'inherited a considerable measure of his untamed spirit' and were 'nervous and queer tempered'. She wrote: 'These two cats will mate, and their offspring are fertile, but the hybrids show almost complete dominance of the wildcat type.'

In 1896 Edward Hamilton concluded after examining many pelts reputed to be of wildcats: 'It seems the original wildcat as it existed in olden days has been almost exterminated throughout Europe. Its place has been taken by a mongrel race, the result of continual interbreeding during many centuries ...' He claimed the offspring *were* fertile, though he does not appear to have given examples of proof, but he went so far as to dub the hybrids *Felis cattus feras*!

In an article that appeared in the March issue of *Scottish Field* in 1984, D. Stephens and D. Jenkins referred to the heterogeneity recorded among Scottish wildcats, and argued that there is no evidence to suggest that the increase in modern populations is due to more hybridizing. Citing upper Glen Esk, Angus, where wildcats have shown a marked increase, Jenkins states:

A census of domestic cats showed of 23 animals only one was partly tabby. If hybridizing had been occurring on an important scale it would be expected that the domestic population would show signs of it and occasional multi-coloured variants might be seen among the wild ones. Since such obvious hybrids have not been seen, it is perhaps reasonable to assume that the variation recorded is characteristic of the Scottish race, although conceivably due to intermittent crossing throughout the recent history of the species.

I would like to make the point that domestic cats gone wild often become as wild as true wildcats, that hybrids often become as untamable as their wild parent (as Pitt confirms), and that therefore neither type would probably be around to show up in a census of 23 domestic cats. Yet, as both authors point out: 'The true picture of in-between cats will never be clear until someone has bred wildcat to domestic, hybrid to hybrid, and wildcat to hybrid.' True, and again, it will only be really clear if this is done with a large number of cats over many years, so that a reasonable facsimile of the genetic pool that exists in nature is achieved. It has been argued that though hybrids often become nearly as ferocious and assume a pelage similar to true wildcats (so how could one tell them at a distance in the wild anyway?), they usually have a fused tail, in that the black rings fuse together, especially on the dorsal surface, and the tail usually tapers.

In an effort to try and solve the mystery, I examined some 88 pelts of wildcats classified as *Felis silvestris grampia* in the Natural History Museum in London, dating from 1867. If Scottish wildcats had been hybridizing significantly during the last century and before, such differences should show up; also a possible gradual decline in size of specimens.

Disregarding zoo and incomplete specimens and what were clearly immature pelts, I recorded all the head and body and tail lengths, and divided the specimens into decades, from pre-1900 to the last dated specimen in the collection – October 1946. Overall there appears to have been a slight decline in size between 1867 and 1946, the lack of more specimens in the last section making the examination on this point inconclusive. There was also a tendency towards more scrawny and fused tails in the modern animals. A far greater range of skins, possibly divided into areas, and including samples from 1946 to the *present day*, needs to be examined for a value judgment. What is conclusive, however, is the considerable variety (within defined limits) of pelage, the proportions of tail to body length, and the weight of wildcats.

Although the wildcat is usually described as short-tailed, there are 51 specimens whose tails well exceed half their head and body length, the longer tails mostly occurring in the pelts dating from more recent years — a slight, though not complete, indication of an influence from possible inter-breeding with the longer-tailed domestic cat. Almost universally, the wildcat is described as having a thick bushy blunt-tipped tail with well separated rings, but there are eight specimens, mainly females, with fused tail rings, plus five specimens with thin tapering tails which, as all other pelage aspects are correct, don't appear to have been wrongly classified.

My opinion is that interbreeding with domestic cats *has* occurred and has had an effect on the Scottish wildcat race. Furthermore, Hamilton's state-ment that it has been occurring for centuries appears to have some validity. Even so, the pure breed most certainly still exists, especially on higher ground, in densest woodland and in its most remote retreats, where feral domestic cats have not yet penetrated, but it is still a relatively rare animal in Britain as a whole.

That is what I wrote ten years ago. Since then new light has been shone on the question of wildcats interbreeding with feral domestics, strangely enough through the solving of another mystery. In recent years reports of the sightings of large black cats have been rife in the Highlands, mostly in the Moray, Torres and Grantown areas. Several readers wrote to me asking my opinion as to what they were. To each I replied that if the sightings were true, I was sure the animals would prove to be not a new species hitherto unknown, as was the popular theory, but crosses between wildcats and feral domestics. The large size would come from a wildcat male and the black colour from a feral female. In 1985 several of these big black cats were shot and one was mounted and put on exhibition in the Elgin Museum. The problem of their genetic origin, however, remained open to question.

In the summer of 1986 one of these readers, Betty Gibson from Hamp-shire, wrote to me that in May she had watched a 'World At Large' pro-gramme on BBC television. She told me: 'They had permission to try and catch one of the big black cats to film, on condition they didn't release it in the same place. The cat was caught, anaesthetised, blood tested, and, as *you said*, found to be a hybrid of wildcat and domestic.'

Gratified as I was by this news, I do not have electricity in my remote home and therefore no television. It was not until early 1987 that I finally managed to watch a video of the programme. It was fascinating. Scientists in the genetics department of Aberdeen University had evolved a system to take blood from a pure wildcat, the usual domestic cat and also from the big black cat, and then, before deterioration set in, to isolate, photograph and compare the make-up of the respective chromosomes. The tests proved beyond doubt that the big black cat was a cross between a wildcat and a feral domestic. It was good, at last, to have proof that the two species interbreed, and to know that my theories of ten years earlier had been correct.

In April 1987 Nigel Easterbee kindly sent me his own summary of the N.C.C. wildcat distribution survey so far:

The wildcat is an extremely difficult animal with which to work, being shy, cryptically coloured and mainly crepuscular and nocturnal, and the survey method had to take this into account. Information on sightings and, where possible, status was collected, mainly by personal interviews with gamekeepers, forest rangers and hill shepherds, who are the most likely people to encounter wildcats. Only direct observations were accepted as evidence that wildcats were present; possible confusion with domestic/feral cats can result if indirect signs such as tracks or faeces are used.

It is hard to say how much the wildcat has spread in recent years since a comprehensive survey of this animal has never been carried out before. However, the picture that has emerged from this work indicates that wildcats are now present in most counties north of a line from Glasgow to Edinburgh, but are absent from the southern parts of Central Region, Fife and the more intensive agricultural areas in Aberdeenshire, Angus and Caithness; they have also spread into the Mull of Kintyre. The main populations of the wildcat appear to be found in east Sutherland, Easter-Ross, Strathspey, Strathtay/east Perthshire and north Argyll. Elsewhere, particularly in the more mountainous areas and in the north and west of Scotland, wildcat occurrence is sporadic, and population density is low. There seems to have been some contradiction of range in the south and west of Central Region, with no sightings reported in recent years whereas wildcats were present twenty years ago. Declines also are reported in west Sutherland, Wester-Ross, parts of Angus, Dumbarton and southern west Perthshire.

No evidence was found that wildcats have recolonised south Scotland and it seems that the relatively narrow industrialized belt between Glasgow and Edinburgh is acting as a barrier to further development southwards.

223

Bibliography

BANG, P., and DAHLSTROM, P., *Collins Guide to Animal Tracks and Signs* (London: Collins, 1974).

BOORER, MICHAEL, *Wild Cats* (London: Paul Hamlyn, 1969).

COCKS, ALFRED HENEAGE, 'Wildcats: Period of Gestation', *Zoologist*, 2nd series, vol. xi, 1876; 'Wildcat Breeding in Confinement', *Zoologist*, 3rd series, vol. v, 1881.

GORDON, SETON, *The Golden Eagle* (London: Collins, 1955).

HAMILTON, EDWARD, *The Wildcat of Europe* (London: R. H. Porter, 1896).

HARPER, FRANCIS, 'Extinct and Vanishing Mammals of the Old World', American Committee for International Wildlife Protection, Special Publication no. 12, 1945.

HARVIE-BROWN, J. A., 'The Past and Present Distribution of some of the Rare Animals of Scotland', *Zoologist*, 3rd series, vol. v, 1881.

HEWSON, R., 'The Food of Wildcats (Felis silvestris) and Red Foxes (Vulpes vulpes) in West and North-East Scotland: Notes from the Mammal Society', *Journal of Zoology*, 200 (2), 1983, pp. 283–9.

JENKINS, DAVID, 'The Present Status of the Wild Cat (Felis silvestris) in Scotland', *Scottish Naturalist*, vol. 70, 1961.

KURTEN, BJORN, *The Evolution of the European Wildcat* (Helsinki University, 1965).

MALLINSON, JEREMY, *The Shadow of Extinction: Europe's Threatened Wild Mammals* (London: Macmillan, 1978).

MATTHEWS, L. HARRISON, 'Reproduction in the Scottish Wildcat', *Proceedings of the Zoological Society*, Series B, vol. 3, 1941.

MATTHEWS, L. HARRISON, *British Mammals* (London: Collins, 1968).

MEYER-HOLZAPFEL, MONIKA, 'Breeding the European Wild Cat at Berne Zoo', *International Zoo Yearbook*, no. 8, 1968.

MILLAIS, J. G., *The Mammals of Great Britain and Ireland* (London: Longman Green, 1904).

MORRIS, DESMOND, *The Mammals* (London: Hodder & Stoughton, 1965).

PITT, FRANCES, *Wild Animals in Britain* (London: Batsford, 1939).

POCOCK, R. I., *Catalogue of the Genus Felis* (London: British Museum, 1951).

RITCHIE, JAMES, *The Influence of Man on Animal Life in Scotland* (Cambridge University Press, 1920).

STEPHEN, D., and JENKINS, D., 'Wildcat', *Scottish Field*, March 1964.

VOLF, JIRI, 'Breeding the European Wild Cat at Prague Zoo', *International Zoo Yearbook*, no. 8, 1968.